PRAISE FOR

RELEASEMENT: LEARNING TO
DANCE WITH LIFE

EVEN AS A CHILD, Lucille Joseph was aware of a tension between her parents' rational, evidence-based approach to understanding, and her own embryonic spiritual aspirations. Lucille would become a respected business and arts management consultant – well known for her role in Luminato Festival Toronto. But even as she addressed corporate challenges, she continued asking the question that occurred to her as a little girl: Am I in the world, or is the world in me?

At the same time, a similar gap was opening in western society. The beliefs of traditional religions were being cast aside, leaving little or no guidance for those who, like Lucille, yearned for meaning beyond the readily explicable.

In *Releasement*, Lucille Joseph bravely uses her own personal experience with her mentor, Kenneth Mills, to illuminate the spiritual quest. She employs the clear, unadorned language of a consultant, as well as the research and analytical skills of her chosen profession, to address the biggest question of all: is it time to rebrand God? A fascinating study of a deeply personal journey within the broad context of massive societal change.

—*David Macfarlane, author* The Danger Tree

A SOUL-STIRRING JOURNEY that beautifully illuminates the path to spirituality and meaning in our modern world. As a fellow seeker and facilitator, this insightful book resonates deeply, providing invaluable guidance for navigating the depths of our own spiritual potential.

—*Harrison Taylor, co-founder of Othership*

THIS IS A PORTRAIT OF A LIFE lived traversing both the physical and the metaphysical. Author and journeywoman Lucille Joseph proposes to the reader that the place of home is a curated space of consciousness. This book is a reminding of what is possible, what is our own potential, within one and a collective of many. Lucille Joseph speaks of the stuff of the universe and encourages us to recall our very being. Through her questing, readers discover the unfoldment of life itself.

—*Michele Chaban, MSW, PhD, University of Toronto*
Founding Director, Applied Mindfulness Meditation Program

LUCILLE JOSEPH HAS ALWAYS been ahead of her time, both as a senior woman in management consulting and as a lifelong seeker after true wisdom. This absorbing book gives us all the opportunity to join her on a quest to lead a truly complete and fulfilling life.

—*Richard Rooney, Vice Chair and co-founder, Burgundy Asset Management*

LUCILLE JOSEPH OFFERS a beautifully written book, drawing out themes of universal relevance in an era of profound change. How do we release old ideas and structures that no longer serve while carrying forward the lineages and wisdom of our ancient traditions? Rebranding God became Lucille's lifelong pursuit as well as the task of the current age as traditional sources of meaning and connection no longer work for many.

Her life journey with the natural sciences, the arts, business, and research became integrated through decades of spiritual practice and study with her mentor Kenneth Mills. Her spiritual path comes full circle in the second half of life as she rediscovers the profound lessons she began learning at the age of eighteen and sees how these learnings clearly fit within the contemporary societal shifts in the landscape. She is a spiritual innovator, finding her voice and platform for sharing spiritual wisdom with a world hungering for depth and meaning. I am excited about the ideas she explores as we collectively reimagine the future of spirituality.

—*Michelle Scheidt, The Fetzer Institute*

THIS BOOK TEACHES ME how to live a creative life. It has reignited my commitment to the internal, and shows me how studying high teaching is practical. The honesty and creativity of her life-long dealings with both the physical and metaphysical world was deeply inspiring, life-affirming and empowering. I loved the way in which she approaches her life: rigour yet play, openness yet discernment, and the courage to go far while staying present. Reading it has rearranged my molecules, just as author Lucille Joseph found that encountering her mentor Kenneth Mills rearranged hers. This is a book I will read again and again.

—*Angela Blumberg, Dancer and Choreographer*

RELEASEMENT
Learning to Dance with Life

LUCILLE JOSEPH

GEM HOUSE

TORONTO, CANADA

Statements made by Kenneth G. Mills are reprinted by
permission of the Kenneth G. Mills Foundation.
Spontaneous Unfoldment and *Unfoldment* are trademarks of
the Kenneth G. Mills Foundation.

ISBN
Paperback: 978-1-7380653-0-1
E-book: 978-1-7380653-1-8
Published by Gem House Productions, Toronto, Canada.
www.gemhouse.ca

Cover & book design: Brian Morgan

Questioner: Is the search worth the trouble?

Nisargadatta: Without it all is trouble. If you want to live sanely, creatively and happily, and have infinite riches to share, search for what you are.

SRI NISARGADATTA MAHARAJ,

I Am That

CONTENTS

PREFACE

WHENEVER life impels us to search for meaning, an answer always appears. It might come from a friend, a schoolteacher, a rabbi, a book, a bird, or a piece of music. On rare occasions it takes the form of one who not only has knowledge of a Higher Way but also is the living embodiment of that knowingness in their spontaneous words and actions. Philosopher and musician Kenneth G. Mills was that answer for me. He appeared in my experience as a living response to a childhood filled with self-enquiry and a deep desire to know. The journey that has become my life would not have been possible without his guidance and encouragement.

Not everyone is open to having a mentor, yet it is a rare aspirant who can truly make the journey alone. Because of my experience, it is obvious to me why living gurus and teachers are the time-honoured way of receiving timeless wisdom.

In the turbulent times in which we live, many of us seek meaning, purpose, equipoise, and joy. Some are turning to meditation, some to creating art. Others are climbing mountains or becoming activists or moving to a remote corner of the world. Delving into what was gleaned from studying with Kenneth Mills has brought a profound release for me. And then engaging with those yearning for meaning today has revealed to me that my individual experience is also universal. The resulting book is about a life because it traces my journey, but it is also about Life—Life as Force, infinite and timeless, the source of the gift of living, and the source of releasement from its boundaries.

What I received from Kenneth Mills, which seemed so radical in the twentieth century, is vital information in our world today. *Releasement* is offered not to promote or attempt to teach his work but to add my voice, as we all must by sharing the wisdom of experience to help restore harmony and balance within ourselves and this magnificent planet.

INTRODUCTION

AT A MUSIC REHEARSAL IN THE 1980s it was my turn to sing a high note, and it came out like a squeak. Conductor Kenneth Mills walked over and stood in front of me. He cupped his hands up to his mouth and tilted his head back, saying, "Tilt the cup to receive the notes. They are not in your voice. All you are doing is preparing to receive them." Imitating his gesture, I cupped my hands and tilted my head back, and sound poured in with an unforgettable surge of energy. "Do it without giving any thought to it. Get out of the way by giving it away." This brief singing lesson has become my lifelong model of what I call releasement.

The word *releasement* can have many meanings, such as a tight muscle finally relaxing, or holding our breath and then letting it go. Releasement can appear simply as the freedom of being able to laugh at the antics of our own minds. Writing this book has been an experience of releasement, being willing to tell my story and getting out of the way to share it.

My first experience of releasement came when I was a small child, dancing around the living room to music. And then in the theatre watching my first performance of the *Nutcracker* ballet, my four-year-old self was completely enraptured. When the male dancer lifted the ballerina high in the air, a bit panicked I yelled out, "Put her down!" Soon afterwards, my parents enrolled me in ballet lessons. It was thrilling to put on the slippers, but somehow, in the classes, that unself-conscious freedom of movement was lost. Thoughts about whether I was doing it right, and the judging eye of the teacher, obscured the music and closed down my lively expressiveness. Nevertheless, my love of dance continued and even came full circle decades later when it was my privilege to serve as chair of the board of the National Ballet of Canada.

As I grew up, the pattern of over-thinking and inner judgement developed in many aspects of my life. The energetic child dancing her heart out with no regard for anyone became shy and reserved as I learned to rely on the intellect and charted a careful life course to pursue success and acceptance. Yet, under the surface I was always looking for that dancing freedom. I didn't know then that many people have this yearning for releasement despite their apparently happy, successful lives.

In high school it was my good fortune to have an English teacher who, in my final year, started to reinvent excitement and unusualness in language. It caused me to wonder what had changed this man from being a conventional teacher into one so inspired, and to look at what now felt like my dull experience and to seek releasement from it.

As a result, in 1974 at the age of eighteen, I attended a lecture by my teacher's teacher, the philosopher and musician Kenneth G. Mills, who turned out to be a man who danced spontaneously and fearlessly in every aspect of life. From Dr. Mills I learned that true releasement comes in freedom from the limitations of the personal self—by no longer identifying solely as that aspect of me that is aging in time and moving around in space. This was an entirely new perspective for me, and it was the beginning of a lifelong journey to establish that fulcrum within myself.

Despite my new commitment to the spiritual path, I also pursued an intense career in business and often found myself with a foot in two worlds: the rational world of material success, and a spiritual quest for releasement. Throughout my career in business strategy consulting, and then in banking, and then in not-for-profit organizations, I lived each part of my life to the fullest—but the whole was missing. I was missing. There didn't seem to be the language or the courage to bring it all together. As a self-conscious young woman, for years I had a tendency to chase success and over-think everything. I was grasping for control while seeking releasement from all of it.

Once I finally followed the impulse to unify my life, I couldn't help but notice that it was matched by a parallel integration happening all around me. Scientists were collaborating with spiritual leaders to understand the nature of mind. Meditation was becoming mainstream, causing a commotion across the full spectrum from medical doctor to spiritual leader. In the last decade, businesses, even consulting firms, have become open to applying ancient wisdom and meditation in the workplace. As a former colleague recently observed, if I were a consultant straddling the two worlds of business and spirituality today, I would be trendy.

Drawn to understanding what was happening, before the pandemic intervened in 2020 I put on my consulting hat and spoke with people from many walks of life, including artists and leaders in business, health care, and the arts. Each leader had a story to tell of attempting for years to quietly introduce spiritual principles and practices into a world that wasn't ready, and then lately finding an insatiable new appetite for this nourishment. I convened a series of focus groups with individuals who had dedicated spiritual practices but were nevertheless yearning for more. There were profound stories of journeys that had started with religion or with atheism and then moved to the letting go of those beliefs, and then the feeling of being somewhat groundless. I understood these junctures well, having been through them over and over again in my own life, confronting my beliefs about materialism and about the concept of God, and having to let all of that go in order to be open to the actual possibility of a higher reality beyond the mind.

I found in the research that, for many, the traditional sources of comfort were no longer satisfying, and that we are not seeking a new belief system; we are seeking releasement, an escape from the conventions that have taught us that the material form is all that constitutes our being. We intuitively yearn for recognition of what we are in totality. The pandemic has only heightened the need for this experience of wholeness.

The promise of our time has been that science and technology, based on the supremacy of the rational mind, are the route to a more enlightened future. Information technology was supposed to provide connectivity and bring us together. Yet society is more fractured and fragile than ever.

Today we live in a world that is seemingly unmoored from any fundamental principles or values, a world in which ego, divisiveness, and digital algorithms are ruling the day with full rein, a world out of harmony with nature and the inherent beauty and goodness of life. No wonder we are seeking releasement. Our essence is the harmony, beauty, and the goodness of life itself. We cannot be at peace in a world that does not evidence this fact.

The philosophical journey that propels my life may seem abstract in the face of the urgent problems facing the world today. Yet I have found it to be the most practical of solutions. A different understanding of what constitutes life itself changes everything for an individual and for a nation.

Releasement is written through the lens of my life and work because any wisdom found here is the result of experience. The timeless truths pointed to in this book have been expressed by many throughout the ages, but what brings wisdom to life in any generation is its realization in the present moment. For those who, like me, seek a solid foundation for their life that is not based on the changeable realm of personality and circumstance, this book includes universal lessons (often hard won) that I received from Kenneth Mills on topics such as self-regulating thought and emotion, meditating, breaking shyness, managing success, imaging and manifesting, healing, and death and grieving. Applying those lessons has released an abundance of energy and opened up wonder, gratitude, love, and compassion.

My life has been one overflowing with what feels like the riches of knowingness, thanks to Kenneth Mills and the community that formed around him. Today, with the world at an extremity in every facet of living, the luxury of keeping journeys like mine private feels selfish. Dr. Mills often said that no one can give you realization; it is an inner individual journey. This book describes how I have worked with what he offered, to make it my own. May you recognize in my journey your own path forward, for this is how we leave footsteps for one another.

We all know the familiar sensation of releasement on an out-breath, the relaxing sigh of letting go. Releasement is also on the in-breath, being open to receiving the breath of life and then giving it away. When we inhale, the breath doesn't let us hold on; we let go, trusting that a new breath will appear. By learning the spirit of releasement, in both receiving and giving, the ineffable and wondrous nature of life that was there all along pours into our tilted cup.

I

AM I IN THE WORLD,
OR IS THE WORLD IN ME?

When you are imagining,
you might as well imagine something worthwhile.

L. M. MONTGOMERY, *Anne of Green Gables*

On the Beach

AT THE END OF THE SCHOOL YEAR we loaded up the station wagon for the trip from Toronto to the west coast of Canada. It was a ten-day drive in the 1960s, everything moved more slowly then, and we stopped often along the way. By the late afternoon, Mum, Dad, my sister Sue, and I had pitched our tent at a campsite, usually near a lake where we could swim.

Counting the tent pegs, checking on the melting ice in the cooler, and curling up in a sleeping bag listening to the sound of rain on the roof, are all regular parts of my childhood memories. But one year, when I was about eight years old, the annual road trip to visit relatives became a much bigger adventure.

It was early in the morning, and my family was still asleep when I crept out of the tent. The air felt fresh on my face as I blinked to see in the partial light. A new day with no mistakes in it yet, as Anne of Green Gables would say. I followed the route down to the beach, past the cold cement-floor washrooms. As the grass became sand, I kicked off my shoes and walked to the shoreline, letting the sand make moulds of my feet. The beach was cool and damp, and I could see the dark outline of the trees circling the lake. While I stood there, rooted in the sand as the sun came up, the everyday world and all the people with all their noise felt a million miles away. Alone, wrapped in nature, a tiny speck but part of something limitless, I was awake to a new beginning.

In the half-light, I looked across the lake at the trees, and somehow the picture morphed into nothing but a shimmering vibration. Then I was in the vibration, and all sense of being a body standing on a beach disappeared. Yet I was still present; in fact I was everywhere. I had never felt so vividly present as I did in that moment. It felt as though I was the creator of this picture and had the power to let it dissolve and to bring it back into form. I was riveted in my spot on the beach and at the same time transported to a whole new place.

The experience was unlike anything I had ever known. Unlike all previous moments of feeling immersed in nature, this was a sudden jolt into a deconstructed reality that seemed to launch me into another world.

Gradually the sensation settled, the lake and trees took shape again, and the picture before me was once again solid. I don't know if it had been seconds or minutes; it didn't seem to have anything to do with time. I stood there for a while, taking it all in, testing the sensation of being in a body. A happiness bubbled up in me, and a surprising feeling of home after years of wondering what I was doing here. I had always assumed that I was just an object *in* the world, but now it seemed like the world was in me. I walked along the beach looking at the sand and wondering how exactly it came to be there when I looked. Then, remembering my family who by now might be looking for me, I collected some treasures on the beach to account for my trip and headed back to the campsite.

I was surprised to see the familiar scene, looking so normal as though nothing had happened: the plastic cloth on the picnic table, the Coleman stove with the kettle boiling for tea, and Mum reminding Sue not to track wet grass into the tent. I hadn't landed in a new universe after all; everything was still the same. Slipping into the routine, I stirred a package of Tang orange drink into the pitcher of water and showed off my pieces of driftwood, perfect chairs for my dolls. I never mentioned what had really happened on the beach. Over breakfast, no one knew that, for a moment, I had disappeared entirely and was now back, doing my best impression of a normal child. But from that day forward I knew something that changed me forever. This world around me that looked so solid was actually just a vibration, and it wasn't separate from some inner power in me.

I now knew that there was "just being," that it was different from "being a kid growing up," and that you could have one of these without having the other. I wondered why people didn't talk about this, why they treated the objective world as though it was real and solid, when it was now obvious to me that it was just a vibration. It wasn't until much later that I realized how rare and precious this moment was, and that all those grown-ups asleep in their tents, or awake but busy with their day, had perhaps never had this experience.

After breakfast we loaded the car and continued on our way. Our first stop was Vernon in the Okanagan Valley, British Columbia, where my father's parents had a ranch. I loved this part of the trip, and not just because we had horses to ride. My grandmother in Vernon was the only grown-up in my small world whose love had no expectations attached to it. I could feel in her hugs, in her homemade applesauce and cookies, that my very presence was a wonder to her. I didn't need to measure up or amount to something in order to be loved. Just being her granddaughter was enough, and I drank in her warmth and affection. Then we moved happily on to Vancouver and Nanaimo to visit aunts and uncles, cousins, and more grandparents.

All too soon I was back in Toronto in Miss Anderson's classroom at John Ross Robertson Public School. As I sat there, supposedly learning arithmetic or the capital cities of the Canadian provinces, I was gazing out the window, preoccupied by a different question: *"Am I in the world, or is the world in me?"*

This question, in these exact words, appeared in my mind soon after the experience on the beach, and it dogged me for years. There was no one to turn to for an answer. The experience was so remote from life with my parents and relatives that it didn't even occur to me to ask them about it. It was obvious they wouldn't understand. At school my teachers and friends never touched on the subject. Our family didn't go to church, and I didn't have a belief system that might have made me comfortable with the discovery of a non-material universe, nor a Sunday school teacher who might have taken my question seriously. No one seemed to be concerned about, or even aware of, the subject that consumed me the most: Am I in the world, or is the world in me?

It was a question that went to the heart of the meaning of life. Are we just physical objects in an objective world? Or are we imagining the world, and is what we see "out there" actually coming from "in here"?

My imagination as a child filled in the gaps. Perhaps the universe was a giant doll's house and there was a God who was to me what I was to my dolls: creator, life force, voice, and animation. Or perhaps the world really did arise in me—a great responsibility for a child. Or maybe this is all a dream, not that different from sleeping dreams, and for a moment I had woken up. I had many theories. I never thought to settle this question by simply acknowledging the wonder of life. My parents were scientists, and I had been taught to use analysis to think through any problem. Accepting that life in its essential nature was a mystery didn't even occur to me.

I didn't tell my family about the moment on the beach or about any of the other unusual experiences that followed. I assumed that they would try to correct my "misperceptions." As biologists, they always had factual explanations that seemed to puncture rather than illuminate my experience. I imagined that they would explain how the retina produces an image and sends it to the brain or how dim lighting can fool your eyes. But I wanted to know what there was about me that was more than a retina and a brain. I wasn't sure if I could even describe to them what had happened. In those moments I hadn't been just a body standing on the beach; I was released into the shimmering whole out of which the entire picture, including me, seemed to emerge. How do you explain that to your parents?

I loved and respected Mum and Dad's appreciation of the natural world and their work as biologists that seemed to wholly sustain and nurture their lives. Who was I to tell them that what they were studying wasn't what they thought it was? From a young age, I was convinced that what I was glimpsing was beyond the understanding of parents and that I would have to explore it on my own.

The early mystical experiences inspired a lifetime of exploring the meaning of life. It was also the beginning of separating my inner world from people around me, establishing a pattern of hiding what meant the most to me. While my inner experience continued to flourish, integrating this knowingness into my daily life and expressing it aloud turned out to be a much more difficult journey.

Red Girl

MY AFFINITY TO THE INVISIBLE REALM, and sense of detachment from the visible, began very early. My parents loved to tell the story of how in my first few years I would come into a room and announce, "Here comes the baby!" Right from the beginning, to me this was all a play and, for some reason, I had the role of the baby.

While I was acting out that part, my imagination was constantly exploring other possibilities. When I was very young, an invisible friend, Red Girl, appeared in my imagination. She took her place at the dinner table and came on those long trips in the car. At first I was very open about her presence, having not yet learned to keep these things to myself. But gradually I realized that to my family, Red Girl was a fantasy. To me, she was as real as they were, although she existed in a different dimension. She did take up space ("Mummy, you can't sit there. Red Girl is sitting there") but she wasn't a child like me. As I look back on this today, Red Girl feels like an energy of solidarity standing with me in my encounters with a strange and stressful new world. It was also the beginning of having to reconcile the inner promptings that pointed to a reality beyond the visible, with being told that this was just my imagination, a quirk of my mind.

A few years later, Red Girl faded into the background, and I moved on to make-believe and testing my parents' willingness to go with me into the realm of imagination. My mother usually played along, perhaps finding my games a fun distraction in her serious life. Each of my dolls had a name, backstory, voice, and adventures. I think I was trying to work out for myself the dilemma of a rich and vivid imagination creating many worlds, and grown-ups around me seeming to believe that only the physical realm was real. Yet the world around me often felt devoid of substance. I would wonder, Do we just make all this up too?

This question was channelled into playing make-believe with my best friend, Mary, who lived across the street. Some of our games became plays that we performed for our families. I was always exploring the boundary between the made-up world of my imagination and the apparently made-up world around me.

One sentence in my mother's "baby diary" explains a lot about the family dynamics in my early childhood. She wrote that I had been a clingy baby but was now more independent, and she was finally able to get back to work at her science laboratory. These words explain my remembrance that when I was strong and independent, Mum was replaced by a caregiver. When I was needy and sick, Mum stayed at home. I was needy and sick as often as possible!

The unspoken message in our family was that playing with children, socializing, and even just having fun interfered with the real business of life—going to work, engaging in scientific discovery, learning something worthwhile, pursuing a career, and accomplishing something important. As a child in this serious environment, I learned to entertain myself and create my own world, which I often found in the arts.

I loved to dance around the house and make up my own songs, as reported by Mum in the baby diary. When Sue started piano lessons, I banged around on the piano keys. There was fingerpainting paper all over the dining-room table, and I often came in from the backyard covered in sand or mud. My mother didn't know how to raise this free-spirited, noisy, messy, musical, dancing child. Her childhood experience of the arts had been in memorizing poems, copying famous paintings, and playing the violin. Wanting the best for me, and perhaps seeing a need to tame an expressive creature who was inclined to show off, she signed me up for lessons.

I started piano and ballet lessons at the age of four. At first it was a grand adventure. I expected to enter the world from which music and dancing came. But piano scales and ballet positions had nothing to do with the spontaneous fun of dancing around the house or hauling all the living-room cushions onto the front porch to put on a play.

I could sense that my mother wanted to know if I had any real talent and whether my artistic nature would amount to anything in future. Music and dance became a test. I wanted to pass and prove her right, but this got in the way of the fun of just doing it. Through the next fourteen years of lessons, which grew to include violin, drama, and performance in musicals, the arts carried a fear of failure. There was no one to tell me that artistic expression is innate and requires no personal effort other than the discipline of practice. There was no one to say, "Don't think about the sing*er* or danc*er*. Just enjoy the song and the dance." I dutifully fulfilled the lessons and exercises but seemed to lose the ability to express through my body a heartfelt response to music. I've been looking ever since for the spontaneous freedom of expression that I had as a young child.

Then there was the problem of "showing off." I was always trying to find the line between just doing what I loved and doing something terrible called showing off. I used to say, "Watching, Mummy? Watching?" desperately wanting recognition and validation of my efforts. My mother, wanting to be supportive but naturally judgemental, tended to temper her applause with encouragement to do better and with reminders to not show off. I was confused and embarrassed that what came so naturally, and felt like freedom from ego, was seen by grown-ups and classmates at school as being egotistical.

Despite the angst surrounding my artistic activities, I was completely open when watching other artists. I loved going to the ballet at Toronto's O'Keefe Centre where at my very first performance I watched the ballerina being lifted high in a pas de deux. Frightened, I shouted, "Put her down!" This embarrassing story quickly became a family favourite. For me, it was the beginning of a lifetime of losing myself in the performing arts.

I also loved going to hear the Toronto Symphony Orchestra, feeling very grown up, taking my seat with my parents in the side balcony and listening quietly to the music. On school trips to Massey Hall, I was always mortified by the kids who didn't know how to behave in a place that for me was already a temple. One evening, in the dim light of its horseshoe-shaped auditorium, another moment of altered perception happened. I glanced across to the balcony on the other side and saw only blobs of flesh sitting in the chairs. The life force was entirely absent. Then, with a blink, the flesh blobs became people again, like a light bulb being plugged in. With another blink, they turned back into blobs. It was a bit frightening but mostly fascinating to my curious mind. Another discovery that no one else seemed to notice or talk about.

My parents took me with them to the Stratford Festival and other theatre productions, as well as to the National Ballet of Canada and the Toronto Symphony. After each performance I left the theatre convinced that I wanted to be on *that* stage, which led to the drama programs and violin lessons, in addition to the piano and ballet.

Through it all, I developed a lifelong appreciation of the arts as a primary connection to a feeling realm beyond my many thoughts and questions. But the feelings and the lessons didn't quell the many "What is it all about?" questions that continued to swirl around in my mind. For as long as I can remember, I have been questioning the meaning of life as though it were a problem to be solved. If I could just think it through clearly enough, I would find the answer.

I was seeking answers while also seeking acceptance and belonging, and I learned to channel my nature within a range acceptable to my parents. Growing up in a family that didn't acknowledge the existence of a realm beyond material existence, and yet feeling that presence constantly, required me to bury these feelings and keep them to myself.

There was an assumption, given my family's scientific world view, that I bought into the proposition that the material world was the only reality. I feared losing the love and nourishment of my parents if I didn't have their approval, and so I never said out loud that my experience told me that the material picture was just an image, a passing show. (And therefore why not make it a stage?) As children do, I knew instinctively that ours was a fragile family unit and didn't want to push the boundaries for fear it would all come crashing down.

My parents—busy with their careers, and having an academic's intellectual view of child-rearing—left me largely to my own devices to figure things out as I grew up. I loved the freedom that I had, in stark contrast to my friends whose parents were constantly telling them what to do and not do. But the lack of direction produced uncertainty and fear of going outside the lines, not knowing exactly where those lines were. I learned to rely on subtle cues instead of direct words and became highly sensitive to the external world, reading the room and predicting the response to words and actions. I believed that my very existence depended on approval and acceptance, while trying to ignore the voice within that knew that gaining approval meant trading off authentic expression.

As I grew up, I hoped to keep alive my inner life while allowing my external world to conform to success as defined by my family and school. As a result, the small child bursting with creativity and expression, with glimpses into an invisible realm, gradually became shy and emotionally withdrawn. At school I was constantly on "high alert" and found unstructured social situations, such as recess, exhausting instead of fun. I became a high-achieving academic pupil, studious and serious.

And the question never left me: Am I in the world, or is the world in me?

Roots in Science

I WAS BORN INTO a multi-generation family of scientists. My father and mother, my grandfather *and* my grandmother, were PhD biologists. Advancing knowledge of the natural world was the family business. Thanks to them, my childhood was immersed in the wonders of nature. In our family albums, in almost every photo we are outdoors. The only indoor pictures were taken with Santa Claus and on Christmas morning.

From an early age my older sister showed an interest in biology. We have a happy picture of Sue with a wild baby bird nestled in her curly hair. Her bedroom gradually filled up with cages and terrariums for guinea pigs, hamsters, salamanders, and other creatures. My bedroom, right next to Sue's, was a riot of stuffed animals, dolls, dress-up clothes, storybooks, and ballerina wallpaper.

Growing up in our house, we had to be careful when rummaging around in the fridge. If I was looking for Cheez Whiz spread or homemade popsicles, I would often find food for various pets, and seed pods preserved from the garden. There might be Dad's film negatives, blood samples from Mum's autism research, or a dead mouse carefully wrapped in Saran plastic for Dad to take to his graduate students to dissect. It didn't occur to me that any of this was unusual until a friend from school asked me why there were holes punched in the top of the mason jar on the kitchen counter. I knew the answer to that one: "So that the insect cocooning inside can breathe." She was never quite as comfortable in our kitchen after that. Her mother's mason jars contained soup, jams, and cranberry sauce. Her parents didn't use the refrigerator as a laboratory cooling unit, or the kitchen counters to teach science. To make matters worse, my mother wore a lab coat in the kitchen. It was practical and suited her better than the frilly aprons of the day. My friends teased me that she cooked dinner on a Bunsen burner, concocting our meals in test tubes.

My mother had learned the lab-coat trick, as she called it, from her mother, Lucy Wright Smith. Lucy was born and raised in Boston, and in 1914 she graduated from Cornell University with a doctorate in limnology. It was there that she met and later married a fellow student, my grandfather Wilbur Clemens, who came from a small town near Stratford, Ontario. They settled in Toronto, where my grandfather began his career at the University of Toronto doing research on freshwater fish. Looking up the word *limnology*, I discovered that my grandmother's speciality had been bodies of water, the habitat of the fish that my grandfather studied. I assume that my grandparents loved each other, but in my unusual family this academic compatibility was perhaps as good as any basis for a happy marriage.

Early in his career, Wilbur Clemens received a call from the Fisheries and Oceans Department of the Canadian government asking him to become the director of the Pacific Biological Station near Nanaimo, on Vancouver Island. My grandfather objected, saying that he was a freshwater fish specialist. But it appeared that no one else in Canada was more qualified. With reluctance, he accepted the position. By then he had two small children and a wife who aspired to her own career in science.

Moving from the bustling city of Toronto in 1924 to what was then an isolated and remote part of Vancouver Island on the west coast of Canada must have felt like moving to Siberia, especially for my grandmother. However, it led to my grandfather's distinguished career as one of Canada's leading west coast fisheries experts. I'm told that the book he eventually wrote is still a reference text today.[1] After running the biological station for twenty years, Wilbur Clemens became the dean of science at the University of British Columbia. There is a room named after him in the biology department.

My grandmother worked with my grandfather at the biological station; I have a precious photo of her peering into a microscope in the lab. An article published about Dr. Lucy Clemens, a newsworthy figure in west coast Canada, described her as "working side by side with her husband," meaning that she was unpaid and without a title. My mother grew up at the station and was driven to Nanaimo every day for school.

Tragically, Lucy died on an operating table in 1937 due to an overdose of anaesthetic, when my mother was just fifteen. From then on, Mum and her brother were raised by their father, a housekeeper, and the young staff at the biological station who took an interest in them. It was a lonely life for a teenage girl, but one that prepared her well for her future as a biologist.

My mother grew up with hardly any religious instruction. She also grew up without the instruction that mothers traditionally give their daughters about how to be a woman. But she knew the scientific method and honed her brilliant mind to be curious and question everything around her.

After receiving her doctorate, Mum began her career as a bacteriologist, developing eye-infection antibiotics at the University of Toronto, which was a cutting-edge field at the time. She then moved on to conducting research at Thistletown Hospital to look for evidence of a genetic basis for autism. In the 1960s, the medical establishment, including the renowned Hospital for Sick Children, blamed autism on what they called "refrigerator mothers" who were unable to establish a loving attachment with their children. This conclusion infuriated my mother, and she was determined to refute it.

The methods available at the time to establish genetic traits were rudimentary. Mum used blood analysis and fingerprint patterns to demonstrate that autistic children had a different genetic make-up. She included my sister and me in the control group, which always caused our father to tease, "How do we know they are normal?"

As I grew up, I came to realize how unusual my mother was and felt very proud of her. Few mothers in our neighbourhood went to work, and those who did certainly weren't biologists in a science laboratory. Mum later told me that she often felt guilty about going to work and leaving her daughters with caregivers for lunch and after school, but she stood by her conviction that one should pursue one's direction in life regardless of whether it fit the norms and expectations of the day.

My mother's research findings did show that there were genetic differences in autistic children, and her results were published in a scientific journal. She loved to tell the story of the day she went to the Hospital for Sick Children to present her report. On seeing my mother in the room, the head doctor demanded, "Who let *her* in here?" On that day, my mother's findings challenged the medical orthodoxy, causing an uproar. Mum liked a good controversy, especially when she knew she was right.

Holmes and Watson

In contrast to my ambitious and fearless mother, my father was a quiet man, absorbed in his work and barely engaged in the day-to-day life of our family. But early on, Dad and I formed a bond over a shared love of words and stories.

He perhaps found it hard to connect with young daughters and wrapped up our relationship in imaginary characters. Dad would call me Holmes and name himself Watson, and together we would solve everyday mysteries. ("By God, Holmes, we're out of milk! What do you make of it?") Dad and I read *The Silly Book* by Stoo Hample, and other nonsense stories, again and again, laughing over nothing and mostly relishing the fact that Mum and Sue didn't get it. When he travelled, he was more communicative in the illustrated letters he sent to me than he was in person when he was home.

Dad seldom gave me advice or involved himself in my life, but now and then he made a gesture that told me he loved me. When I had my tonsils out, for example, he drew a marvellous cartoon book, which I have still today. When I was older, he sent flowers on the opening night of a school play in which I had the leading role. He once attempted to help me with shyness by saying, "Man is a social animal." He perhaps felt he was providing the information necessary to solve the problem, even though it didn't help me deal with the cruelty of kids at school. Other than these occasional interventions, he left our upbringing to Mum, much to her endless frustration.

While my mother was drawn to medical research, my father was always happiest outdoors in nature. In my lifelong image of my dad, he is tramping through the woods, binoculars around his sunburned neck, carrying a small leather-and-canvas knapsack, which contained a note-book, stubby pencil, magnifying glass, laboratory jars for samples, and markers for writing on the jars. I still have most of those items today.

When we walked in the woods together, now and then he would stop to listen to a birdsong. The presence of that bird, and where it was, gave my father clues about the health of the whole forest. Or he would turn over a piece of rotting wood, and we would crouch down, staying very still to watch the community of insects and plants thriving in an apparently dead tree branch. This was Dad's way of seeing through a superficial view of the objective world and appreciating the whole ecosystem. He seldom talked about it, but I learned just by being there with him that a forest was an intricately connected organism, alive and evolving every moment. To Dad, the forest was a microcosm of the integrated nature of all things, including *Homo sapiens*.

Sometimes we waded in streams, collecting samples to look at under the microscope in Dad's biology lab, or bringing home tadpoles in a jar to watch them start to turn into frogs. I never did develop Dad's scientific interests, perhaps to his disappointment, but he gave me the gift of wonder and appreciation of nature. Because of him, the natural world is a place where I always feel completely at home.

Dad also passed on to me his atheist world view, which he had learned from his father. Back a few generations, the men on my father's side of the family were Church of England ministers in the Salisbury area of England. By the early 1800s, they were also missionaries in India. My great-grandfather grew up in India and stayed on to work for the East Indian Railway Company. His son, Jack, my grandfather, also grew up in India and was horrified by the cultural superiority of the English imposing Christianity on the Indian people whom he greatly admired. He left at a young age to go to boarding school in England. At seventeen, he left England and India behind and moved to Victoria, on Vancouver Island in Canada. It seemed to me that he ran as far from his parents' world as possible, stopped only by the Pacific Ocean. Had he gone further, he would have found himself approaching India from the other side.

Jack joined the Canadian armed forces and fought in the First World War. As a veteran, he received a tract of land from the government to establish a ranch near Vernon in the Okanogan Valley. By then he was married to Hilda, who would become my beloved grandmother. Jack ordered a house from Eaton's catalogue and assembled it with help from the neighbours. (The house is still standing today.) For decades my grandparents' daily life was an endless round of milking cows and delivering milk. One of their goals was to make sure that their children were educated and would not have to work on the farm.

Jack also made sure that his children—my father, David, and his younger brother, John—were raised to have nothing to do with the "blasted Christian church." The lesson was well inculcated. A generation later, I still feel an instinctive negative reaction to the Christian church and especially to missionary work, even though I have never known a missionary or a recipient of their efforts. My reticence to share what I have found of value in my life in spiritual teachings may stem, at least in part, from this family heritage.

While Jack wasn't an academic like my mother's father, he was a natural scientist in every respect. He was always identifying birds, collecting butterflies, and showing us insects and plants and was a keen fly fisherman. His affinity with nature was shared by my father, who knew from the time he was a boy that he would have a career in biology.

At the University of British Columbia, Dad became a student in Wilbur Clemens' biology class and started dating the professor's daughter. Mum and Dad went on to do their doctorates at the University of Toronto and married in 1947. My father began his career at the Ontario Department of Lands and Forests and then became a founding professor of York University, where he had a distinguished career in environmental science.

Somehow into this family, brimming with biologists and academics, was born a daughter who loved make-believe, stories, music, and ballet and had a natural affinity with the non-material realm. Years later I would tell my mother that I was "just there for variety."

Encounters with Religion

My parents' combined expertise could explain almost anything observable in nature, but that didn't help answer the question that had arisen ever since my experience on the beach: "Am I in the world, or is the world in me?" It also didn't explain why, when I gave my dolls a name, voice, and backstory, they seemed to become more lifelike. If they were made of atoms and molecules like I was, what was it about me that made me alive?

Most children in the 1960s were given answers to questions like these at church and Sunday school. I was aware that my family was different, and I adopted a child's view that we were more up to date than our church-going neighbours.

In 1961, according to Statistics Canada, 96 per cent of the Canadian population belonged to a religion. There were fifteen Christian religions listed on the census form, and the only other choices were "Jewish" and "All other religions." The census didn't even offer the option of "No religion." It was assumed that everyone had one. Even so, about 1 per cent of the population created their own category. I can picture my father doing this, adding "None" in his careful writing, and checking his own box.

I don't remember any argument against God because the topic never came up. Reading between the lines, I understood that God was a kind of hoax that people believed in until they became scientifically enlightened like my parents.

My father's atheist views were learned from his father and reinforced by his career as a biologist. The concept of God to my Dad would have been like a plug number in the equation of life. As soon as all the variables in the equation were known, we wouldn't need a plug called God anymore. To Dad, like other scientists of his generation, the observed world was not the work of a Creator or the evidence of a grand design, but the result of the survival of the fittest. Darwin's one-hundred-year-old theory of evolution, reinforced by more recent genetic research, was incompatible with the Biblical creation story. If all of creation can be explained by incremental adaptation from early life forms, humans do not "have dominion over" the birds, animals, and plants but are made of the same substance, derived from the same origin.

My father instilled in me the beauty of this unifying theory and, at the same time, its absence of inherent meaning. As his contemporary, Nobel Prize–winning scientist Francis Crick, famously put it, "You, your joys and your sorrows, your memories and ambitions, your sense of personal identity and free will, are in fact no more than the behavior of a vast assembly of nerve cells and their associated molecules."[2] This sentence now feels like a heartless, vacuous definition of life, but to people in the 1960s shaking off religious beliefs, perhaps it felt like a bracing blast of fresh air.

Crick's view was only the latest in a long line of scientific thought dating back to the Enlightenment. In 1748 the Scottish philosopher David Hume wrote: "If we take in our hand any volume of divinity or school metaphysics, for instance, let us ask, Does it contain any abstract reasoning concerning quantity or number? No. Does it contain any experimental reasoning concerning matter of fact and existence? No. Commit it then to the flames, for it can contain nothing but sophistry and illusion."[3]

This was the unspoken context at home when I was having moments of altered perception—experiences that I knew would never meet this test. No wonder I kept them to myself.

My father's views were influenced, as we all were, by the first images of Earth beamed back from space. Mankind woke up to a new perception of home with those first pictures in August 1966 of a small blue planet floating in space. Like a child leaving home for the first time, we experienced our planet as just one of many—an insignificant object that we needed to take care of in order to have a habitat in which to live. I was ten years old at the time and still remember the eye-opening experience of seeing the "blue marble" on which I lived.

For grown-ups, perhaps seeing Earth from the perspective of the moon made them feel part of a much larger universe and at the same time made human conflicts, and the industries that threatened our planet, look petty and small-minded. It was the moment that sparked the global environmental movement, which became the focus of my father's career. For others, it perhaps changed their perception of religion: What did it mean to be Christian versus any other religion in a vast universe of planets and stars? From a cosmic perspective, like everything else on Earth, it now looked like just "local culture."

The images of Earth from space perhaps brought mankind closer to a feeling of oneness. Yet we couldn't help but ask, Would this vast, unfeeling universe even notice if the entire human population disappeared? Our significance as a species seemed to further decrease. We were not only the random outcome of an evolutionary process but now also just a blip in a dumb, uncaring universe. I wondered and wondered, Is that really all I am? And if so, how am I able to think about this problem? Can a bit of random flesh floating in space do that? I found no answers to these questions.

My mother approached the question of Sunday school with the same pragmatic openness, curiosity, and experimentation she used throughout her life. She wanted her children to be exposed to all possibilities and make their own decisions. She also wanted us to be involved in the neighbourhood where most of our friends went to Sunday school. For a while, we went to St. George's United Church. My Dad would stand at the door as we were leaving on Sunday mornings and say, "Church is for the birds." My recollection of my brief time in Sunday school is mostly of confusion. Who were these people travelling on journeys, and where were they going? What is a Holy Spirit or an original sin? In my recollection, the United Church experiment was short lived, as was our membership at the First Unitarian Church. There, my mother found that the absence of any philosophical underpinning left her with only the adage to "be nice and do good deeds," which she found unsatisfying. Even though I had loved singing in the church choirs, I had no context for what I was learning in Sunday school and was glad to let it go when Mum stopped taking us to church.

I've since talked with many people about their childhood experience of church and Sunday school. My friend John Donald, a businessman who is not religious today, told me that Sunday school was the anchor of his childhood. "The outstanding feature of my childhood was perfect attendance at Sunday school. It was a supportive community; everyone was kind and friendly. It gave me an anchor of security in contrast to the dodgy world of the schoolyard, the vagaries of family life and academic achievement. Where do young people today go for that kind of foundation in their life?"

In the 1960s, going to places of worship gave children and adults alike a publicly sanctioned, respected place in which to acknowledge a spiritual basis of life and to learn a moral code. Whether or not those in the pews accepted all the beliefs associated with their religion, it was a time set aside every week when people turned their attention away from their personal life and focused on something they called divine. No doubt some people were also thinking about what to make for lunch or why their son hadn't phoned lately or whether they would get that promotion. But just being there was a tangible reminder to reflect on a higher purpose and meaning of life. It was an implicit acknowledgement that there is more to me than an intellect and a body, that life includes acknowledgement of God, mystery, and wonder, and love of my neighbour. Places of worship were also active communities based on these shared values. These well-developed institutions, with distribution systems into neighbourhoods across the country, were designed for offering spirituality to the "mass market" of worshippers.

Since the 1960s, these places of worship have seen a steady decline in attendance. Where will society turn in future to acknowledge being more than a body and a rational mind? Instead of church, what is a new context in which to have this conversation, to openly acknowledge—or even question—the existence of anything beyond the physical and mental realms?

Parents to whom I've spoken in doing research for this book face the same dilemma that my mother had in the 1960s: how do I instill in my children enduring principles and values without indoctrinating them in a religion? This urgent question remains unanswered, not just for children but also for adults who seek a foundation rooted in philosophical enquiry rather than a religious belief system.

When I was a child, with or without church, Christian morals and values were all around me. Every day at school we said the Lord's Prayer. Girl Guides taught me to "help other people every day especially those at home." My family was like any other in Canada, in that we lived by a moral code that reflected religious values.

We have perhaps underestimated the effect of becoming a non-religious country, with no replacement to provide a moral foundation for society. We are seeing today the fragility, uncertainty, and fear many are feeling in the face of the pandemic, climate change, and global unrest. There is a tendency to lash out at individuals and organizations in an effort to exert force and regain control. Later in the book we will explore how philosophical attainment, which can seem so abstract in the face of "real-world problems," can actually be the most practical of solutions for individuals and nations.

Perhaps in part due to my shaky start in churchgoing, over the course of my life I have never found my place in institutional religion, although I have come to respect deeply the wisdom underlying all religious traditions. I'm grateful to have grown up without being indoctrinated into a belief system (other than mid-twentieth-century science). However, I had no grounding for the questions I was asking, or for what I would now call mystical experiences. There was nothing I learned from my parents or from my superficial understanding of religion that explained what happened on the beach or on the balcony in Massey Hall. I continued to question the nature of me and my world but still hadn't found any answers that were satisfying.

Blossoming

WHEN I WAS TEN YEARS OLD, my life changed. My father became the first biology professor at the brand-new York University, and in addition to being one of thirteen founding professors, he was appointed master of Vanier College. This appointment required that our family live at the new campus on the outskirts of Toronto, which at the time seemed to be in the middle of nowhere, surrounded by fields and industrial buildings. Mum worried about a repeat of her lonely childhood at the Pacific Biological Station, but I was excited about this adventure. Our new home was a beautiful log house nestled in a woodlot, on a campus still under construction and surrounded by windswept fields. I was beginning grade six, and the move gave me a fresh start in a new school. The four years of living on the York campus were happy ones for me.

Shortly before the move, Dad came home from a press conference announcing plans for the new university, looking very pleased. A reporter had asked the incoming president, Murray Ross, what religious affiliation York University would adopt. Dr. Ross, having never thought about it before, replied, "None." His answer apparently surprised the reporter and offended some advocates for the new university. At the time, most universities in Ontario were affiliated with a religion. However, the president persevered, and York University became an institution without any religious ties.

It is hard to imagine today just how much one's religious beliefs, or lack of them, mattered in Canada in the 1960s. The church, the school, and even the hospital you went to was a public statement of identity. Whether as an institution or an individual, not being affiliated with a church required an explanation. In my case, saying "My parents are biologists" seemed to explain everything.

Not being affiliated with a religion gave York University the freedom to teach the subject of religion from a non-denominational, and sometimes radical, perspective. I've since met former students who had benefited from York's openness in the religious studies department, as well as in other faculties. The late 1960s was a time when many people believed there must be better ways to do things, and new ways of living. The new university took full advantage of this trend.

The spirit of newness and adventure spread to other levels of education as well. In grades eight and nine I attended Jane Junior High, a new experimental, "child-centred learning" school. I brought home report cards informing my parents that I had "blossomed." Despite the teasing this produced, everyone acknowledged that I was finally coming out of my shell. I was concertmaster in the school orchestra, excelled academically, and had the lead in the school play. I had come into my own as a performer and had discovered that I lost all shyness and feeling of being self-conscious when I was on the stage. This was a remarkable discovery, one that drew me to performing in plays throughout my high school years.

At Jane, we had no classrooms, few regular classes, no set textbooks, and no required courses. We worked with teachers to develop individual learning programs based on our needs and interests. I was energized by making choices and decisions about my education, while my parents made sure that subjects such as science, mathematics, and French stayed in the program—otherwise I might have only read books, played musical instruments, and acted in plays. Although the arts was an easy choice, selecting what part of history to learn or which books to read was an impossible task for a twelve-year-old child. Just like at home, I felt the freedom of making my own choices but without a clear foundation on which to do this.

I realized, many years after we moved away from the campus, how living at York University had drastically compromised my mother's career. She had become our chauffeur and social convener, making it impossible for her to continue to work downtown. After bridging the gap as best she could for four years, she made sure that we moved to the growing village of Thornhill on the outskirts of Toronto as soon as my father's term ended as master of Vanier College.

No doubt there had been tension between my parents about the move to York University. My mother's acceptance of her role to raise the children and give priority to my father's career must have caused resentment. But we never talked about these things as a family. In fact, there was very little communication about subjects like love, relationships, and commitments to one another.

I never doubted that my parents loved me, but they never mentioned it. Love seemed to be part of a messy human world they preferred to avoid. I noticed that the family dog received most of the physical affection.

The depth of my parents' reticence to express love became clear to me many years later on the porch of my uncle's home in Nanaimo. My mother and her brother, Alvin, hadn't seen each other for decades, and it was now late in their lives. They just stood there, two small people gazing into each other's eyes, their bodies almost quivering with excitement and happiness. Yet they couldn't bring themselves to actually embrace. My aunt Florence finally came to the rescue, warmly welcoming us into the house and putting on the kettle for tea.

When I think back to my father's biology lab at York University, it too feels like a place comfortably secure in knowing that subjects involving love, personal relationships, mental health, philosophy, or religion were located in other buildings on other parts of the campus. The long black counters in the antiseptic laboratories, with the whiff of formaldehyde, was a place to hide from the unpredictable realm of people and feelings. I grew up in that world, one that barely acknowledged, let alone celebrated, aspects of being that couldn't be measured or found in a test tube. Where or what is love, in this world view? The organized, classified world of science didn't admit such intrusions.

The repression of feeling that seemed to go with a materialist world view was perhaps a side effect of trying to find meaning and purpose only in physical laws. The entire realm of invisible, subjective experience was missing, and with it, any acknowledgement of a source of life other than what could be found in the material world.

New Perspectives

WHEN I STARTED HIGH SCHOOL in the early 1970s, it wasn't hard to concentrate on getting my homework done. My whole family was doing homework every night. My sister and I were doing school assignments. Mum had become a high school science teacher, and she and Dad were both marking papers. One day my father picked up my science textbook and looked at the chapter on atoms and molecules. He dropped the book on the table and said, "They are teaching this subject as though these are objects. Atoms and molecules are a way of explaining behaviour; no one has ever seen one." The distinction was a mind-opening revelation to a young teenager who thought textbooks were always right. It was also a brilliant one-minute science lesson that increased my respect for my father.

Occasionally, when doing science homework, I made the mistake of asking my father a question. Forty-five minutes and half-a-dozen reference books later, I would be pleading that I only had a few lines to fill in and another ten questions yet to go on the assignment. My father was having none of that kind of superficial education. If I wanted to know something, I had to go all the way. He would do anything but just tell me the answer. To survive, I learned to ask my mother these questions; she was equally knowledgeable and as a high school teacher she understood the exigencies of a student's time.

Throughout high school I continued with piano lessons and performed in numerous musicals at school, at an arts summer camp, and in a local amateur theatre group. Nevertheless, I decided that I didn't have the talent or confidence to become a professional artist. Yet I always felt a thrill walking into a theatre and thought that it would be a wonderful place in which to work every day as an arts administrator. I also considered a career in broadcast journalism. CBC Radio was always on at our house, and broadcaster Barbara Frum was a hero to me, doing her job as my mother did, without drawing attention to her gender.

During my high school years my father went to Europe for the first time to attend an international science conference. It was an eye-opening experience for him, and he came home determined that his daughters would not wait until their forties to make this journey.

My first opportunity came almost immediately: a trip to Italy in grade ten. Dad was right—the ancient city of Rome opened up new perspectives for a Canadian girl. In particular, the cathedrals and the Vatican with its painted ceiling caused me to wonder about the people who had dedicated their lives to conceiving and constructing these huge sacred places, and painting, worshipping, and making music there.

My mother was one of the parents on our school trip. One day an Italian asked my mother, in all seriousness, if he could marry me. Mum called Dad and asked if he thought this was a good idea, or if I was perhaps a bit young at the age of fourteen. After that, whenever things got difficult during my teenage years, one of my parents would wonder aloud if they had made the right choice: perhaps they should have accepted the offer.

A second opportunity to go to Europe appeared the following summer, to travel with my friend Diana. Her family had immigrated to Canada from Holland and brought with them traditions and Christian religious beliefs that went back generations. The relatives in Holland wanted to meet the daughter who was growing up in Canada. I was happy to go with her, and not just for the chance to see Europe again. Diana and I had frequent conversations about atheism versus religion that always stimulated new ideas for me.

I was still questioning the nature of life and wondering about the word God. It puzzled me, in studying great civilizations in history class, that some form of acknowledgement of a source or power beyond the material world always played a central role. Similarly, many popular movies, cartoons, and books—and even Santa Claus—featured realms and beings that were outside the confines of the three-dimensional world. Where did this impulse come from and why was it so universally expressed? My father would have said that people had a need to explain their world and, in the absence of facts, they made things up. But almost all cultures throughout history seemed to make up essentially the same thing: a higher realm, not subject to the limits of time and space. I was curious about the source and reliability of this universal impulse. Perhaps the people who put forward these ideas had had experiences similar to mine.

Outside of the many arts programs, I was quite passive in my teenage years, as though what happened in the three dimensions didn't really matter. I knew it wasn't as real as it seemed to be, and had convinced myself that it was therefore inconsequential. I continued to hide anything that smacked of spirituality and left these considerations unexpressed. It seemed to me that that was okay because those experiences were not in the external world anyway. As a result, within myself I had one realm of experience as I continued to enquire deeply about the nature of reality, and with my family and at school I acted out a different realm. This split had become normal for me, and I seldom even thought about it.

In high school I learned about symbolism, which added to my theories for answering the question "Am I in the world, or is the world in me?" Perhaps the whole world is symbolic, and we are the translators. Maybe it isn't really substantial in itself at all; it just symbolizes something else. More speculation, with not much to go on. I don't think I even tried explaining this one to Diana.

Diana was sometimes annoyed at my lack of understanding and respect for religion, but I could tell she was as interested as I was in debating the subject. I would say, "God doesn't speak English, you know. He's not a person like you. When you pray to Him in English, what makes you think your message gets through?" She would quote from the Bible and talk about the Word of God and try to explain prayer to me. One day, walking home from school, I inadvertently said out loud, "If religion isn't real, why do people all over the world feel inclined to go to church?" To which she replied, "Well, that proves it! Religion is real." We never felt the need to convince each other, perhaps because we both knew that our opinions were due to our upbringing and that we hadn't yet arrived at an independent point of view.

For me, however, neither religion nor science provided the answers I was looking for. The archetypal stories of Christianity that I had assimilated only on a superficial level seemed preposterous: that Jesus rose from the dead, that he died for our sins, that Mary was a virgin, and that, after we die, we go to a place called Heaven which is where God is. None of it seemed remotely plausible to me. I was aware that there must be a deeper significance to these stories, but with a teenager's assurance I dismissed them as outdated and irrelevant.

In addition, my parents' scientific view also seemed incredulous: that the realm of intelligence, awareness, and love, and the ability to observe my body aging in time and moving around in space, were actually all in the circuitry of the brain in my head, which itself was aging and moving in space. Furthermore, if we were just decaying pieces of matter, wouldn't we feel comfortable and accepting of death? The proposition that life, my life, was just a random accident of molecules in a physical universe that could have just as easily not produced life at all, made no sense to me.

Meanwhile mystical experiences continued to appear unbidden from time to time, reinforcing an innate knowing that "this" is not all there is. For example, I sometimes felt a presence at the foot of my bed at night. It was never frightening, even though my mind thought it should be. It felt comforting and calm.

Between the scientific world of my parents and my vague notions of Christianity, I found nothing that accounted for my actual experience or satisfied my growing list of questions. Surely, somewhere there were people who questioned life in the way I did, people who also had experiences that couldn't be explained in logical terms. For now, Diana was the only one on the receiving end of my enquiry.

In the summer of 1972 Diana and I embarked on a month-long trip to Europe. To balance out weeks of visiting Dutch relatives, my father arranged for us to stay with his cousin, John Sawtell (another scientist), who lived just outside Oxford in England. At fifteen, we were a bit younger and more cautious than the surge of backpackers with their sewn-on Canadian flags heading off to explore Europe. Nevertheless, it was an eye-opening trip.

While staying at the home of Diana's grandmother in Holland, I was fascinated to be in a family where socializing—just sitting around talking to each other—was the priority. It occurred to me that my family was perhaps the outlier. These people were deeply connected and didn't hesitate to express love for one another, whereas at my house we were always focused on doing something productive and tended to avoid messy human contact. Watching Diana and her cousins constantly being told what to do, what was right and wrong, and what to believe, I noticed that it gave them a confidence and certainty about life that I didn't have. According to my trip diary, I eventually dismissed all this in favour of my family's world view that everything is relative and one needs to make one's own choices.

After three weeks in Holland and a week in London with my relatives, we returned home to Canada. My diary concludes: "I'm getting used to being sociable but I still don't enjoy it." A sentence I could as easily write today.

Watching Europe's international travellers, many of whom were just a few years older than I was, was the beginning of opening my eyes to possibilities other than choosing between science or religion. The hippie movement was morphing into the New Age movement with its spiritual imagery and language. The countercultural activism of the 1960s with its message of "tune in and drop out" was being replaced by the "feel-good" vibe of the 1970s. The musicals *Godspell* and *Jesus Christ Superstar* appeared in 1973, presenting spiritual themes in a new way. I went to them more than once, soaking it in, looking for new perspectives and, possibly, answers.

The social transformation of the human potential movement was underway, changing organizations and shifting power to the individual. Religious institutions were losing adherents and moral authority, while new, trail-blazing leaders and authors were gaining prominence. A blend of psychology, personal development, and spirituality was emerging that combined personal actualization with spiritual attainment. Although this movement remained on the fringes in a long gestation period, these were the seeds of the rapid growth in spirituality outside religion that we are seeing today.

With the rapid decline in the attendance and authority of religious institutions, the magnitude of the change seemed to imply a deep shift, one that couldn't be easily explained by church scandals or changing attitudes. Some people, including my parents, believed that the decline in religion was making way for a purely secular society firmly based on science. But that didn't appear to be happening either. Something new was taking shape that incorporated science but pointed beyond its traditional scope.

Meanwhile my conviction that there is no right or wrong, that everything was wishy-washy and relative, was about to be challenged as I returned to Thornlea Secondary School in September. Like Jane Junior High, Thornlea was a free school with lots of scope for a creative education. This time I found it not in the arts programs but in English class with Mr. McGrath.

English Class with Mr. McGrath

I LEARNED to sit near the back in Terry McGrath's grade-ten English class, hoping his bright, penetrating eyes wouldn't land on me when he turned from the chalkboard to pose yet another impossible question: "What's the difference between classical music and pop music?" This time Terry didn't wait for an answer; he covered the entire blackboard with two words: "IT LASTS." With this as introduction, he played a portion of Richard Strauss' *Salome*. Learning about the music, the storyline, and the concept of leitmotif somehow became English literature, the intended subject of the class. Terry would quote, "All arts aspire to the condition of music," and then challenge us to explain why this was so.

I barely hung on through my first term with Terry, by turns fascinated and frightened by this brilliant, mercurial teacher. English had always been my favorite subject at school, but it had never been taught like this before.

We studied Mozart's fortieth symphony, read books by R. D. Laing, Allen Ginsberg, and other authors, ancient and contemporary, whose work was far outside the standard curriculum. Decades later I caught up on *To Kill a Mockingbird* and *The Catcher in the Rye*, books that everyone else had read in high school.

Terry wore, in effect, a school uniform. From September to June he wore Birkenstock sandals with white socks, blue jeans, and a black, baggy, crewneck sweater over a white T-shirt, giving the effect of a clerical collar. With his long hair and casual appearance, he was very popular with the cool kids in the school.

Being on the receiving end of Terry's intense classroom questioning was made easier by his genuine love of words and music. He wanted to know the answers as much as we did. He took us along for the ride, but his main sparring partner seemed to be the English language itself. He would review a passage in a book we were reading and then look up the Greek and Latin roots of the words. Suddenly the meaning was illuminated in a whole new way. Terry's excitement was infectious, and we all found a new appreciation of what we were reading. I soon bought an etymological dictionary and was doing the same at home.

Most of the time, I found the performance that was Terry's English class stimulating and entertaining. Occasionally he was fierce and unreasonable, even mean. He would say, "Anyone who can't identify this piece of music will fail the course," and try to enforce his threat. Sometimes he seemed to sink into a low mood, and even Mozart couldn't rouse him back to his lively self. Nevertheless, I would not have traded the wild, unpredictable ride with Terry for the pedestrian English literature class going on across the hall.

Thornlea Secondary was a school that didn't grade students other than "fail," "pass," or "honours." The report cards were primarily designed for the teachers to write notes about the student's performance. My first term in Terry's class earned me a passing grade and three words: "Who are you?" I was mortified that after a whole term Terry didn't know who I was. I was also surprised that if he really didn't, he would admit this on a report card. I even wondered if he was posing a philosophical question. My parents were alarmed: English had always been my best subject, and as academics they read my report cards carefully. I worried they might want to meet with Terry McGrath, which, in my teenage opinion, would make matters worse. They would never understand this brilliant and inspiring English teacher.

In fact, it was the difference between my parents and Terry that made the class so attractive to me. He opened up a whole world I didn't know existed. For the first time, I had a model of someone living in a world of philosophical enquiry and artistic expression, someone who drew on more than just intellectual learning.

Despite the less-than-encouraging start to my first term in Terry McGrath's English class, I continued to sign up for his class every term until I graduated. By then I knew what to expect, and Terry definitely knew me. (And he knew that my parents were academics who read my report cards.) I was one of the quiet, unhip kids in the school, but he recognized that I shared his love of ideas, words, and music. Now I was sitting at the front of the classroom.

Terry made every other adult—and my own life—seem dull by comparison. I didn't know it was possible to colour so far outside the lines. His unusual presence paved the way for more to come.

At the beginning of grade thirteen Terry shocked our class by walking into the room wearing a suit and tie—and shoes. His hair was cut, and he looked very professional. He announced that we were to address him as "Mr. McGrath." We were used to Terry's changeable nature, but this was something new. Some of the boys tried to mock him back to his former familiar relationship with them, but he was firmly in a new place. As far as I can recall, he never provided any explanation to the class for his sudden transformation. It was obvious he was happier, more relaxed, and more comfortable in his interactions with us.

As the fall term continued, we realized that in many ways we had a new English teacher. Terry's behaviour had stabilized; every day he was articulate, energetic, and emotionally balanced. He was attentive to individual students and had a sparkle about him that we hadn't seen before. I could talk with him and feel his genuine interest—in me as well as in the subject. He laughed easily and seemed much less intense about things that used to set him off. His standards and expectations were higher than ever, and his language was different. Today I would say that his presence exuded love, although in high school the word *love* had a different meaning that none of us would have associated with Mr. McGrath.

In our graduating year each student met with a school guidance counsellor, Colin Morrison, who advised us on post-secondary education and career plans. Colin was an excellent listener. Despite being constantly confronted with a parade of teenage angst and hormones, he was unflappable, kind, and unfailingly polite—a rock at the centre of the storm. When I first met with him, I asked him how he was able to be so stable and calm. He paused and then said, "I have a teacher." The world stopped for a moment. Not knowing what else to say, I asked, "What's his name?" "Kenneth Mills."

A thought appeared: *This is what I've been waiting for all my life.* As an anxious teenager who over-thought everything, I was surprised by my certainty. Furthermore, I had never been aware of waiting for anything. Later, my mind tried to dismiss my response as irrational. Mills is a common enough name. What's the big deal? But something more urgent pushed these thoughts aside.

I went back to see Colin to find out more. It turned out that Kenneth Mills was a piano teacher who lived in Willowdale, a few blocks south of my home in Thornhill. He was also a philosopher who gave a lecture every weekend at one of the hotels in Toronto. "What does he talk about?" I asked Colin.

"He talks about the fact that we are unlimited as the love that we truly are." That didn't mean much to me, but the effect on Colin was obvious.

Then I guessed, and Colin confirmed, that Kenneth Mills had recently become Terry McGrath's teacher and was the source of his sudden transformation. Now I was really intrigued. I had gone to see Colin to discuss university, but now the education that interested me was whatever was at the source of these transformations. Terry and Colin were reticent to discuss the subject because of their role as teachers in the public school system. However, the beneficial effect of their study with Kenneth Mills on their work with students was self-evident.

I asked Mr. McGrath how I could go to one of the lectures. He responded that if that was something I wanted to do, nothing in the universe could stop me. Colin was more helpful. When I told him I wanted to attend a lecture, he quietly gave me Kenneth Mills' phone number. When I called, the person who answered the phone told me that Dr. Mills was in New York and the next lecture in Toronto would take place on March 24, a few weeks' away. My family was going to Paradise Island in Nassau for the school break that week, and so I arranged to come to the lecture in the following week.

Mr. McGrath's response to this arrangement was, "Why would anyone go to Paradise Island when they have the chance to hear Kenneth Mills?" What a strange comment. Why would anyone give up a fabulous trip to Paradise Island in order to attend a lecture that apparently happened practically every week? But his provocative words have stayed with me to this day.

I did go to Paradise Island, my family's first and only Caribbean vacation. Even though we were supposedly "in Paradise," I had nightmares every night and couldn't enjoy the days. My whole inner world seemed to be turned upside down, and every possible emotion was coming to the surface. I didn't tell my family about my plan to attend the lecture, or about the nightmares. This was my own experience, and it was the beginning of moving in a new direction that was entirely my own.

II

THE JOY OF BEING

In the effulgence of Being Consciousness,
unconfined by thoughts of being mortal,
I find no shadow to dance with me,
but only the joy of Being at one
with the burst of the sun upon the mountains within sight.

KENNETH G. MILLS

At My First Unfoldment

I BORROWED MY PARENTS' CAR and drove downtown to Toronto's elegant Hyatt Regency Hotel. It was a quiet Sunday evening in March of 1974, except on the second floor of the hotel where hundreds of people were gathering in a ballroom.

At the registration desk, I learned a little more about Kenneth Mills' lectures, or Unfoldments,™ as he called them.* I agreed to attend a rehearing class to listen to a recording of the spontaneous lecture that Dr. Mills would give that evening. They confirmed that I was eighteen (as of a few weeks before), which was the minimum age to attend an Unfoldment without written parental permission. Payment was optional.

I was ushered into the room. There were hundreds of people sitting in silence in rows of chairs facing an empty podium. Their attention was focused, but nothing was happening. To a high school student, it was a remarkable sight. I had entered a different world. I selected a seat and tried unsuccessfully to relax into the group's quiet, meditative state. We sat there for what felt like an eternity, probably ten or fifteen minutes. Suddenly the door opened and Kenneth Mills came in with the purposeful stride of a seasoned concert artist walking onto the stage.

Dr. Mills was elegantly dressed in a suit and tie and seemed to be about the age of my parents. He looked around the room, greeted a few people, and swung the microphone in front of him. He sat quietly for a few moments, his eyes gazing down, then raised his head and began to speak. After a few opening comments about flowers, Dr. Mills launched into spontaneous rhythmic and rhyming poetry, which continued almost uninterrupted for the next thirty minutes. In the poem he described his recent trip to New York. The story seemed allegorical, apparently pointing to some larger philosophical truths. I couldn't follow most of what I heard, but strangely enough, that observation didn't concern me. The setting and language were foreign, but something about the Unfoldment was familiar. It felt like home.

---

* See the appendix for an introduction to Kenneth G. Mills.

As I listened to Kenneth Mills that first time, I was not thinking, "Do I agree with this?" or, "Does this fit with my beliefs?" I was thinking, "Oh, he mentioned God. Perhaps God does exist." "So this is what it's going to be, listening to these poetic lectures. I like this." I was an intellectual teenager who thrived on debate and analytical thinking and was surprised by my own response. I had been raised on the scientific method. But with the dawning of a heart response, all of that rational logic suddenly seemed irrelevant.

After the formal lecture Dr. Mills opened the floor to questions. His responses were as eloquent and poetic as the formal lecture and obviously spontaneous. How was this possible? And how was it possible that I had been so moved, just sitting there listening to something that intellectually I didn't even understand? This man seemed to be able to put into words what had been for me inchoate feelings and impressions. I had no context from my background for understanding what Dr. Mills was saying, but it felt like my own heart was speaking, even though, to my mind, phrases like "harmonic state of Being beyond the mind" sounded like fantasy.

I couldn't deny a deep recognition, and that guided me, regardless of what my mind was thinking. Despite the unfamiliarity of the setting and the language, somehow I knew that I had found my tribe. The questions that had occupied my mind for years seemed less daunting, and even secondary to what I was now discovering.

This profound experience of intuitive knowingness, distinct from thinking something out and coming to a conclusion, had begun when I first heard Kenneth Mills' name in Colin Morrison's office. In description now, this kind of certitude can sound like being taken in by someone. In experience, it was and is the opposite. It comes from an inner impelling that is free from the influence of anyone's judgement or thoughts about it, including my own. Uncovering this faculty of intuitive knowing felt somewhat destabilizing at first, and yet it was undeniable and a powerful force of calm conviction.

A few days later I went to a house in Willowdale (a suburb of Toronto) and picked up a verbatim transcript of the lecture. Paging through it, I could hardly believe that the many pages of rhythmic and rhyming poetry had been given spontaneously, but I knew it was true because I had been there. Years later I learned of the oral tradition of spontaneous poetry and prose that has appeared at rare moments through the ages, most famously with Rumi. It seemed I had encountered a modern-day expression of the tradition, this time in the Western world.

I looked through the transcript for passages in which Dr. Mills spoke about God, the word that had attracted and repelled me all my life. The concept of acknowledging God seemed old-fashioned to my mind. Wasn't this a new, forward-looking philosophy not based on religion? I found a reference to God as "Father-Mother," which felt even worse. At eighteen I was ready to leave parents behind. Now I was being told that I had other parents that I didn't know existed. What did it mean to be the child of *Father-Mother*, capitalized? In my conception of me and my world, I was firmly at the centre and possibly even the source of this picture. I didn't want to know that I wasn't in charge. Despite these thoughts, I was deeply drawn to the concept of God. It was obvious that I was going to have to grapple seriously with this to continue to attend the lectures.

Later that week, at a rehearing class (gatherings in small groups to listen to and discuss an Unfoldment), we learned that Kenneth Mills equated the word *God* with many synonyms, including Mind, Love, Consciousness, Self, and Principle.* These words had no preconceived thought associations with God in my imagination. Dr. Mills apparently preferred the word *Principle* "because you can't dress it up in the likes of you." His use of *I* was also explained. We were told that the *I* or *I AM* in his lectures referred to the infinite, the eternal, the unchanging. According to Dr. Mills, the I AM is our true identity,† what we really are.

---

* Mary Baker Eddy, the founder of Christian Science, identified in her work seven synonyms of God: Mind, Spirit, Soul, Principle, Truth, Life, and Love.
† In this book I have adopted the capitalization used by Kenneth Mills in his Unfoldments and have capitalized words that point to an unchanging Reality beyond the mind.

When I first went to a rehearing class, I assumed that acknowledge-ment of God was natural to the majority of listeners because they would have grown up in Sunday school, church, or temple. Dr. Mills' use of Biblical language and imagery was a bridge from their heritage and from Dr. Mills' heritage to his message today. It seemed to me that they must have an advantage in understanding what they were hearing. It was all new to me, both the Christian references and the Unfoldment. But Kenneth Mills' use of the word *God*, and his inter-pretation of the Bible, challenged equally those with religious beliefs and those without. He claimed for one and all the statement of Jesus, "I and my Father are One," changing it to "I and my Father *is* One now and not 'shall be.'" This non-dual standpoint, expressed in the words of Jesus, was provocative to those for whom this statement applied only to Jesus.

Gradually, after attending several Unfoldments and rehearing classes, I came to understand the essence of Kenneth Mills' message in non-religious language: Man's true nature is conscious-awareness Being, inseparable from the source, Consciousness. We are not limited to the body-mind we seem to be. As he put it, "You are not a human being; you are Being, appearing human." In this language, his words exactly matched my experience of standing on the beach years before.

Kenneth Mills not only talked about this beingness; his very pres-ence exuded a rarified state of Being. When giving the Unfoldment, he seemed to be simultaneously beyond the visible world and acutely observant of every detail in it. He was not in trance and yet had an elevated awareness that I had never known was possible.

Coming away from my first Unfoldment, and the many that fol-lowed, I too was in an elevated, altered state. The sky pulsed, the clouds seemed to breathe, and the whole world was vibrant and more colour-ful. My body felt lighter, more alive, and only after my facial muscles started to tire did I realize that I had been smiling for hours. Most of all I felt a new calmness, a relaxation, a feeling of home. Listening to Dr. Mills stirred a curiosity and yearning to know more about this inner home and how it was furnished in the realm that I was now conceiving beyond the intellectual decor of logic. A place within myself that had been silent and unformed was now awakening. It felt like I was coming alive. The thirst to be around Dr. Mills and hear the Unfoldments wasn't about handing myself over to someone else and being in his thrall. As he often said, "Everything you see in me is all within yourself." I was starting to build a foundation in my own experience that I could stand on and be whole.

Naturally my parents were curious about what I was into. We were an uncommunicative family, and this topic was particularly sensitive. When I would return home from a lecture, Mum or Dad would ask, "What did he talk about?" A simple enough question, but one that I found impossible to answer. I would make an attempt to explain the Unfoldment, but it always came out garbled and sounding like I was avoiding the question.

Some of the people attending the Unfoldments at that time promoted the view that what we were learning was so radical that we had to be very selective in whom we spoke to about it and what was disclosed. This was nonsense, especially for a teenager living at home with worried parents, but I didn't know that. Dr. Mills himself was a distant figure, not someone I would actually speak to, especially about anything as prosaic as dealing with parents.

Sometime later, when I did have a conversation with Dr. Mills, he was very interested in my parents and even offered these words to say to them: "You empathize with the natural world outside yourself, while I empathize with the natural world within my own Selfhood. You look without with eyes open, and I look within with eyes shut to see from whence comes the Light of sight."[4]

I never did say these words to my parents. The pattern of non-communication about Dr. Mills had already been established, and besides, I couldn't imagine myself uttering such sentences. Looking back, it's unfortunate that someone didn't help me translate Dr. Mills' words into language that was natural to me, that I could actually say to my parents. It might have been a first step in breaking the communication logjam. His statement captured in an elegant and poetic way the essence of the difference in my parents' perspective and what I was learning from Dr. Mills. To Kenneth Mills, no further explanation or translation was needed; he saw me ready to receive these words and to say them, whether I intellectually understood them or not. However, I was far from being willing and able to do this, and as a result, statements like these remained in a kind of catatonic state for years.

My parents allowed me to attend the Unfoldment without interference. Whether it was trust or a conviction that an eighteen-year-old needs to figure things out for herself, they never said anything disparaging to me about it, and as far as I know, they didn't even investigate this man or ask to meet him. While this gave me the freedom to follow my own impelling, without their endorsement or involvement I was, as always, fearful of fracturing the bond with my family.

Those early attempts to speak with my parents about what I was doing were the first steps in trying to explain to a not-understanding world the attraction and fulfillment of studying with Kenneth Mills. This became a lifelong challenge as I immersed myself in something that was so natural to me that it needed no explanation, and yet it seemed to be opaque to others. From the outside, it might look like a cult or a waste of time or simply repetitive to continually attend lectures by only one speaker, but in the experience it was an unfolding, it was growth, it was releasement, and it was fun.

The 1970s when I met Dr. Mills was a time rife with speculation about cults. Spiritual teachers outside of established religions were appearing, some with behaviours that raised public concern. Dr. Mills was tarred with the same brush, which led to a few of his students' meeting with a government commission, which quickly determined that his students were not being mesmerized. But reputational damage had been done. Years later, during an interview for a film about his life, Dr. Mills was asked about his experience of being labelled a cult leader. He said:

> Today's world seems to be very much in stress, and there is a need to search for a meaning higher than the habitual that evolves from everyday experience. Many start the search, but almost with trepidation and fear because there are so many people speaking about spirituality today. When there is

power and force present in the appearance of an individual, the fear that people sometimes encounter is dealt with by labelling that individual and calling him a cult leader—which, understandably, terrifies everyone.

The followers of a cult leader are those who seem to be mesmerized, whereas the path of the Higher Way asks each one to consider deeply the basis of their belief and the basis of their identity. This involves the willingness to find that Point that is unchangeable, and then living and moving from that realization.

I have been called a cult leader, and unfortunately the name brings such fear with it. It has been something that has really marred my life and its offering of nearly thirty years. It should be noted that anyone who comes to hear me speak has asked to come. I have never asked or advertised for anyone to be part of my lectureship. The reason people gather is because like attracts like.

The mark of my work is to release in the individuals their own worth by correct identity. That identity is not achieved by me telling them anything; it is achieved by them being willing to associate their thoughts with something they might term perfect, something called God, the Source, the Self, or Principle. It is this Principle upon which man bases his life, and this is what has been offered in my lectureship during the past thirty years.[5]

Releasement of my own worth by correct identity was the mark of my experience with Dr. Mills. Furthermore, not once in the thirty years that I knew him was there an encounter that was other than proper, gracious, focused on the purpose of the visit, and completely without sexual innuendo. I recall a phone call with him in the 1990s when I proposed flying to the Caribbean where he was staying, to meet with him to discuss a project he was doing. The idea was natural to me, since as a consultant at that time I often flew to other cities to meet with clients, but he was appalled that I thought I would just come down alone to see him. What would people think? We did the meetings by phone, and I didn't get a holiday in the sun.

Unlike most spiritual teachers of the 1970s, Dr. Mills lived a formal, disciplined life. This was all new to me, and the opposite to my upbringing. He loved elegance and beauty, having grown up in very modest circumstances and then been taken as a young man under the wing of Guy Murchie, a wealthy American who lived an almost Edwardian lifestyle. Kenneth Mills had found that adopting elegance was transforming, and he saw it as an expression of the abundant nature of life itself as expressed in the Biblical statement "All that I have is thine." However, like most academics, my parents viewed dressing-up as superficial and self-indulgent, the opposite of a serious philosophical pursuit. But I had seen the change in Mr. McGrath and how his decision to dress professionally helped him maintain emotional stability and balance.

I said to my mother, "If you found a scientist whose field of research was exactly your interest and they had achieved a remarkable breakthrough at the cutting edge of the field, you wouldn't stop to worry about whether you liked them or agreed with their lifestyle choices. You would want to work in their lab. I may not be comfortable with Dr. Mills' mode of dress and living, but that makes no difference to the value I gain from studying with him." She understood.

I also asked my mother if she believed in God. She replied that she was a sun worshipper. At the time, I was frustrated that she took my serious question so lightly. However, a conversation with Dr. Mills much later in my life caused me to admit that perhaps she wasn't so far off, after all.

In my final year of high school, it was time to choose a university. Up to this point my family and I had assumed I would go away to university and had considered several Canadian and international options. Now, for me, there was no possibility I would leave Toronto. The choice of university was secondary to studying with Kenneth Mills. My poor parents! University was the happiest time of their lives, and my father had dedicated his career to building a university. I eventually chose York University over the University of Toronto because of the arts administration courses, and so I went to the "family university" and obtained a degree in English and in arts administration.

While I tried to share my parents' love of academia, I found studying English literature at university very dull in contrast to studying with Dr. Mills. One meant analyzing on paper something written in the past, and the other was alive and direct, an outpouring of spontaneous wisdom. To me, Kenneth Mills was in presence what a university could only talk about.

Meeting Kenneth Mills at the age of eighteen forever changed my relationship with my parents, pulling us apart and yet giving me the opportunity to find my own way and finally take a stand for my own convictions. It required me to introduce into the family dynamic the most difficult subject, religion and spirituality, as well as another unspoken one, love. This led to a moment in my teenage bedroom with my mother in which I asked her the most urgent of questions: "If I become philosophical, will you still love me?" I don't recall her answer; it was probably a mother's instinctive "Yes, of course." She didn't say, "Let's sit down and have a good talk about what you're learning, and why it means so much to you, and how I can support you in this new interest." As always, I felt both respected in my freedom to make my own choices, and a bit at sea.

My question had been heard, however, and Mum soon showed her support in a tangible way. I had received an Ontario scholarship for university, and my mother said, "We had set aside money for your tuition. We consider this money now to be yours if you want to use it for something else." We used part of the money for me to attend Kenneth Mills' summer festival in Muskoka for two weeks in August 1974. My mother wrote the cheque and signed it. Dr. Mills' bookkeeper, who was also attending the festival, addressed me, when I met him, as Ann Fowle, my mother's name, because it was the name on the cheque. It was a jarring moment but also perfect in its way, briefly bringing my mother into this realm in which I had assumed she had no part. It was a flicker of integration in a divided world.

Do What You Don't Want to Do

NOW THAT I WAS ATTENDING Unfoldments every week, I hoped to hear answers to my question, "Am I in the world, or is the world in me?" The premise expressed in every Unfoldment that "Consciousness is fundamental" gave me new words for thinking about those childhood experiences, and those words would eventually mature into a new perspective. But at first they were only words, an intellectual step that didn't bring a sense of resolution. A meaningful answer required summoning the courage to ask Kenneth Mills my question directly and work with his response.

My first summer festival, in August 1974, could have been an opportunity to do this, but I was much too shy. Those two weeks were my first time away from home with adults rather than teenagers. I didn't know what to pack, what to wear, or what to expect. When I checked into my room at Clyffe House Resort in Muskoka, I felt very grown up and more than a bit nervous. The events that followed were a blur of unfamiliar experiences. In between the Unfoldments, classes, and afternoons for swimming and relaxing, I heard about Zen Buddhism, numerology, Christian Science, dark forces, and many other topics that were way outside my small world. At times I wondered what I had gotten into.

Surprisingly, the Unfoldments with Dr. Mills were the most familiar events in the schedule. I had been attending these for several months, and it already felt like home. However, Dr. Mills on the dock in his bathing suit talking with people, or in the lake leading a water meditation with a group of swimmers, or stopping to chat with someone as he walked around the property was unsettling. I had put him on a distant pedestal, and now here he was, in the flesh and very present.

I did speak with him once, among a small group sitting on the on the lawn chairs overlooking the lake. I told him that I had just finished my grade-nine piano exam at the Royal Conservatory of Music while completing my final year of high school. I wanted him to know that I was a piano student. I was probably also looking for recognition, having found it challenging to do both at the same time. He asked me about my piano teacher, whom he knew. From there, my recollection is that Dr. Mills dismissed my accomplishment as a very ordinary level of effort. He described his own schedule, when he was my age, of nine high school subjects plus three hours of piano practice a day to win a scholarship to go to university. This short conversation was my first glimpse into how my life looked in light of Dr. Mills' standard. Remembering it today, it was also a glimpse into his integrity. He did nothing to make me feel more comfortable speaking with him, or to ingratiate himself with a new student who was finally speaking up. He simply replied honestly based on his own experience.

When Kenneth Mills gave an Unfoldment, he often opened the floor to questions at the end. There were several hundred people in the room, all of them older than I was. While many were in their early twenties, to me they seemed very mature and worldly. They were not shy about making the most of the journey they were now on. They asked questions, checked their practices, and shared their life experiences, and Dr. Mills would respond with lengthy, insightful, poetic, and sometimes life-changing answers, regardless of the nature of their questions.

I wanted to have this experience but was afraid to open my mouth. I had had a lifetime of keeping things unexpressed; speaking out loud about my inner considerations or even about my life was a huge hurdle. Plus, asking a childhood question that sounded ridiculous was too embarrassing in front of this accomplished group of people (*Does she really think the world is in her?*). And I certainly wasn't going to talk about my experience of living with my parents and going to high school.

I did ask one question, a simple question for clarity based on something he had said in the Unfoldment. I was so nervous, I didn't hear a word of his response, and when I heard the recording later, I still didn't understand it. But it got me over the hurdle of standing up and opening my mouth for the first time. What I did understand, and which has stayed with me ever since, was the story Dr. Mills told immediately after answering my question. He described some men in the fraternities at his school who were so smart, they could just cram for the exams without really learning the material. It concerned him because some of them were medical students:

They were awfully bright, but they didn't know the material at all. I just thought, "What an experiment that they are going to use when they are dealing with people and trying to offer a healing to a solution that they themselves have never found." It's the same thing in this group. You start to find how to use the words, and it sounds impressive to people not in the group, and rather distressing when your actions speak so little compared to your words. So, which is empty, your words or you?

A fair warning to one very capable of cramming for exams, who had a habit of impressing others with being smart, who was enjoying discovering new words, and who could easily neglect the interior work that was the only real attainment. Dr. Mills concluded a second story by saying, "After all, I had to live with myself, not with them," pointing again to inner integrity rather than outward impressions. It seemed to me that he had somehow picked up on a tendency to prioritize making a good impression. Navigating the world successfully had become such a big priority for me that it could overtake a focus on inner enquiry. I vowed in that moment to not become like those fraternity students, but it took years to actually achieve freedom from the thought habit of seeking outward success via a well-honed intellect. Humility, inner integrity, and a return to the heart without mental interference came much later.

The following summer, in 1975, I finally began to have a more natural relationship with Dr. Mills, and this resulted in receiving instructions that became foundational in my life. To take this step I had to let go of identifying as a teenager who didn't know anything, and accept my experience in the moment as a legitimate basis for spiritual practice and transformation. It seemed that Dr. Mills took the initiative to make sure it happened.

That year's summer festival was held for the first time at Sun-Scape Inn, a resort property on Sparrow Lake in Muskoka, Ontario. I signed up to attend for two weeks and this time arrived as one who had already been to a festival, unlike the many first-timers who had met Dr. Mills within the last year. My greater confidence, however, did not erase all moments of teenage emotion and angst.

One day, soon after arriving at Sun-Scape Inn, I was sweeping out the cobwebs on the wraparound porch of the building in which I was staying. We all had chores like this to maintain a high standard of order and beauty, despite the aging buildings and diligent spiders. While my hands were moving the broom, my mind was elsewhere, ruminating about what someone had said to me that morning that was causing me emotional upset.

Dr. Mills happened to walk down the path next to where I was sweeping and noticed my state. He stopped to talk and, without asking what the problem was, offered a solution: look in a mirror and laugh. Surprised and embarrassed, I thanked him, and he continued on his way. I went right upstairs to the washroom in the old white clapboard building and, still upset, peered into the ancient, peeling mirror. I forced myself to laugh, and it broke the spell immediately. It was a revelation to see how flimsy the apparently strong emotions actually were. I had to admit to myself that I was choosing to indulge in them. Thanks to the mirror, observing from a distance the antics of my own mind for the first time was like discovering a superpower. I could choose not to get caught up in an emotion, and looking in a mirror and laughing was the perfect method. It was obvious in that moment that I wasn't the emotion; I was the one looking at a face in a mirror taken up by an emotion. I knew that Dr. Mills' summer festival wasn't about indulging in emotions and that I needed to let this go in order to be fully present at the festival. With a few return trips to the mirror, I was able to do it.

Many times over the decades since that day, I have returned to the mirror to laugh at emotions and ego. And I still associate it with sweeping away cobwebs. Dr. Mills had endless ways of holding up mirrors to enable us to see ourselves more clearly and to sweep away cobwebs. Mine began with an actual mirror and broom.

Along with the negative emotions, I had also been feeling much more energy in the form of joy, passion, and conviction, apparently just from being around Dr. Mills and studying the Unfoldments. It was as though I had woken up; I was much more alive and engaged. Since childhood I had indulged a habit of retreating into my imagination, but now the world around me was pulsating with vitality and significance. I felt strongly about everything and liked this new sensation. I was stretching into feeling confident about my own convictions. With the mirror exercise I had found a method to stop directing that energy into negative emotions and ruminating. But I was still startled by my own forcefulness and worried that I was harnessing this new-found energy for personal benefit and becoming willful.

Soon afterwards, Kenneth Mills spoke about willfulness during an Unfoldment and pointed me out as one exhibiting this trait. I asked him how to break willfulness without becoming passive. He said, "Do what you don't want to do, and don't let anyone know that you don't want to do it."

This sounded to me like instructions from a parent, whereas I had been hoping for a "real" spiritual practice. Furthermore, it was not a message I wanted to hear, especially because I interpreted it to mean doing everything "right" even if you don't want to. "Do what you don't want to do" were radical words to a teenager in the do-your-own-thing generation. I had grown up in an environment that emphasized discovering what you do want to do.

However, I adopted the exercise. I discovered that doing what I didn't want to do meant eating what I didn't want to eat, and replacing bread or dessert with vegetables or fruit. It meant initiating conversations and being sociable. It meant getting up every morning in time to study and meditate for an hour before breakfast, and staying up a half-hour at night to do the same before bed. The clincher was not being able to tell anyone that it was not my natural inclination—no chance to complain or be a hero, no recognition for making the effort.

I had had six years of going to free school ("What do you want to learn?") combined with my academic parents' laissez-faire approach to child raising ("What do you want to do?"). At nineteen I was finally attempting to learn self-discipline. This practice often required me to not act on my thoughts, because they were always telling me what I did want to do. Until this moment I had implicitly assumed that I *was* my thoughts. Now I had to manage my thoughts and accept the proposition that thoughts, like emotions, could be rejected and replaced with other thoughts. I started by replacing thoughts such as "I'm tired, I'll skip studying and go straight to bed tonight," with telling myself, "I want to take the next half-hour to study." With practice, I started noticing other thoughts such as "What if they don't like me?" or "They are not doing it right," and was able to say to my own mind, "I'm not going to think about that." It wasn't easy, and I often fell back into the habit of simply accepting whatever was in my thought as "real." But after a while I grew to recognize old thoughts patterns that I had come to dislike, and whenever they came up, I was able to just notice them—"Oh, you again!"—and say goodbye.

This practice of watching thoughts brought to life what I was hearing in the Unfoldments: just because a thought occurs in the mind, it doesn't have to be adopted and lived out. It was the act of accepting the thought that made me subject to it, and if I didn't want to accept it, I had the choice and the power to kick it out.

Eventually, doing this practice gave me a new level of freedom over my thought field. I became more adept at observing the thought stream and identifying as one watching the thoughts instead of as one being the thoughts. By doing this, I became less attached to the "me" that was serious, had strong opinions, was too shy to be sociable, disliked housework, needed lots of sleep, and so on, and I was more open to trying other modes of living and being. It was never easy, but I was carried by a strong intention in those early days to grow into my full potential by studying with Dr. Mills, even if the purpose of the exercise I was given wasn't clear to me at the time.

Reflecting today on Kenneth Mills' advice to me to "do what you don't want to do," I see that this exercise can also be approached simply by trying new things, being less stiff and rigid, and flowing with the moment—anything to loosen the attachment to the self-created identity of "me" and "my" and be open to new possibilities. I approached the exercise with great diligence and angst, which was my nature then. The practice was very valuable, especially given my lack of discipline while growing up. It was a great gift to finally have someone putting a demand on me to replace personal preferences and mechanical reactions to situations, with a clearly defined intention.

These exercises of watching thoughts and emotions, of simply observing the mind and releasing attachment to the personal self, are universal ones, practised by every aspirant. I was beginning to learn the art of living based on a philosophical ideal, rather than allowing circumstances, thoughts, and emotions to rule my world. My footsteps to accomplishing this were specific to Dr. Mills' unique way of teaching and to my ability and willingness to receive and adopt what I was given. But the journey is a universal one, and it is an inner journey, only represented by an external teacher.

During the summer festival of 1975, Dr. Mills gave a lecture out on the lawn at Sun-Scape Inn that came to be known as the "Imagination Unfoldment." In response to questions from individuals who were building their careers and businesses, he talked about how to image employment and prosperity and said, "The position you seek is seeking you, but you have to be willing to be found ready." Enrolled in a university, I wondered how this applied to being a student. I asked Kenneth Mills, "How is being a student impersonally done?"

He replied, "Oh, by rejoicing in the ever-newness of Being! This is great fun!"

It was a marvellous and memorable answer that has stayed with me ever since. I was so serious and cautious, diligently practising doing what I didn't want to do, that I needed to be reminded of the joy of the ever-newness of Being. And that this was fun! Friends who were there that day still occasionally say to me, in fun, "Rejoice in the ever-newness of Being!"

Fun—including being able to laugh at myself—became a leitmotif in my conversations with Dr. Mills over the years. I learned to take things more lightly and not invest so much in the unreliable world of circumstances, but to take time and turn my attention to enjoying the newness and lightness of just Being. Years later, after I had thanked Dr. Mills for some wise words, he said, "Oh, it's fun! There is nothing serious about it at all. It's the most fun thing—the Truth is fun. What's heavy about it is your thought."

When Kenneth Mills appeared in my life as a living answer to my years of self-enquiry, at first there was a tendency to simply enjoy his Unfoldment and bask in the energy and clarity of his realization. But the point was not to follow him or merely witness his realization. It was to do likewise, to take the journey within. These exercises were the beginning of that journey.

What Is Real?

IN THE SUMMER OF 1975, I moved from my parents' home into an apartment with friends, and subsequently, during my twenties, I moved several times, as young people do. Sun-Scape Inn in Muskoka was the constant and became like a second home. For fifteen years it was the location of Dr. Mills' summer festivals and workshops and of many projects and events.

I had discovered to my surprise that I liked community living. At Sun-Scape Inn, people who had very little in common on a personal level came together as a community. There was a feeling of purposeful living—taking the time to not rush through the day on the way to somewhere else but to savour every moment and live in a way that reflected an elevated state of awareness. We got to know one another not just on a personal level but as fellow travellers on the Path. Becoming part of this community greatly alleviated the shyness and anxiety I still felt in unstructured social situations. Like acting in a play or employed in a job, there was a purpose for being there, which helped to dispel any worry about what other people thought of me.

Kenneth Mills had designed Sun-Scape Inn to be unlike any spiritual retreat. In fact, it resembled the Algonquin Resort in St. Andrews, New Brunswick, in the 1940s where he had performed as a young pianist, more than it did any spiritual gathering, with elegant meals, formal attire in the evenings, afternoon tea on the lawn, impeccable manners at all times. We learned table etiquette, including how to host a conversation at a large dinner table. Then, changing roles, we learned how to properly set a table, wait on tables, wash dishes, and clean the kitchen. As a result, we learned how to live harmonically and rhythmically and to appreciate beauty and the satisfaction of actions completed to a high standard of perfection.

Still in my early twenties, I was sometimes assigned the role of maître d', overseeing the dining-room staff and the flow of the dinner service. Those older than me perhaps had their own lessons in being gracious and letting me take the lead. Together we focused on moving seamlessly as one body by anticipating each other's needs and being sensitive to the rhythm of the kitchen and the dining room.

Sometimes I was assigned to the team that cleaned the kitchen after dinner. This sequence is still seared in my memory. The kitchen had to be spotless. We would race to finish washing and drying the pots and mopping the floor. Then we ran down to the lake for a quick swim before dashing to our rooms to change into something elegant for the evening's Unfoldment. I always made it, just barely, and was more than alert for the evening program.

By trying on these different roles, we learned to serve one another with formality and grace. When those of us who shared this experience get together today to help one another or do a project, we always marvel at how quickly and easily we complete the work.

In the fall of 1975, Dr. Mills held a series of weekend workshops, the first one taking place in early September. We carpooled to Muskoka on a Friday afternoon, letting the two-hour drive from Toronto release our day-to-day thoughts and prepare us to enter a different world. By evening we were all assembled in the Unfoldment Hall, a white clapboard building with a long porch overlooking the lake. After giving the Unfoldment, Dr. Mills opened the floor to questions. I finally summoned the courage to say something related to my childhood question. I raised my hand and said, "Dr. Mills, sometimes I feel that I'm all there is and there is no one else as real as I am, and yet there seems to be others to say, 'I am here.'" Here is part of his response:

They could not help but say, "I am here," when you consider
yourself to be Real in the framework of your mentality.
"You" are never Real. If you were Real, you would be unchanging. . . . If you are changing and can note the change,
then find the note, the Pitch that is the Light that enables
you to discern the change. For I AM changeless, even in
the midst of the apparent change.

In the moment, the lengthy answer to my question went right over
my head, but I did hear the shortest sentence of all: "You are never real."
The centrepiece of my puzzle, me, that seemed to project the world
and occasionally cause it to become just a shimmering vibration, was
actually not real at all, let alone more real than everything and everyone else. This required a major realignment in identity. Nevertheless,
hearing this answer was thrilling and gave me a knot in the pit of my
stomach, as I became aware for the first time of the possibilities of
being more than me and my changing world.

It was time to make the leap and accept that "me" is not the centre
of the universe, and acknowledge that there is a reality, the Light or I
AM, beyond me and my mind. The nature of that reality, according to
Kenneth Mills, is that it is fixed and unchanging. Therefore, it is not
found in the objective world, because that is always changing. The
unchanging Light is what enables me to discern the changing.

Dr. Mills pointed out that there must be a fixed point in order to
discern the changing, as illustrated in Einstein's famous moving-train
example. If the train and the scenery were moving at the same speed,
the passengers on the train wouldn't know it was moving. This concept
made sense even to my changing mind.

I knew from the practice of watching thoughts that there is an
unchanging observer that is not the thoughts; it is the watcher of the
thoughts. I was attempting to identify as this fixed point of observation rather than as the changing stream of thoughts, and tended to
think of it as "the real me." But was this unchanging observer an aspect
of me, or was it evidence of this higher reality? These considerations
were taking me in the direction of acknowledging the Source, which

meant confronting the question of God. I lay in bed at night trying to reconcile the world view that I had learned growing up with this new standpoint of an unchanging Light beyond the mind. Every time I got to something that smacked of the *God* word, my mind objected and eighteen years of conditioning took over.

I was like Galileo discovering that the earth revolves around the sun rather than the other way around. I had grown up believing that higher-order qualities such as wisdom, insight, love, wonder, joy, musicality, creativity, and awareness were personal human traits, and I felt the pressure of having to produce them. Attributing these to an unknown God felt anthropomorphic, mentally projecting my nature onto a thought construct called God. Yet there must be something greater than me and my world.

For those of us who did not grow up with it, God is a difficult concept to wrap your mind around, harder than the word Consciousness. After decades of being in charge of me and my world, I found the notion of God quaint and outdated, even oppressive. But without my coming to terms with finding meaning in the word God, my conception of Consciousness, or the oneness of all life, remained more of a super-human state, with me still very much at the centre. Awareness of this shift in standpoint continued throughout the years with Dr. Mills and beyond.

On the second day of the September 1975 workshop we reconvened in the Unfoldment Hall. This time I tried on one of my theories of life. I asked, "Are life experiences symbolic?"

Dr. Mills replied, "Yes." Pause.

Hoping he would speak further, I said the only thing that came to mind in that moment: "All of them?"

"Sure." Another long pause.

"So translated they can point in meaning?"

Dr. Mills responded: "And translated you find Life as it IS, freed from the belief of symbolic. Very good, out of the mouths of babes."

Life experiences are symbolic! A piece of my mental puzzle had been solved. To this day I don't entirely know the full implications of this except that it means our lives are never just on the level of the material, no matter how the picture appears. It is a conscious experience primarily, and the apparent objective points symbolically to a higher level of awareness.

Towards the end of the class I said to Dr. Mills, "It's interesting what you said about 'out of the mouths of babes' because I've been feeling very uncomfortable in that disguise."

He replied: "Oh, don't worry. You're an old hag, dear, but smile! I mean you are so old, you should be grateful the fashion designer for the Age gave you such a gorgeous presence defined. It is a great camouflage until you have the strength to take over the craft."

It was thrilling to finally be speaking with him sincerely, and to have overcome the sense of being a stranger in the room, listening to other people talking with their mentor. I still wasn't fully understanding his answers, but even before comprehending the language, I knew that I had had a new experience and had received something significant. Later that day someone brought me a typed excerpt of my questions and answers, and I studied them word for word.

Dr. Mills' "out of the mouths of babes" phrase, with its praise and recognition of my youthfulness, was gratifying but also an indication of things to come. I soon learned that I had to get over the need for praise, to stop identifying as young and inexperienced, and to claim a new standpoint of being complete now. Nevertheless, I was glad to hear—as one who never felt like a baby or a child—that I was really an old hag!

It was a great gift to receive many points of guidance before fully embarking on adult life, yet being old enough that the encounter was my own impelling and not due to my parents or family. These foundational moments became the backdrop to my entire life and set me on a new path of self-enquiry, one that was now open to the concept of acknowledging God.

A New Name

WE ARRIVED for the final 1975 workshop at Sun-Scape Inn at the end of October. The air was crisp, and the trees were vibrant in fall colours. The cold air outside made this workshop even cozier as we wrapped ourselves in warm sweaters and gathered around the fireplaces.

On Friday evening, about sixty people were in the dining hall after dinner. Dr. Mills came in and greeted each one by name. He passed over one of the women without saying anything. He later turned his attention back to her, commenting that her name didn't suit her vibrationally. After a moment of silence, in which he appeared to be listening intently, he proposed the name Katrine. (This woman later told me that she had always disliked her birth name and didn't feel it suited her at all. She was thrilled that Dr. Mills had somehow picked up on this, and she immediately loved the name Katrine. She felt so at home in it that she adopted it as a new name for herself, which she has used from that day forward.)

Watching the scene in the dining hall, I was intrigued with the possibility of changing my name. Up to this point in my life, my name had been Elizabeth, a name I didn't like at all. It was long and formal, and I had a slight lisp as a child, which made it difficult to pronounce. Because of the glamorous young Queen Elizabeth, it was a popular name when I was born. There were three of us in my grade-one class, and the teacher called us Beth, Liz, and Elizabeth. I got Elizabeth, and I can still feel the struggle of printing all those letters with my left hand. At home my mother called me Elizabeth, my father called me Lizzie, and my sister called me Liz. Over the years I had experimented with Liza and Lizabeth. None of these felt like my name.

So, as I sat there in the Sun-Scape Inn dining room, I prayed that Dr. Mills would comment on my name. He continued greeting people, without commenting on their names. Then it was my turn: "Yours is another name I find hard to remember. Elizabeth suits you ..." There was a long pause and it seemed that I would be keeping the name Elizabeth. Then he continued: "Elizabeth suits a stiffness about you. It doesn't suit the fun that you have found." Another long pause, which felt like forever to me. "Lucille is nice. It's a good one. Lucille. It's very flowing. And let them call you Lucy."

I immediately loved the sound, and the meaning, "light." The vowels had a musical quality that seemed to even improve my last name at the time (Lucille Fowle). I was excited by the idea of adopting Lucille as my name—it would be a new beginning as I embarked on adult life, rather than using a name my parents had chosen. Dr. Mills later gave me a very unusual spelling of the word, just for my own use, which helped me to hear it as a sound frequency rather than a conventional name. This sound later became part of a mantra and is not something that I share.

I lay in bed that first night in my cabin at Sun-Scape Inn, picturing a clothesline with everything I had ever imagined about me hung on the line. Elizabeth was the clothesline. Changing my name meant releasing everything—a frightening but attractive prospect. What did it mean to be Lucille? It felt like a clean slate, starting from a sound frequency rather than family heritage. Who is Lucille?

It was difficult to tell my parents that I was considering changing my name, and I expected that they would find the name Lucille strange and inappropriate. My father was initially disapproving, but later referred to Lucille as my "professional name," a phrase that seemed to satisfy us both. He continued to call me Lizzie or Elizabeth for the rest of his life, and my sister still calls me Liz.

But when I sat down to talk about the name with my mother, over a cup of tea in the kitchen where we always had our chats, she told me a remarkable story. There was a rare tear in her eye when she explained that, when I was born, she had wanted to call me Lucy, after her mother. This was the first time I had ever heard her mother's name; Lucy Clemens had died decades before I was born. Mum said she had decided that the name Lucy Fowle sounded awful, and named me Elizabeth instead. She said that the name Lucille hadn't occurred to her, and she acknowledged that this version of the name worked well with our last name. As I write this, I wonder why I didn't pick up on the cue from Dr. Mills to "let them call you Lucy" and suggest to my mother that she call me Lucy. It feels now like a missed opportunity to be called by my mother the name she had wanted to call me since birth.

My mother's words helped me to claim the name as my own. In addition to being a sound that felt like home, it was almost the name my mother had originally chosen, and it honoured my trail-blazing grandmother. I had already discovered the lightness and fun in the name Lucy, which a few friends had started to use and, with time, my mother and my friends became comfortable calling me Lucille.

Despite an inner decision to adopt the name, it was still a difficult transition. Lucille was an outdated, old-fashioned name and the name of guitars and country music songs. Becoming confident with the name Lucille despite all of its connotations (to this day, people occasionally sing, "You picked a fine time to leave me," when they first hear my name)[6] was good practice in learning to stand by my convictions. I was also uncomfortable with the association with Lucille Ball, even though I was a fan of the *I Love Lucy* show. The zany red-headed comedian was still very prominent in popular culture in the 1970s. Now I find it hard to imagine a better role model for an overly anxious young woman learning to have fun than the fearless actress whose brilliance made us all love Lucy.

A few months after I had adopted the name, Dr. Mills told me that he had known a Lucile. Lucile Pillow was a philanthropist from Montreal with an astonishing art collection. She and her husband, a very wealthy businessman, Howard W. Pillow, spent their summers in St. Andrews, New Brunswick, where Dr. Mills as a young man had given concerts at the Algonquin Resort. The Pillows were part of a group of patrons who had supported his piano studies. Dr. Mills said that Lucile Pillow was a brilliant woman whom he had always admired. His affection for her was evident years later in his memoirs, which included stories and even a photo of her note of appreciation following a piano recital.

I did some research and discovered to my surprise that her given names were Lucile Elizabeth, which was now also my name, as I had moved my first name to be a middle name. I appreciated having the image of Lucile Pillow to hold as I adjusted to my new name. Little did I know that years later I too would marry a businessman and become a patron of the arts—although nowhere near the level of the Pillow family.

It is still unfathomable to me how Kenneth Mills picked this name, seemingly out of the air, and it turned out to be the name my mother had chosen for me—something that neither he nor I knew at the time. This was one of many mind-stopping moments over the years with Dr. Mills when his remarkable words caused me to admit that I really didn't know the magnitude of this experience called life.

Meditation

MEDITATION IS ANOTHER FACET of the early instruction from Kenneth Mills that is foundational in my life. Dr. Mills had learned to meditate in the early 1960s, receiving private instruction and a mantra directly from Maharishi Mahesh. For several years he meditated for hours every day. He realized in doing this that the state he entered in meditation had to be a constant, regardless of what he was doing. Eventually he let go of the daily sitting-meditation practice and his life became a constant meditation, as is evident in the spontaneous Unfoldments.

When someone asked Dr. Mills in 1975 what types of meditation practice he found valuable, he said:

> The best way to meditate is to be consciously aware of tying your shoe or to be consciously aware of cleaning your teeth— of doing everything you do—of taking someone's hand, of putting your arms around someone. That is meditating. But if you are thinking whether or not you want to take someone's hand or embrace someone, why, you are leaving so much in the way of a "tracing" (your mind and its workings) that your action doesn't have power.[7]

In the 1970s Dr. Mills also gave us instruction for a breathing meditation practice. We were to sit quietly, breathe slowly, and count the breaths from one to ten, for up to five sets, without losing track of the counts. If our attention wandered and we lost the count, we had to go back to the beginning and start again. Dr. Mills emphasized that this was only an exercise to settle the mind and focus the attention. After completing the counting, we were to "sit with an air of expectancy with the mind disengaged and yet engaged, as intuition dawns."

My early attempts to meditate often left me hyperventilating from too much oxygen. I still have notebooks documenting my early efforts, which read like a teenage diary mixed with the earnest attempts of a spiritual aspirant. At the time, I was reading *The Three Pillars of Zen*,[8] which was very inspiring but set a standard that was more than a little daunting.

To check our meditation practice, Dr. Mills gave brief one-on-one encounters (adopting the Zen Buddhist term *dokusans* for them) in which the student presented their meditation practice for the teacher's adjudication. These meetings were my first private conversations with Dr. Mills. I would go to his home in Willowdale and wait in the anteroom for the bell, my heart pounding in anticipation. Here are a few excerpts from one of my dokusans:

> LUCILLE FOWLE JOSEPH: Where should I focus my attention in meditation?
>
> KENNETH G. MILLS: On your Self. The best way to prepare the focalization is by asking, "What am I?" or "What is I AM?" There will be no answer, because an answer would be intellectual. There can only be experience.
>
> LJ: I want to strive more in meditation, in being attentive, and I feel as though I'm fighting an enemy, and yet I can't find an enemy.
>
> KGM: That is right. It's conjured up, as if you could strive. You are the strife and the striver. Could I AM strive to be I AM?
>
> LJ: No. When I feel detached and watching the meditation go on, then there's no striving.
>
> KGM: Are you able to stay on the counts?
>
> LJ: Yes.
>
> KGM: Regardless of your thoughts.

LJ: I am able to keep the count, but often my attention wanders.

KGM: That is the thought-projection. The thoughts are trying to get you to bow to them instead of acknowledging the Fact and see the Watcher. Be one with the Watcher, or one with the Watch, and that is uncontaminated with strife, striver, counter, and let all the others seem to happen until the Watch is won.

In the winning all the struggle fades out, for where is there a striver to be found, a meditator thought-bound, when the goal is won, the inner accomplishment is due to One, and that is why "won" is "Now" when seen from the other side of the suggested three-dimensional realm [i.e., when spelled backwards].

"Won" is what a winner wants. He wants to win so others will say he has won. But from that state of the Watch, won becomes Now and all is done. Done: the Divine One. I AM . . . Now . . . done.

LJ: Does it matter in meditation whether the eyes are open or closed?

KGM: Yes. It's easier to keep them closed. You have enough thoughts about what you don't see. I can't imagine how many you would have if you opened your eyes and thought you saw as you are trying to meditate. You might as well pull the blinds on the suggestion that outside of you is the world.

Looking back on this exchange now, I can't help but wonder: How did Dr. Mills, barely knowing me at all, identify these aspects of my nature that would become the areas of focus in his mentoring of me over the following decades?

One particular aspect was that of winning. In my meditation practice I began to repeat the phrase "I AM . . . Now . . . done," but the idea of "Won is what a winner wants; he wants to win so others will say he has won," had to be confronted in daily life. As long as I felt the need to prove myself, to validate my identity through "winning," and have others verify it, I wasn't the Watch, the observer in the world but not of it. Feeling insecure, I had invested far too much credence in the opinions of others, measuring my self-worth in their eyes. Seeing through a need to win was to be one of my greatest lessons from Dr. Mills.

The meditation practice of counting the breath is very valuable and something that I continue to do to this day. It brings my attention home, into the present, reduces anxiety, and quiets the ruminating mind by focusing on simply counting and being aware of the breath.

Although Dr. Mills encouraged us to meditate, the primary daily practice learned from him was not meditation; it was watching my thoughts and aligning them, along with my language and actions, to what I claimed as an Ideal. As Kenneth Mills once put it:

> When you feel moody, ask if God could feel moody. If God can't feel moody, you are living a fictitious existence if you are moody. ... If [you are] feeling depressed, or feeling happy and joyous and the whole world [your] oyster, ask if God could feel joyous and the whole world His oyster, or would He feel the Power that could support the world in the Light of His Awareness?[9]

Daily I studied passages such as this in the transcripts that we received after each Unfoldment. I'm particularly grateful now for the passages and poems from Unfoldments that I have memorized over the years. These have become an inner tuning fork, a way to realign my attention to a higher state of awareness and be open in any moment to unlimited possibilities.

Dr. Mills began an Unfoldment in 1980 by saying: "We are in that position of receptivity in which the possibilities of Being are more and more clarified as we stem the tide of thought which would have us primarily human." The radical idea that we are not primarily human grabbed my attention, and decades later, every time I hear it in his Unfoldments, it still takes my breath away.

Blanket of God-Consciousness

DESPITE THE FOUNDATION I was building through daily study and practice, and the occasional moments of inspired realization, in 1976, when I was twenty, some of the newness, surprise, and delight of the early encounters with Kenneth Mills seemed to fade. Such is the changeability of the human mind.

When I was listening to an Unfoldment or talking with friends who were also studying his work, the truth of Dr. Mills' message seemed self-evident. But later, when I was alone or with family or with friends at university, I wondered what I really believed. I had always been good at acting and going along with the people around me. Perhaps I had slipped into that pattern again? Did I really believe anything Dr. Mills was saying?

I did fully accept his assertion that the changing three-dimensional realm is not the primary reality. Childhood experiences had already shown me that what most people take as reality is not actually reality. I observe the changing; I am not the changing. It was far more challenging to acknowledge an unlimited, unchanging Reality beyond the mind, called God, a standpoint that required no longer attributing to my personal self the life force, perception, awareness, energy, creativity, and insights that were my experience.

Kenneth Mills had accepted as a boy in his Baptist family that "I of myself can do nothing; it is the Father that doeth the work." But just because Dr. Mills declared this to be true didn't make it true for me. It felt like being asked to give up control, handing my life over, to an imaginary "Father" that I didn't trust was actually there. Why should I become like a submissive child who could "do nothing," when I was feeling so much energy and finally entering the adult world? I knew there must be something beyond my puny existence, but my mind was unwilling to come to terms with the implications of that acknowledgement.

For Dr. Mills, the answer to what's beyond it could be expressed myriad ways, but most fundamentally it is Consciousness. He based his life on the premise that "Consciousness is fundamental and what you are conscious of as Principle constitutes your Real experience." He expected us to adopt this premise and to discover through practice and experience the meaning of the statement. I was making some effort to do this, but it felt forced and unnatural to me.

Nevertheless, I went to the summer festival at Sun-Scape Inn in 1976. Once there, however, I found that I had reached an impasse in which I was not understanding or appreciating anything Kenneth Mills was saying, including the "Consciousness is fundamental" premise of his work. I was ready to leave the festival and get on with my life, but it didn't feel right to leave without first going to see the host of the event. Whether it was good manners, or a desire to state my convictions, or an intuition that this was not the end of the journey, I wanted to voice my doubts, rather than simply leave.

There were hundreds of people at the festival, and I was shy about speaking with Dr. Mills in a class, let alone paying him an unscheduled private visit. The fact that I did this reminds me of the dire state I must have been in. I walked over to where he was staying on the campus and found him about to go down for a swim in the lake. He was gracious as ever and stopped to talk with me. Thanks to his associate Jaan being there with the tape recorder, the conversation was recorded. I don't recall if I told him that I was leaving the festival or that I did not understand and accept the premise of his work, or perhaps I said nothing at all about the purpose of my visit. It was obvious that I was at an extremity of some kind, spiritual and emotional, with a heightened clarity of purpose and a need for resolution.

Neither the words on paper, nor the audio recording I still have, capture the transforming encounter that followed, and the lightness and clarity I suddenly experienced. This was a much more honest moment with Dr. Mills than any previous conversation and marked a new phase in the relationship with him.

Here is a short excerpt from our conversation when we were sitting on the Muskoka wooden chairs overlooking Sparrow Lake:

> KGM: Did you ever see perception in a piece of wood?
> LJ: No.
> KGM: That's right. That's why you are more than meat.

You are Consciousness, and that embraces your mind and you and your chair. It embraces your mind, your awareness, your perception, and your comfort appearing as you having a chair to sit in and having the mind present to declare it is a chair.

If you sit under this [*Dr. Mills put one end of his beach towel over his head and passed the other end to me*]—put it over your head. We're both under the same garment of Consciousness. Are we separate under this? We can appear to be separate, but are we?

LJ: No.

KGM: Exactly. This blanket could be called God-Consciousness. You can appear to be you, I can appear to be me, but are we separate in the Light of God- Consciousness?

LJ: No!

KGM: That's all there is to it. Look at you! You're happy and free. An awful lot of cobwebs blew away that time! What a different face! It doesn't take time; I knew you could do it. No one has gotten at it with that intensity. Now you can date, you can have a beautiful home, family, and everything, but at least you know how it happens: one Consciousness appearing diversified. But in reality is it [diversified]?

LJ: No!

KGM: That's it. If this isn't a miracle!

LJ: It is!

KGM: Ask and you shall receive. That's part of the law of the Light. Go down and have a swim.

I walked back to my cabin, floating in an altered state, alive with energy and possibility, the sky pulsing. Something had happened between the words that had transformed my whole being. Taking Dr. Mills' advice, I didn't think about the conversation; I just went for a swim. The water was delicious as though I had never felt water before. The blanket of God-Consciousness took on a new form as the lake in which I was both separate and enveloped. It reminded me of the moment on the beach many years before as I relaxed into its embrace.

As a result of this conversation I finally realized that acknowledgement of God-Consciousness was the resolution to my question "Am I in the world, or is the world in me?" In my childhood conception there had been two players—me as the viewer, and the world as the object viewed. It seemed to me that one of these two had to encompass the other. It never occurred to me that both subject and object arise within a single body of Consciousness into which this apparent duality disappears. Without acknowledgement of God-Consciousness I had assumed that the awareness of the objective world I experienced was an attribute of me, putting myself in the position of God. I now knew that the innate knowing that I am, the thought "I" that we all share, is due to the shared light of Consciousness. I felt a new awareness of being connected to a greater whole, of Oneness, instead of being personally in charge of me and my world.

In his distinction between the wooden chair and me, Dr. Mills had even offered an answer to my childhood question about what makes me more alive than the dolls and objects around me: awareness lighted by Consciousness.

Dr. Mills used in this encounter the term *God-Consciousness*, a phrase I seldom, if ever, heard him use again. It bridged for me the more neutral and scientific terminology of *Consciousness* with that thorny word *God*.

I didn't leave the summer festival that day and floated through the week that followed, feeling the lightness and grace of the experience. A happiness often welled up for no apparent reason, and new insights suddenly appeared unbidden. Small obstacles and inconveniences over the course of a day barely registered in my attention, while the fragrance of a flower or a phrase of music captivated me completely. Approaching any event, I could see the overview and the detail all at the same time, and all of it was just a picture appearing on the screen of attention. Whenever this heightened state of awareness seemed to fade, I returned to the moment under the beach towel and re-entered the feeling of the blanket of God-Consciousness.

In the months and even years that followed, I often returned to the feeling of releasement in this moment as my first touchstone of knowing that there is a realm beyond the mind. This was finally an experience, not an intellectual assertion.

The encounter with Kenneth Mills that day didn't mean that my commitment to studying with him was never to be challenged again. It is in the confrontation of the ego that spiritual growth really happens, and more of those challenges were right around the corner. There were many more layers of meaning yet to unfold, but I had finally made my own the journey with Dr. Mills. It brought a new level of honesty to my relationship with him and unified my childhood mystical experiences with my new experience of the Unfoldment.

After so many years of my speculating alone as a child, and then attempting to understand his work, it was a great gift to have Dr. Mills present, willing, and able to offer not only words but also instantaneous transformation in the form of a felt experience. It is hard to put on paper the difference between being led point by point to arrive conceptually at this premise, and having the sudden blast of knowingness that came in the moment under the towel. This is the magic of a Teacher whose very presence can open the awareness of a student who is ready.

This story and its importance in my life cause me to reflect on what it means to have a teacher. Most people are uneasy about putting someone on a pedestal and letting them have such an influence in their lives. There are many accounts of people being taken advantage of by charlatans and of the effect of an egotistical teacher whose presence diminishes, rather than elevates, the students. However, there are also many accounts of those on an independent path who find themselves stalled, listening only to their own mind and yearning for more. I'm grateful for my experience with Dr. Mills who opened the path of wisdom for me in the classical way of gurus and teachers through the ages.

While we are rightly horrified by individuals who misuse power and authority, the opposite—a feel-good relationship that only reinforces the ego of the student—is of no value. It seems to me that there is a risk of this today as "spirituality" becomes more accepted, even trendy. This greater acceptance is a positive development, yet the word *spiritual* sometimes strangely lacks meaning and the potency that it once had. Radical ideas of past decades have been softened, which allows for broader appeal to a mass market. It has become less of a mind-stopping confrontation with a new and uncomfortable truth, and more of a tool for personal development.

The relationship between speakers and spiritual aspirants today is often indirect, at conferences or via the internet. Ubiquitous cameras and recording devices that can take words out of context and post them to the world perhaps constrain spontaneous encounters. This can protect against egotistically motivated teachers and the ulterior motives of listeners. However, without a more direct connection, there is no challenge to the ego, and the teaching remains on the level of the intellect.

Listening to someone speak to you about the insubstantiality of the ego is not the same as having your illusory world punctured by someone willing and able to see through it. Unless the ego is at risk, it will continue to parade as though it were real and to take over the field of the vision and action with a convincing message that "thanks to some new knowledge I have become enlightened." From my own experience, confronting the lifetime of assumptions that we have built up about ourselves and our world happens most readily in the presence of one who is standing before you with the peaceful assurance that transformation is possible and is in fact already the case.

The new modes of spiritual search available today, via the search engines of the internet, make it possible to privately and directly listen to many great teachers, past and present, who are offering much needed wisdom. The more people take advantage of this, the more hope I have for the world. And yet, reading, watching, or listening to a speaker on the internet does not equate to a single moment in front of a living master, when your heart is pounding, you can't think straight, and you suddenly know something deeply and feel a releasement and joy beyond words.

Where Success Belongs

IN 1977, I graduated from York University and began working as assistant to the theatre manager of Toronto's St. Lawrence Centre for the Arts. I was excited to have a job in the arts but frustrated to be doing only clerical work.

Working in a theatre caused me to think about the new music ensemble that had formed around Kenneth Mills. Christopher Dedrick and his sisters Sandy and Ellen were the successful pop group the Free Design, whose music still has a following today. Chris had composed some original songs to Dr. Mills' poetry and had asked him to help them with their performance. This was the beginning of what became a twelve-voice vocal ensemble called the Star-Scape Singers conducted by Kenneth Mills.

When I learned that one of the halls at the St. Lawrence Centre was often used for musical debuts, I wrote a letter to Dr. Mills, suggesting that Star-Scape might make its debut there. Soon afterwards, I received a call from Chris, telling me that Dr. Mills loved the idea and that I should "organize everything." It became clear to me in listening to Chris that "everything" was much more than my role at the theatre of preparing a contract and marking a date in the calendar. Dr. Mills, an accomplished concert pianist who had performed to critical acclaim in Canada and the United States, was entrusting the debut of this new singing group to a twenty-one-year-old whom he barely knew, who had just graduated with a degree in arts administration and had almost no work experience. I was thrilled and scared to death.

Fortunately a friend, Janet, who was also studying with Dr. Mills, worked nearby. Janet was six years older and much wiser than I was. We met for lunch in the park between our offices and worked on marketing, ticket sales, the program, public relations, and so on. Dr. Mills oversaw our progress. It was the first time I had worked with him on a project and I was eager to prove myself. Every phone call, usually made from the pay phone in the theatre lobby, produced many pages of scrawled notes. I was way out of my comfort zone but coming alive with the excitement and tension of my first professional assignment.

The Star-Scape Singers' debut at the St. Lawrence Centre in January 1978 was a huge success. It sold out quickly, and a second night at another theatre was added. The concerts launched the career of these singers who went on to perform all over the world.

Decades later, when Kenneth Mills was writing his memoirs, I reminded him of this story as an example of how he sponsored young people by giving us opportunities to grow, doing projects beyond the scope of what anyone else would have given us at the time. He added the story to his manuscript, and I reviewed what I thought was the final draft. When I opened *The Candymaker's Son*, which was published posthumously in 2007, I discovered to my surprise that he had added a sentence in the middle of the paragraph:

> Years later Lucille told me how amazed she had been when I had told her to "organize everything" for the debut, which was such a contrast to the limited role she was allowed to fulfill in her job as an entry-level employee. *It gave her a start in breaking her shyness of dealing with people, for she never would have entered the career she eventually entered if she hadn't broken the impediment of otherness.* This is one of many examples of giving the young people who came to hear me speak their start in what was to become their career.[10]

"Broken the impediment of otherness." A parting gift from Dr. Mills in the form of a perfect insight. To Kenneth Mills, getting over shyness wasn't about changing personality or gaining confidence. Feeling shy is the evidence of incorrect identity. The solution is the standpoint of one Consciousness, knowing that there is none other.

When I was growing up, the word *shy* appeared regularly on my report cards, in parent-teacher interviews, and at music recitals. As an adult, I almost forgot about this dreadful word that had defined my childhood. This was largely because, until I read this sentence, Dr. Mills hadn't once in the thirty years I knew him used the word *shy* with me.

Not that he didn't work on it. For example, one evening in the 1980s, I had a brief private meeting with him just before a Star-Scape Singers' musicale at his home. After the meeting, the audience of about seventy people was already quietly seated for the concert, and I stood in an anteroom, planning to slip in as the concert started.

I heard a whoosh behind me and turned to see the line of twelve singers, followed by their conductor, sweep through the anteroom and make their entrance. Suddenly, Dr. Mills took my arm and placed me in front of him on the way through. In the few steps between the anteroom and the music room he whispered, "Walk into that room just filled with delight that all of these people are looking at *you!*" On the word *you*, we were already in the room. I was shocked and scared but had no time to think. I followed his instruction and somehow made it through the room as the audience applauded the entrance of the artists. I smiled, looked people in the eye, and pretended that walking in with the conductor was the most natural thing in the world. When we arrived at the podium, he subtly gestured to me to sit down, which I gratefully did, sinking into the nearest chair and hoping that everyone's attention was now on the singers.

On the night of the debut concert of the Star-Scape Singers at the St. Lawrence Centre I was intensely alert to every detail. Until the applause ended and the audience had left, I was completely absorbed in making sure everything ran smoothly and was not thinking about me at all. I was surprised and pleased to be invited to a reception at a private home after the concert. At the reception Dr. Mills publicly acknowledged my contribution and spoke about the "transpersonal attention" I brought to the work on the concert; he said that when my attention was focused in the same way on the Self, "it would be the same." Later that evening he pointedly asked several singers if they had sent me thank-you notes.

The next day on the telephone Dr. Mills expressed some criticism of the singers, while praising me to the skies. It completely went to my head. Overnight I went from being almost oblivious of taking any personal credit for the concert to being so personally involved that I believed I was perfect and could do no wrong. All thoughts of acknowledgement of God-Consciousness disappeared in the gratifying moment of receiving Dr. Mills' validation of my presence and capabilities.

A few weeks later, in February 1978, I went to my first workshop with Dr. Mills at his home in Tucson, Arizona. This "Wordshop" (as he called it) has since become famous in the annals of events with Dr. Mills as the most grueling, challenging one that ever took place. Everyone found themselves turned inside out. By the end of the week all participants were made whole again but could still feel the quick, sharp shock of the verbal *kyosaku* of a living master. Every participant except for me, that is. I was still luxuriating in the gratifying experience of Dr. Mills' praise and support.

All week I had been afraid to open my mouth and reveal that I wasn't actually perfect, and thereby bring an end to Dr. Mills' confidence in me. It was as though I believed that having won his praise and endorsement, my journey was done. The need for acceptance that had defined my childhood took precedence over any spiritual quest.

Dr. Mills had none of these illusions. In fact, he used to say that the quest often happens "through the negative." Challenges from the teacher, and negative thoughts arising in one's own mind, are bound to happen when one is grappling with questions of identity, and the ego is trying to maintain its position. It is an indicator of the hard work that is actually being done to dispel a false sense of identity, rather than just bathing in the vibratory frequency of someone else's realization. Kenneth Mills never hesitated to say or do what came to him to offer to someone as commensurate to Principle. He never ingratiated himself or shied away from a confrontation with ego:

> The moment you face Truth, "you" are in disturbance
> because your identity is all based on a supposition that you
> are primarily "this." I don't know why most people consider
> knowing Truth is going to be a blissful state. Knowing the
> Truth, or experiencing the Truth, is one of the most athletic
> experiences you can have. It's confronting the entire univer-
> sal concepts surrounding Being.

Puncturing the supposition that we are primarily "this" (the mortal body-mind) was at the heart of Dr. Mills' teaching and the hardest to understand and accept. It is an "athletic experience" to confront this belief and re-identify primarily as Being, and only secondarily as this person that we seem to be. Listening to Unfoldments transported us to a place where this truth was self-evident. The practice came afterwards when we seemed to land back on earth, once again grappling with mentality.

On the last day of the Wordshop, after everyone else had had the humility to receive teaching, Dr. Mills offered a statement to each one of us. His statement to me was, "Continue to wear the garment of constancy and keep all success where it belongs." Still in the fog of personalization, I interpreted this to mean that I would have lots of success in my life and would need to keep my priorities straight— which turned out to be true, but there was so much more to learn from his statement. Protecting an illusion of success had become front and centre, ruling my world. Was that where it belonged? It was preventing me from receiving any further guidance from Dr. Mills, and from looking less than perfect in the eyes of others. It had taken the place of inner integrity.

Somehow, in parallel with a sincere desire to penetrate the mystery of being and know only Oneness, there was an ego looking for recognition and afraid to fail. As Dr. Mills had said to me in my first dokusan, "Won is what a winner wants. He wants to win so others will say he has won." There it was in one concise sentence: winning, and then the "otherness" of seeking praise and recognition from others.

Dr. Mills had had his own experience of learning where success belongs when he was a teenager. He told us the story of a winter day when he played the piano at his church and received many compliments. After the frosty walk home he huddled with his parents around the kitchen stove, talking about his playing. His father said, "Aren't you forgetting something? I'm glad you played so well tonight, Ken, but do you think you did it? Always remember to give credit where it's due: *I of myself can do nothing. It is the Father that doeth the work.*" This statement made such an impression on young Ken that it became the basis of his life and, ever since, as he put it in his memoirs, "Nothing that is achieved is ever accepted without recognizing the Source."[11]

As I came to realize what I had done, it was embarrassing to see how my behaviour revealed that, despite moments of realization, in activity I was still not acknowledging the Source and was attributing success to me alone. I later learned that Dr. Mills called these experiences "being given enough rope to hang yourself," which is exactly what I did. While mortifying in the moment, it was the best thing that could have happened to me.

"Keep all success where it belongs"—or, as Dr. Mills later rephrased it, "to Whom it belongs"—became a vital charge for change. To Whom did it belong? The only solution to the cul-de-sac of personalization in which I found myself was to return to sincerely and deeply acknowledging God-Consciousness. Despite the transforming experience under the beach towel representing God-Consciousness, this humbling new experience showed me that in activity my mind was still conceiving of the Self as "my higher being," with no real acknowledgement of a transpersonal Reality beyond me and my world. It was a sobering experience and a valuable reminder that one moment of realization is not enough. Constant practice, constant remembrance, constant discipline is necessary. As Dr. Mills put it:

> Remember, a revelation is a *recurring event.* One revelation doesn't do it.... It's the same with Enlightenment. Enlightenment is not just one moment; Enlightenment is many! There are many levels of Enlightenment, just as there are many levels of Realization. Work, work, work! [12]

Dr. Mills had endless ways to inspire us to work, including giving us enough rope to hang ourselves. In his lectures he constantly brought new facets of identity to our attention, using sound, metaphor, poetry, diagrams, charts, and stories to loosen our attachment to the personal self and remind us of our true nature as one with the Creative Source. He offered many practices and set a high standard for our daily living.

Over the years, Dr. Mills returned to the subject of success with me again and again, finding new ways to expose a limiting personalization of allowing personal insecurity and need for success to overtake an acknowledgement that "I of myself can do nothing." It wasn't enough to have lofty considerations of acknowledging

God-Consciousness in the privacy of my home while studying in the morning. I had to put it into practice as I ventured out every day, including in the business world.

Dr. Mills' freedom was my example. He had no fear of failure and was always the student, learning something new. In his seventies he took up weight lifting and painting and taught himself to compose on the newly available electronic keyboards. Furthermore, throughout his life, he remained vividly true to what he had arrived at within himself regardless of the views of those around him, and with no concern about how he might appear to others. And he never neglected to acknowledge that "I of myself can do nothing; it is the Father that doeth the work."

Choice

"AHHH . . . YAHHHH. . . ." "Ahhh . . . yeeee. . . ." My whole being poured into these sounds. It felt like calling across centuries, across galaxies, as pure sound—transpersonal, fluid, a wave of energy glancing across time and space. Dr. Mills was standing in front of me, giving me sounds to imitate, and I was doing what I had dreamed of all my life: singing with a free and open voice. It felt completely natural and so much fun. Singing is an activity that apparently makes many people self-conscious. For me. in this moment it broke that barrier completely.

I had always wanted to sing. When I was a child, my mother had offered me every alternative: piano lessons, violin lessons, ballet and jazz lessons, and drama classes. She never told me her reason for not letting me take singing lessons. Maybe she didn't want to put up with my practising, or perhaps she had been told by our school choir conductor that my voice stood out and wasn't always on pitch. In the elementary school choir, to my shame, the teacher had told me to mouth the words in concerts.

Nevertheless, the desire to sing was always there and had been heightened by the debut of the Star-Scape Singers. When a choir formed five years later at the 1983 summer festival at Sun-Scape Inn, I was in the front row, eager to give it a try. Dr. Mills dropped by the Unfoldment Hall to listen to us and almost immediately picked me out as a "wobbler." Here we go again, I thought, kicked out of the choir already. Instead, he worked with me, and it was magical. He made a sound and told me to imitate it, which I did without thinking about it. My focus was entirely on making whatever noise was necessary in order to release the sound. I felt a deep impelling to do this, as strong as the original impulse to hear Dr. Mills speak. Within minutes of imitating sounds back and forth, my body vibrating in the powerful energy field, a beautiful open and free voice was heard.

A week or so later, at a Star-Scape rehearsal, Dr. Mills looked at me and said, "What's she doing sitting there? She's a contralto." I stood up and sang some notes for Dr. Mills, who determined that I had a soprano range but an alto sound. "Why not learn both the soprano and alto parts and we'll see how it goes," he remarked pleasantly. Reeling from the unexpected opening I had just been given, my mind raced with the thoughts of learning the mountain of Star-Scape music—twice, and after one five-minute singing lesson! I began attending Star-Scape Singers' rehearsals and learning the music. While it was a relief a few weeks later to be assigned the second soprano part, the energy engendered by the attempt to learn it all propelled me quickly to a whole new level. The beginning stages of standing in the line and becoming comfortable with such a radical change in activity were passed over more easily with my attention focused on the attempt to learn the music and engage the totality of the experience.

Rehearsing as an understudy with the Star-Scape Singers was richly gratifying physically, emotionally, artistically, and intellectually. It was also daunting—several of the singers were professional musicians, and the group had been rehearsing and performing as a vocal ensemble for years and were already touring internationally. Occasionally during a rehearsal I received a few minutes of individual instruction from Dr. Mills, imitating his sound, which helped me to find my own. I would go home and practise for hours, learning to stabilize the placement in exercises and then in the music.

One day, when I was attempting to sing a note, only a squeak came out. Dr Mills said, "The voice was never supposed to sound like a squeak. It shook the world into form." He walked over to me, tilted his head back, and cupped his hands at his mouth, saying, "Tilt the cup to receive the notes. They are not in your voice. All you are doing is preparing to receive them." I imitated his gesture, and a huge sound poured in, a vibrant illustration of the same instruction he had given me since we first met: be open to receiving rather than personalizing. "Get out of the way by giving it away."

On another occasion Dr. Mills pressed his fingers on my jawline, and instantly my jaw relaxed and the sound poured in. It felt like a lifetime of pent-up tension had been released. A few days later I was in his music room, standing next to the piano. Dr. Mills sat at the keyboard and walked his fingers up the notes of the high soprano range. High C, and several notes higher, were effortless. I had somehow acquired almost a whole new octave of soprano range.

This newly opened voice gave me more confidence standing in the line with the Star-Scape Singers. I relished the moments of being part of that tower of sound, pure energy, boundary-less, vibrating in a sphere much less dense than Earth. There was nothing personal about it. This releasement, this shift in identity to being sound, was immediate and completely natural. It was a visceral experience of what Dr. Mills said in his Unfoldments: we are Sound Being in essence.

After about a year of attending rehearsals as an understudy I had developed some technique and had learned much of the repertoire, but I was still a long way from being ready to perform. The gap was heartbreaking. From the first moment he heard me sing, Dr. Mills claimed the possibilities that he heard in my sound as complete and perfect now. Nevertheless, years of work are necessary to fully realize it. His ability to open the voice, and his endless images and metaphors, greatly accelerated my learning. I could imitate his sound and walk into a new vocal palette. In the moment it was magical and exciting. But just hours later, back home at my piano, attempting to replicate what I had done, I learned that this gift did not alleviate the need for long hours of daily practice.

The Star-Scape Singers had learned to hold the pitch with extra-ordinary accuracy through long pieces of unaccompanied music. Accomplishing this was my greatest challenge, and I learned from Dr. Mills that it stemmed from a familiar stumbling block: "The lack of pitch is usually too much concern over giving a sound instead of *hearing it* before you give it, because you can't give what you haven't got." He continued in poetry:

> So hear the sound that you wish to impart
> In the joy of singing with an open heart.
> And then the pitch will conform as planned
> To the harmonic structure of a Song to be sung for Man.
>
> The pitch is elusive when the attention does start
> To dart from head and then to heart.
> But when the attention is caught in wonder,
> You'll find there the Pitch, the Source, the evidence, Wonder.

This spontaneous poem was applicable to all aspects of my life. Dr. Mills' musical instructions were never only about learning to sing. Listening for the Pitch, for the sound that goes with an open heart, rather than being concerned about giving a sound, was the key to my entire life. It was the lesson of releasement.

To achieve their goal of performing in Carnegie Hall and touring the concert halls of Europe, the Star-Scape Singers practised on most evenings and on weekends, while also working in full-time jobs. It was clear that in order to achieve this level, I needed to work much harder and release the obstacle of personalization and over-thinking, and even then there was no guarantee of making the grade.

My logical mind, fear of failure, and need for success—and likely my family's definition of an acceptable career—all came to the fore. Given the choice of a growing business career that was already showing promise or a long-shot chance to be part of a world-touring singing group while working other jobs, I didn't abandon the career. In the end, it seemed to be Dr. Mills who made the decision. He reminded me of the value of the volunteer work I had been doing previously, transcribing the Unfoldments. We both understood that for me to sing with Star-Scape required a commitment and a leap beyond what I was willing and able to do.

For a year I had taken the risk and become immersed in music, doing what I had loved most as a child. Continuing the journey would require letting go of things that seemed necessary for survival and success. It was a stark, difficult choice of heart and mind, and I still wonder today what my life would have been if I had chosen my heart. Even if I hadn't made the grade, going for it and giving it my all would have derailed my well-ordered life, but at the same time it would have given me the fruits of following a purity of intention. Instead I made a choice on the side of compromise and conformity, for something that I already knew I could do well.

No longer singing, I reluctantly returned to the typewriter and remembered that I loved translating the sound of the Unfoldments, heard through the headphones of a Dictaphone machine, into sentences on paper. Shaping the spontaneous language of an Unfoldment into recognizable English grammar was far more creative than transcribing a normal lecture. It was almost like translating music from sound into notes on a score. And it was something I could do in my own time while also pursuing a career.

I continued to organize concerts for the Star-Scape Singers in Toronto and, in the years that followed, had a few brief opportunities to join the line and sing for a while. However, each time I took this step, something "big and new" opened in my business career. I never did make the grade, nor did I make the choices to enable that to happen.

The Star-Scape Singers went on to perform in New York's Carnegie Hall and on many other stages around the world. I made a small donation towards their first tour of Europe, even though at that time I was barely making enough money to support myself. As soon as I did this, my world opened up. Instead of it being limited to paying rent and meeting other personal needs, it now encompassed a European tour. By simply writing a cheque, I included in what constituted my experience something as grand as performing all over Europe. While the amount on the cheque probably had no effect on the tour, it was transforming for me. I had discovered that making donations to support something meaningful is a marvellous way to engender a more expansive and inclusive outlook, and I continue to do so today.

Many times throughout the 1980s and 1990s the Star-Scape Singers toured Europe, performing in festivals, in cathedrals and concert halls, to rave reviews. They toured Eastern Europe several times even before those countries were fully open to the West, and they sang to great acclaim in the Soviet Union. Musically literate audiences in Europe were deeply appreciative of the sound and the technique of these singers. We were often astonished to observe how, in the wake of their performances, borders came down and countries opened up to democracy and freedom.

It was an honour to have briefly stood in the line with the Star-Scape Singers, and it was the fulfillment of a secret aspiration ever since their concert debut. It gave me the raw, direct experience of knowing that I am Sound Being in essence, and only secondarily a material body. Energy, vibration, and sound are my essential nature. To this very day I cherish the gift received.

On my music score during a rehearsal I jotted down this statement made by Dr. Mills: "If God ever had an image, His form would be sound."

Master of Being an Ass

A FEW YEARS after the opportunity to sing with Star-Scape, I was at an Unfoldment enjoying listening to Dr. Mills speak and was jolted by some startling words: "master of being an ass." It turned out to be Dr. Mills' definition of an MBA.

By then I had been working in publishing for several years, starting as an assistant acquisitions editor. Soon after joining the publishing firm, I was asked by the CEO, Warren Bingham, to provide administrative support to the management team that was developing a strategic plan. Warren noticed that I had an aptitude for strategic thinking and sent me to take strategic planning courses. I was soon fully involved in the project.

The final plan called for adding a conference business. The opportunity to start up and run this new division was offered to me and became my first taste of business management and entrepreneurship. I was so excited that what had been just an idea on paper was attracting customers and generating revenue that I wanted to frame instead of process the first registration forms and cheques. After a few years of my successfully building this business, Warren encouraged me to do a master's degree in business administration (MBA).

A business degree was the logical next step in my growing career, but to friends studying with Dr. Mills, it was an odd choice. Why go back to university and plunge into the business world, which would undoubtedly draw me away from the Unfoldment and deeper into the realm of personal success? It was a good question, and one that I still ask myself today, but at the time, the question seemed small-minded, limiting my future possibilities. I expected to work for a long time. Why not have an interesting, well-paying career doing something I was good at and enjoyed?

Someone must have told Dr. Mills of my plans, which prompted the "master of being an ass" phrase. Group dynamics being what they are, I was soon receiving advice from others at the Unfoldment that day that I shouldn't do the MBA. Fortunately I decided to ask Dr. Mills about it directly. I don't recall his exact words, but from our conversation I understood that he was not advising me whether or not to go back to university; his intent was more fundamental. If his definition of an MBA had irritated me, it was an opportunity to observe, within myself, a false sense of identity at being enthralled with having an MBA. As long as I could see through any position that might appear in my experience and not personalize it—and be able to laugh at the joke—there was no right or wrong about it.

This exchange gave me a lens through which to view Dr. Mills' comments over the years and to counter the all-too-human tendency to want to hand over responsibility for life decisions to someone else. Dr. Mills would never tell me what to do, and he reminded me not to interpret his words in that light. It taught me to use his sometimes irritating comments for my own self-examination, as well as for guidance in arriving at my own decisions. Rightly or wrongly, I decided to do the MBA and make the business world—a world consumed by the logical mind and personal success—my gymnasium in which to practise being in the world but not of it.

When preparing for the MBA, I was living in a large house in downtown Toronto with three friends who were also studying with Dr. Mills. On a Friday night we hosted some international guests and held a reception in our home following a Toronto performance of the Star-Scape Singers. I was scheduled to write the four-hour MBA graduate management admission test (GMAT) early the next morning. Having barely slept a wink, I wondered if in my sleepless state I would be able to sit, let alone pass, the exam. When the results arrived in the mail, I was surprised and happy to find that I had received a very high mark. My father was thrilled, and on the very same day that I received the results, he took the whole family out to dinner to celebrate. I'm sure he was relieved to see a future for me in other than studying with Dr. Mills.

Remembering my father's uncharacteristic, spontaneous gesture that day still moves me to tears. I loved being my father's daughter, and my choice to dedicate so much of my life to studying with Dr. Mills felt like a betrayal to him—a rebuke even—to choose metaphysics over science. We never talked about it, leaving us both with unresolved feelings. I wanted to please him but could not abandon what I knew had to constitute my life. I wonder today whether a large part of my motivation to do the MBA was to prove to myself and my parents that I wasn't a flake, that I had a sharp intellect and could use it, just as they did in their careers.

The adjustment of going back to university in 1984 at the age of twenty-eight was much bigger for me than it was for the other students. In addition to the reorientation to schoolwork, I had a major reorientation to my peers, who had spent the last decade very differently.

Until I went back to university, I hadn't realized how much I had withdrawn from the world. An MBA involves considerable group work, and there was no avoiding social relationships amongst the students.

I don't know what they thought of me, but I felt like a visitor from another planet. In addition, I had moved back in with my parents to save money, an arrangement that required adjustment for all three of us. It took time to find my footing, reintegrating life at home with my parents, doing the MBA, and continuing my dedication to the Unfoldment. In typical fashion I pursued each of these three separately and didn't attempt to bring elements of any of them into other realms where I knew they would not be readily accepted.

The dramatic change of going to university and living with my parents was a shock, but I could feel that it was good for me. I thought, "If I am finding it hard to function in the world after ten years with Dr. Mills, how would I be able to function after twenty or thirty years?" It was not that Dr. Mills required his students to live set apart in an ashram type of existence; it was the engrossing nature of the Unfoldment and its surrounding activities. The reintegration required me to learn to function again in the rational, secular world in which I had grown up, but now with a new appreciation of the true nature of Being. It gave me the intention to learn "be in the world but not of it"—to fully engage in the world as it appears, while maintaining the inner distance of being the observer, aware that this is just a passing show.

The decision to get an MBA changed the course of my life. Ever since, I have had a foot in what at the time were two separate worlds. Friends on each side of the "divide" found my interest in the other side very puzzling. In the 1980s, on the one hand, few people could see a place for philosophical insight or meditation in the workplace. On the other hand, most people on a spiritual path found the business world foreign and distasteful. It was a lonely choice and one that often left me feeling that I was not bringing my whole self to any aspect of my life experience. However, although my life had become divided, I was convinced that bringing these together in some form of integration was possible and even necessary.

Wisdom Isn't Clad in Form

AFTER GRADUATING with an MBA in 1986, I joined the Canada Consulting Group, which soon became part of the global firm the Boston Consulting Group (BCG). My social education continued, learning to integrate with my peers, along with learning the craft of strategy consulting. For the next twelve years I enjoyed a career at BCG, working with brilliant and insightful colleagues and clients. It was such a set-apart, immersive environment that there were times when I thought, well, now I've joined two "cults," the Unfoldment and BCG.

I had put myself into two worlds and had chosen extremes in both cases. Studying with Dr. Mills and being part of the group that surrounded him was a deeply immersive experience. At the same time, strategy consulting was an intensive career that was its own rarified world. One world was about going beyond the logical mind and experiencing our true nature as Conscious Being; the other was about using the mind to develop strategies and plans for success in the material world. But both sought the underlying ideas behind the appearance, and both relied on the persuasive use of language to alter thinking and thereby circumstances. These were perhaps the common elements that drew me to strategy consulting.

BCG was a very enticing environment. We worked on projects in Canada and internationally that were important enough to "keep the CEO up at night." There is a theory that consulting attracts insecure people who have a high need for praise and validation, people who are willing to work extremely hard in order to be seen as smarter and faster, as brilliant and insightful, offering indispensable advice to the client. That motivation doesn't apply to all the consultants I knew, but it did to some, including me.

Joining BCG was a leap straight into the realm of winning, and helping corporations win, despite all the warnings and opportunities I had received to take a different course. Dr. Mills never questioned my choice and he took a great interest in my career, as he took an interest in everyone who studied with him.

My decision in the mid-1980s to pursue a business career after years of prioritizing the spiritual path reflected a shift in society that was happening at the time. Despite the flowering of spirituality and the search for meaning in the 1970s, the quest had shifted by the 1980s to achieving material success and wealth. Consumerism was enthusiastically embraced, and the balancing factor of religion and spirituality was losing its sway. The religious beliefs that had given us our moral values were falling away, and there appeared to be no new basis for civil society other than competition and winning. The Western world turned to the rational mind as the new god, the source of knowledge and authority. Facts and logic were the antidote to the faith-based beliefs that people were rejecting and to the New Age movement, which now looked like a passing fad. Science and engineering, and especially information technology, were the route to a more enlightened future.

In business, as in science, these were decades in which we seemed to believe that the intellect, if pushed far enough, could provide the answers and even the sense of meaning and purpose that in the past had been sought through religion and spirituality. Analytical professions, such as the management consulting career I chose, were greatly valued. Financial services organizations grew exponentially in size and stature. Business leaders and digital entrepreneurs were highly compensated and recognized for their work. Working long hours at the office was a badge of honour. Business success and wealth was implicitly the basis for a life well lived.

Nevertheless, I was determined not to identify with what was written on my business card, but to remain positioned, knowing that I am conscious being primarily and only secondarily a person having the fun of working as a consultant. This standpoint is fundamental to practising being in the world and not of it. When we do not appreciate our significance as one with the Source, Consciousness, we tend to puff up our material existence to seem as real and important as possible. From the start of my career I knew that any sense of identity based on circumstances and personality was ephemeral and ultimately unsatisfying—even while I was drawn to the image of being a business professional.

I continued to meditate and study, attended the Unfoldments whenever I was in Toronto, and used my vacations to attend Dr. Mills' workshops and festivals. I attempted to fulfill, at the most basic level, Dr. Mills' words to me to "continue to wear the garment of constancy and keep all success where it belongs." I would wake up early in whatever hotel, in whatever city it may have been, and set myself for the day. Soon I was at work as a consultant, sharpening the analytical skills of my mind.

It sometimes seemed that I had recreated the dichotomy of my childhood, only this time I was playing both parts: the scientist and the mystic. I felt the pressure and compromises on both sides. On the one hand, I missed events with Dr. Mills and time with my friends who were studying the Unfoldment. On the other hand, I didn't develop deep friendships with colleagues at work or take full advantage of all the professional opportunities now available to me. It was a divided world, with me running back and forth between the two. But I was finally maturing, with many stimulating and challenging opportunities to grow.

It didn't help that at this time the corporate world and the world of wisdom teachings were miles apart. Spirituality outside of religion was still seen as a cult or as New Age pablum for those who couldn't make it in the real world. Although there were meditation programs that didn't fit either category, at best corporate business viewed meditation as removing competitive edge, making people passive and less productive.

The combination of business and spirituality was made even more difficult by the fact that, at that time, any spiritual quest had to be a public activity. People attended lectures and meditation gatherings, and some travelled the world to find spiritual teachers. In most cases they were expected to sign up, become students of a teacher, or join an organization. The only private way to learn about spiritual teachings was to read books that could be found in obscure, incense-soaked stores, in between the crystals and the beads. Today's concept of a self-directed path, with access at home to spiritual teachings via the internet, was still decades away. While I was working at BCG, the nature of spiritual teachings—in content, format, and access—was so remote from the business world that few people working in business, including me, were open about their commitment to a spiritual path. I often felt uncomfortable about my ongoing study with Dr. Mills and what people might be thinking about that. As much as possible I kept it to myself, rather than breaking through the suggestion of "otherness" and having the courage of my convictions.

I noticed that even religion had become a private matter, rather than the public statement of identity it once was. We brought only our body and mind to work; feeling, intuition, wonder, and other non-rational aspects of being were kept to a minimum. This required inventing a persona for working in business. When I spoke with people who chose to leave the business world, they often said it was the inability to bring their whole self into the workplace that caused them to change careers. I too felt this way but had a forum through my ongoing association with Dr. Mills for the non-rational aspects of my nature. And dividing my life into separate buckets had become normal for me.

One of my first clients at BCG was the newly created Ontario Premier's Council, a panel of prominent Canadians advising the premier on strategy for industries in the province of Ontario. Our consulting team conducted research and analysis and developed draft recommendations for the panel. Since this was a public project, one evening over dinner I spoke with Dr. Mills on what we were learning about the competitiveness of Ontario industries. He was strongly in agreement with the concept of competition, whether it be in organizations, in a province, or between countries. He said, "A society that loses a competitiveness of excellence—when you have no competition, no contest, no battles raging in the realm of excellence, you have a nation of people going to sleep." We could have put that on the cover of our report.

The work done by our consulting team led by BCG partner David Pecaut was made public and was very well received. One memorable day the Premier's Council and another project on which I had worked were both featured in the daily newspapers. I told Dr. Mills about the articles and said that I wanted to find a way to bring this type of activity and accomplishment in my life into harmony with my dedication to the Unfoldment, otherwise I felt divided.

Dr. Mills replied, "Oh, no, no, no, no. You don't try to make 'this' harmonize with 'That.' Don't feel that false sense when you're in your office and in the work that you're doing with the government. Remember that your work is to be true to your Self. You deal with what appears as your office as best you can, but remain positioned in what you know to be true."

After this conversation I became more relaxed about the combination of career and study of the Unfoldment and went to the office every day to simply do my job to the best of my ability, while remembering that my real work is to be "true to the Self." Although this form of "work" sounds abstract, I found that simply by claiming it, it was stabilizing, and my approach was no longer so caught up in the triumphs and trials of the consulting world.

Dr. Mills also gave me valuable guidance as a woman in business. I had told him that I was frequently the only woman around the table in client meetings. My upbringing as the daughter and granddaughter of women in science had prepared me well for navigating the largely male world of professional work, but I was still finding my feet in how to be a woman working in business in the 1980s and 1990s. Some women adopted a masculine style of behaviour and dress and were more aggressive than the men. Others accepted a submissive relationship to their male colleagues and found themselves second-class citizens. Dr. Mills gave me a simple statement that became my guideline: "Don't draw attention to difference." Applying this principle, I realized that both accentuating feminine attributes and attempting to imitate masculine ones drew attention to difference. Adopting a standpoint of unity, I focused on what was undifferentiated and on our shared purpose in the work for the client. I found that when I did this, the men in the room did the same, and it had the remarkable effect of eliminating much of the tension. I've since passed on this advice to many young women in business who have also found it of value.

In 1991 at a gathering at a friend's home with Dr. Mills and a group of people who were meeting him for the first time, he turned to me and said:

> So many are constrained by the social encounter and its demands for achieving success on the broad scale of social acceptance. The only acceptance you must find is yourself accepted in the light of that which is termed the divine Principle or the divine Ideal. You can't expect to find yourself accepted in the sight of those who are still trying to create

an impression and dominate others in your social environs. You don't have access then to the higher potentialities at all, because those are closed to egotistical involvement. As long as you are egotistically involved with one-upmanship, then you are closed to those higher promptings which would exculpate you from the situation.

When chaos seems to surround you, know that if you perceive it as chaos, you have nothing to be concerned about because God lives as your very presence in the perception of the lack of rhythm, the lack of harmony, and whatever the lack is that confronts you. It's all a suggestion that there is a creation apart from That Which IS.

So wherever you're working, wherever you be, you can imagine the wonders of knowing this. You're in a world in which the social environment is such that most people are just wrapped up in being the vendors of their success, whereas you are not "vending" anything. You are only venting the great zephyr of knowingness that comes with the magnification of what you know to be Real.[13]

It was wonderful advice that gave me great stability in navigating the environment in which I found myself. However, as I continued in consulting, the pressure to succeed and consistently deliver outstanding results only increased. One project was particularly difficult and often left me emotionally drained. This led to the following conversation with Dr. Mills. His vivid description of armour melting was exactly what I feeling at the time.

> LJ: I start off in the morning poised and together, having studied and being set, and then become what I'd describe as "frozen in the headlights," feeling it is too much and I can't cope, and end up in an emotionally negative spiral. Professionally as well as personally, it is not an attractive situation to be in.
>
> KGM: That's good, though, it's a wonderful exercise for you. What you are facing is a situation of intensity which will make you grow, it's a positive step. You are responding

to the intensity of a business situation and you find that you have to put on armour to protect yourself, and then the armour starts to strangle you. Then when the situation is released, the armour melts and you are just left vibrating with nothing to hang on to and you call it an emotional strain. It's because you have moved into a personalization of the wisdom of your offering.

LJ: There is a tendency to go into mental overdrive and not be able to sleep and have images and things carried with me from work—

KGM: Don't. That is the residue of personal involvement. Don't have your wings clipped by emotionality. You can laugh at it, you can say anything you like from the standpoint of the vigilant one, but you can't say anything to it if you get caught in it and hallucinate about it. Stay within your heart where you are feeling the Authentic.

Remember, Wisdom isn't clad in form. Wisdom uses the form as a voice piece into a dimensional experience. In other words, intelligence uses the non-intelligent for an entrance into the world that is receptive. Intelligence uses a non-intelligent state. Intelligence has never been found in a body.

This was a transforming and healing conversation that deepened my feeling of the Authentic and my commitment to acknowledging the Source of wisdom. My work at BCG was not just a job; it was a continuous lesson in not personalizing. The statement "Wisdom isn't clad in form," and the advice again to laugh at emotions and treat it lightly— between the words as well as in them, I found great wisdom, wisdom that appeared to be clad in form as Dr. Mills but is never found in form.

I began to choose projects at work that interested me, regardless of whether they were on the track to partnership. These usually had a social or civic value such as an internship program or support for scientific research in Canada. I monitored any sense of emotional pressure as a signal that I was taking things personally, and I would reorient my attention to knowing that "Wisdom isn't clad in form."

The Science of the Invisible

WHILE I WAS WORKING OUT the apparent dichotomy between my job and the Unfoldment, in another part of my life the philosophical divide that I had felt with my mother was starting to close.

One day at my parents' house in the early 1990s I was very surprised to find, next to the usual stack of scientific journals, newsletters about energy fields and dousing addressed to my mother. But then Mum had always been fearless about exploring new frontiers of knowledge. Throughout her life she hadn't fit in easily with other women of her generation and had carved her own path.

As soon as my sister and I were old enough to have our own summer activities, my mother began what became twenty-five years of solo adventure travel all over the world, often joining scientific expeditions as a research volunteer. She learned to scuba dive and went on marine biology expeditions, well into her seventies. After I started working in business, Mum and I enjoyed a mother-daughter role reversal: I would drive her to the airport in my business suit on the way to the office, and drop off Mum in her jeans, with backpack and diving gear, heading off to explore another part of the world.

Mum's training as a scientist, and the lack of traditional female role models in her life, made her an unusual mother. I loved and respected her deeply, but my inner journey away from our family's reliance on intellect and into dedicating much of my life to exploring awareness beyond the mind, had driven a wedge into our relationship. It often seemed that either I was a living challenge to my parents' belief that there was nothing beyond the material body and its brain, or I was evidence that they had failed as parents, with a daughter immersed in the kind of beliefs that my grandfather had worked so hard to dispel. Unlike families in which this kind of rift is debated and challenged, we never discussed these differences and they were left to fester, almost as though if we didn't talk about it, they didn't really exist or at least not enough to harm our fragile family unit.

Reflecting on this, I wondered how society, and especially families like mine, had arrived at the assumption that science and religion (or spirituality) were opposites and incompatible. The divided world view that separates science and religion can be traced back centuries to the Europe of Galileo and Newton. When science presented new and dangerous challenges to the primacy of religion in the sixteenth and seventeenth centuries, the Church, in a kind of power-sharing arrangement, allowed scientists to continue their work as long as they confined themselves to the laws of the physical world. The Church maintained its authority over the non-material world and all that it encompassed such as heaven and hell, love, beauty, morality, and justice, while leaving facts and theories about the nature of the material world to science.[14]

By the time I was growing up in the mid-twentieth century, people seemed to have accepted the proposition that there actually *were* two realms—a physical world analyzed by scientists and a heavenly realm worshipped in church. Some religious adherents chose only religion and rejected science. Materialists such as my parents chose science and rejected religion, assigning anything in the non-material realm to unsubstantiated religious beliefs or to not-yet-understood chemical reactions. This created the need for a world view in which life and consciousness arose from a non-sentient physical universe. The accompanying belief that the rational mind was the only legitimate source of knowledge led to a society in which inexplicable, non-rational aspects of human life were often viewed as suspect or were ignored entirely.

It seems to me that my parents' insistence that reality is solely material was derived at least in part from their avoidance of anything that was in the domain of religion. If religion hadn't occupied the space on the non-material side, scientists might have colonized this territory earlier.

But by the 1990s, while I was spending long days at BCG, my mother was redirecting her sharp scientific mind and research skills to the invisible realm. Her change in perspective had begun with a health challenge. Soon after she retired from teaching, Mum developed rheumatoid arthritis (which remarkably barely slowed down her travels and scuba diving or the hours in the garden at her home). Traditional medicine seemed to do nothing for the pain or the progress of the disease, and she began to explore alternative treatments. Mum figured out through trial and error that she was sensitive to mould, and once she had eliminated mould from her diet, changed her gardening habits, and limited her exposure to dog and cat hair, her symptoms improved. From there she went to an energy healer, bringing samples of mould and pet hair, and to her amazement the treatments eliminated her sensitivities entirely. After this experience she had to admit that there was more to life—more to what constituted her beingness—than her scientific training had revealed.

Mum continued to investigate energy fields, which led her to dousing. At a grocery store my mother would surreptitiously douse with her pendulum the fruits and vegetables to determine which ones didn't have mould. She claimed to be accurate and used this method to manage her diet. Then she began using the dousing pendulum to answer questions about other aspects of her life and was amazed that the "guidance" she received proved again and again to be accurate. Her lifelong belief that it was necessary to think through every problem had to be re-examined. She had discovered a precognitive level of knowing, one that was available only by bypassing logical thinking.

One day in 1996, Mum fell while taking her dog for a walk in the ravine. She forced herself up and walked back up the hill and through the neighbourhood to her home, where she called my sister. When Sue arrived, Mum insisted on a cup of tea before leaving for the hospital, knowing there would be a long wait in the emergency room. When the doctors finally diagnosed a severely broken hip, they were amazed at her endurance. Mum told me later that when she fell, Dr. Mills suddenly occurred to her. As she struggled to get up and make the long walk home, she felt his presence. She attributed her ability to get home and calmly drink her tea to this feeling. I was amazed by this, and so was Dr. Mills. She had only heard him speak once, in 1978, and had barely shown any interest in him since.

Around her family and friends Mum was cheerfully open about her new "woo-woo methods" as she called them and about the "eye of newt" conferences that she had started to attend. Watching my mother balancing her lifelong rational outlook with undeniable glimpses into a higher realm was inspiring to me. Dad and Sue were very disapproving of these developments in Mum's life, and they did their best to discredit her methods and discourage her explorations. But Mum relied, as she always had, on her own experience, which was telling her that information and change happened first on an energy level and then manifested on a physical level.

My mother's explorations into the non-material realm coincided with a fundamental change taking place in the scientific community in the final decades of the twentieth century. The split that had begun with power sharing between religious authorities and scientists was finally breaking down. Spiritual leaders were overseeing joint research with scientists, based on the premise that were not two realms but only one; the laws of the universe had to apply in every mode of existence. Science can no longer ignore the subjectivity of the person conducting the experiment. Religion can no longer ignore the findings of science. No belief system—religious, spiritual, or scientific—can be satisfying when it ignores entire realms of existence.

We are no longer seeking the comfort of a belief system in an unknown universe, but neither are we satisfied by exploring only within the limits of the rational mind. We are seeking direct knowledge of what we are, incorporating both the visible and the invisible, the objective and the subjective, matter and energy, the material world and our non-material nature.

By the end of the twentieth century, physicists and neuroscientists were working right at the edge of reclaiming the territory of the invisible and exploring it with scientific curiosity and rigour. In quantum physics the false barrier between the invisible and the visible had already come down. The famous double-slit experiments with electrons in the 1970s and 1980s had led to further, even more puzzling, findings such as entanglement that continue to baffle scientists about the nature of reality.

One of the most exciting scientific discoveries I came upon had to do with the nature of light. For decades, experiments in quantum physics had found that light converts back and forth between behaving as a stream of particles and behaving as a wave. Scientists in a lab in

Italy in 2017 finally proved correct Einstein's claim that light doesn't convert back and forth; light is always both wave and particle.* This deep insight has profound implications for understanding life itself as both wave and particle, both energy and matter. As soon as I read the article, I jumped up and said, "That's it! That's what we are, both wave and particle!" Here was scientific language describing the mystery of the coincidence of the invisible and visible, and the releasement of energy that happens when we no longer identify only as the particle. Our nature as simultaneously wave and particle perhaps explains why healing can begin in the realm of thought, which is an energy wave, and bring about a corresponding healing in the body, the visible particle.

At the same time, breakthrough discoveries in the field of neuro-science were changing our understanding of the brain. The concept of brain plasticity was first proposed in 1890 by William James in *The Principles of Psychology*, but it was not taken seriously until the 1970s. By the 1990s, it had become a widely accepted fact. New medical imaging technology had demonstrated that altering thinking, attention, and emotion changes the physical brain. Further research showed that these changes in brain chemistry in turn alter the chemistry of the body, which can bring about physical healing. Increasingly, the evidence shows that long-maintained thoughts of, say, fear or resentment about the external environment cause the brain, and then the body, to react appropriately to the perceived threat, even when this threat is only in thought. Similarly, releasing long-held thoughts and beliefs (such as the "impediment of otherness") also releases fear and changes the brain's chemistry, which signals to the body that it is safe from harm.

Richard Davidson was a key pioneer in the field of brain plasticity. He famously monitored the brain activity of meditators, which demonstrated in Western terms the value of meditation for health and well-being. These findings opened up more mainstream acceptance of

---

* "A research team led by Fabrizio Carbone at EPFL have captured, for the first time ever, a single snapshot of light behaving simultaneously as both a wave and a stream of particles" (Ecole polytechnique fédérale de Lausanne, EPFL, 2017).

meditation and of the mind-body connection—with the mind leading the way.

Seeing these developments in science made me think that perhaps I could have become a scientist and stayed in the family business while exploring my affinity to the Invisible.

My mother seemed to have picked up on the new openness of scientists to exploring the non-material realm. This was gratifying and healing for me, and it brought us closer together in the last decade of her life. By her actions she encouraged me to stand by my convictions and to be open to new possibilities, while rigorously testing everything. My mother found a lightness and joy in her life in those later years and made new friends of all ages. She was able to laugh at her own reactions to discoveries that refuted a lifetime of scientific learning. As always, she took an individual path with no regard for whether or not it fit anyone's expectations of a scientist, a wife and mother, or a tiny woman in the final years of her life. She was a great example to me, as only mothers can be.

Discovering Branding

WHEN I FIRST JOINED BCG, I had imagined that consulting work primarily involved research and analysis to think logically through any business problem. With experience I learned that this was only an input to the real work of consulting. The essence is working closely with the client to reconceive what is possible for their company and vividly evoke this vision through description, facts, models, imagery, metaphor, and rigorous plans, to replace old thinking with new ideas and bring them to life. This does require research and analysis but also imagination and being comfortable with ambiguity. We were working in the realm of ideation, intention, and possibilities and never had all the facts or a situation of certainty.

This broader understanding of consulting had a parallel in what Dr. Mills was doing. All these years, I had been learning from him how to redefine the possible. Rather than identifying solely as an aging body with a rational mind attached, Dr. Mills presented the vision of being Conscious-Being primarily, inseparable from unlimited God-Consciousness, with all the freedom, inspiration, and co-creative responsibility that implies. This is a vision that requires correcting fundamental misperceptions about what is going on here as we live our lives. Like consulting clients, we have to do our own work of implementing a new vision.

I became fascinated by the parallels between what I was learning from Dr. Mills and what I was doing in consulting. I even made a presentation at Kenneth Mills' 1992 summer festival on how management issues could be addressed by drawing on the principles of wisdom teachings. When I made this presentation, I was in my thirties and had gained some confidence and expertise from working in business. It was gratifying to finally make the leap, in the eyes of Dr. Mills and those attending the summer festival, from being a young aspirant to being a mature individual contributing what I had learned in my own life experience. While savouring the newness of this step, I also laughed to observe within myself that the old need for success and approval was being satisfied that day. Dr. Mills saw me anew, and I could feel his respect for my accomplishment. He responded enthusiastically to my presentation and even proposed that I start a consulting firm on this basis.

While I could imagine the potential of a consulting firm offering this advice, actually presenting principles of high teaching as my mode of consulting was way outside of anything I was willing to attempt at BCG, let alone setting up my own firm. In the business environment of the early 1990s, I didn't have the fortitude to introduce these principles explicitly into my consulting work, even though it was always implicit. Had I not been so reticent, I might have anticipated the trend twenty-five years later of bringing mindfulness meditation and timeless wisdom into the boardroom. Today, at BCG's arch-rival, McKinsey & Company, several senior partners are doing exactly this integration, and an increasing number of boutique consulting firms are offering it as their primary service. Dr. Mills, as usual, was way ahead of his time.

Working with clients at BCG, I gained an understanding of branding. This too seemed to translate across to other aspects of my life. It gave me a conceptual framework to reconcile my deep affiliation with spirituality on the one hand, with being so uncomfortable about it on the other. It seemed to me that it was the brand image of spirituality that was unattractive, even though I was constantly hungry for its substance. I didn't find anything attractive in the brand image of the New Age movement or in contemporary spiritual teachers as they were portrayed at the time. Yet my life was dedicated to something that seemed to fit this category. The dilemma was frustrating because I was still caught in seeking validation and didn't have the language or an image to describe what I was doing in a way that would satisfy both my inner integrity and a need for acceptance.

Reflecting on this, I became interested in how the brand might change without changing the essence. How would you take one of the oldest brands of all—the concept of God—and remake it for a new day?

Applying this framework, I realized that "rebranding" was what Dr. Mills had been doing for me. I was never going to accept my concept of the God of the Christian church that had meant so much to my earlier ancestors, nor could I accept the materialism of my parents and grandparents. Dr. Mills offered what he had arrived at, a standpoint in which acknowledgement of God was central, without a religious affiliation. My educated mind, taught to resist the word *God*, had rebelled, but from the beginning I had a deep sense of knowing, especially when expressed in other words such as *Consciousness* or *Source*. Dr. Mills' unique use of language, and his unique life in which he defined himself as "spirited, not spiritual," was a powerful example of what was possible. Dr. Mills had been rebranding the concept of God for me in every Unfoldment and interaction. I began to think about how I would do this in my own life, taking cues from what I was learning from Dr. Mills.

It seemed to me that many people may have this branding problem. They are drawn to the same essence, but negative thoughts about religion, the word *God*, or the New Age movement obscure a deeper response. How does someone like me, who grew up without religion or spirituality, express an inner knowingness that they didn't create themself, that there is something greater than "me and my world"?

I knew firsthand from working with clients that changing a brand requires changing language, imagery, and emotional affiliation in order to change the way we think about something. Could these techniques be used to get us past intellectual reactions and reconnect us with an innate inner yearning? We would need new language and imagery, unaffiliated with any religion or the New Age movement.

It didn't feel right to just invent new words and images and try to impose a new brand by manipulating thinking, as happens in consumer branding. Could a new brand emerge organically, globally, without any institution, leadership hierarchy, ritual, or even doctrine and become integrated into the mainstream? Once this question had occurred to me, it never let me go.

Some of us had had a taste of a new brand of spirituality in the 1970s, but during the following two decades spirituality had been largely swept aside in the drive for material success and reliance on the logical mind. It was assumed that these were incompatible with a serious quest—you couldn't have one without sacrificing the other. Surely the new brand would have to encompass both.

The growing exchange between East and West was already a core element of this new brand in a blend of Eastern mysticism and Western pragmatism. My favourite book at the time was *Autobiography of a Yogi* by Paramahansa Yogananda, a yogi who had arrived in the West in 1920. Other remarkable Eastern teachers including the Maharishi Mahesh, the Dalai Lama, Trungpa Rinpoche, and Thich Nhat Hanh had come to the West, and their work also helped shape my appreciation of the spiritual path. For many of us, the presence in North America of these leaders fundamentally shaped the changing brand in the West. Spirituality outside of religion was fuelled by globalization, as thousands in North America adopted Eastern ideas and practices without adopting the religion. In particular, the Maharishi's provocative decision in his Transcendental Meditation program to separate meditation from religion opened the door for the multitude of secular meditation and yoga programs that followed and changed the brand of meditation forever.

Despite the negative climate at the time, there were unique and courageous individuals from the West who, along with Kenneth Mills, were altering the brand image of spirituality and pointing the way to a new convergence. The work of Dr. Jon Kabat-Zinn stands out for me as central to the revolutionary change. As a scientist conducting research on relieving pain in patients, and as a meditation practitioner, he applies both logic and love in his methods. He began his career as a molecular biologist at the Massachusetts Institute of Technology (MIT) and then became a student of Buddhist teachers Philip Kapleau and Thich Nhat Hanh and a founding member of the Cambridge Zen Center. In the basement of the University of Massachusetts Hospital in the late 1970s, Dr. Kabat-Zinn began teaching meditation and mindfulness techniques to patients experiencing pain. Even in the 1990s there was still skepticism about the value of this endeavour, although his techniques codified as Mindfulness-Based Stress Reduction (MBSR) were benefiting an ever-growing number of people. While not identified as "spiritual," these techniques take practitioners beyond purely mental exercises as their awareness opens up to identifying as the observer of thoughts, pain, and the body, rather than identifying with the object observed. His assertion to patients that as long as you are breathing, there is more right with you than wrong with you, set a new framework for managing pain. Discovering his work had a profound effect on me, and he continues to be a powerful voice in shaping a new brand that is integrated with health care and science.

During these years another pioneer, Oprah Winfrey, was changing the brand image of spirituality with the books she championed for her book club and by interviewing spiritual teachers on *The Oprah Winfrey Show*. When she first introduced the word *spirit* on her program, ratings dropped and she was under pressure by her network and the media to not challenge the religious status quo. But she persisted and went on to have enormous influence on the development of spirituality outside of religion. She recommended Eckhart Tolle's book *The Power of Now* to her book club soon after it was published in 1997, and it remained on Canadian bestseller lists for almost two decades. When

I read it, I was amazed by the synchronicity with what I had learned from Kenneth Mills. When Oprah interviewed Eckhart Tolle on her television program in 2008, millions watched. This scale of interest and engagement in spirituality outside of religion had been unheard of up to that point.

These individuals were inspiring to me, extending spiritual principles and practices into a world that so obviously had need of them at a time when accusations of cults were still in the air. Their courage opened the door for all who follow, and began to change the brand image of spirituality away from institutional religion and away from exotic and dangerous cults into something new with the potential for broad acceptance.

The growing body of work of neuroscientists, quantum physicists, and other scientists was also a core part of changing the brand, bringing the visible and invisible worlds back together in a new convergence, one that was acceptable to the Western mind.

I was witnessing in the 1990s these early brand changes from my ringside seat of having a foot in the corporate and spiritual worlds. I could see that both spirituality and secular society would have to change to birth something new and that the seeds were already being sown for a new, more integrated brand.

III

LIFE-GIVING FORCE

The Life-giving Force must be a consideration to you. What in your life can you control that is essential for life? What in your life are you master of that is Life-giving? And you deny a primal Source? Or allow it to be considered non-present? There is no one who is capable of controlling the Life-giving Force that sustains what appears as you and your world.

KENNETH G. MILLS

A Chapter on God

AS THE YEARS WENT BY, I had set aside my childhood question and moved on to new considerations. But during the 1990 summer festival I finally told Dr. Mills the story of what had happened on the beach when I was a child and the burning question that had occupied so much of my childhood. Here is an excerpt from that conversation:

> LJ: As a child I used to wonder, "Am I in the world, or is the world in me?" How would you respond to that question?
>
> KGM: That's very beautiful, you as a child wondering whether this world was in you or you were in the world. Now the question comes to give itself up when you realize that the suggestion that "I am in the world" is perceived as a supposition, and the world being in you is a supposition that such a gigantic concept could be within you. So, neither is actual.
>
> LJ: Yes, they are both incomplete.
>
> KGM: Yes. The world is not in you. The greater cannot be put into the lesser. You perceive that the world exists outside of you because you are cognizant of it within you.

His words confirmed what I now already knew: the greater cannot be put into the lesser. The moment on the beach that had shaped my life arose not within me but because the thought "me" was released, allowing for experience without an experiencer.

It feels so arrogant now to think back on the years when I was reluctant to acknowledge anything beyond me and my world, as though I believed that I had created myself and sustained my own existence, as though my personal sense of self was the source of life. So many of us seem to have this arrogance, to the point that acknowledgement of God can be seen as weakness. Richard Rooney, a Protestant Christian and a senior leader in Canadian finance, described his experience to me: "People seem to equate believing in God with being a little thick, a little slow. They tell me that they wish they could have faith like I do, implying that to do so, they would have to give up all rational thinking and intelligence."

Canadian poet and singer-songwriter Leonard Cohen expressed his comfort with the concept of God in an interview with Michael Harris:

> I think there really is a power to tune in on. It's easy for me to call that power God. Some people find it difficult. You mention the word God to them and they go through a lot of difficult reactions, they just don't like it. I mean that there's certainly no doubt about it, that the name has fallen on evil days. But it doesn't have those evil associations or those organizational associations for me. It's easier for me to say God than "some unnamable mysterious power that motivates all living things." The word God for me is very simple and useable. And even to use the masculine pronouns He and Him, it doesn't offend me as it offends many; so that I can say "to become close to Him is to feel His grace" because I have felt it.[15]

According to various market research surveys, 70 to 80 per cent of Canadians believe in God. But what do we mean when we ask and answer the question, "Do you believe in God?" Perhaps we are asking, "Are you still in agreement with what you were taught about God as a child?" Or perhaps, "Are you comfortable with the belief of God in your mind, or are you yearning for more?" Or "Are you willing to acknowledge an unknown Source of life?" When we say, "I don't believe in God," perhaps we are saying, "I no longer believe in the concept of God that I held in the past."

Neither choice—I believe in God or I don't believe in God—is attractive to me. How did a word that is presumably describing a state fundamental to my very existence become tangled up with a word as flimsy as *belief*? I think we can agree that if God is anything, it cannot be a belief.

Regardless of our thoughts about the word *God*, we dream constantly of escape, of going beyond the limits of space and time, and of mortality. Our movies and books are filled with these dreams—cartoons, superheroes, science fiction, space travel, fantasy. Even Santa

Claus comes from this impulse. As Dr. Mills said, "It is so sad when you realize that Santa Claus has been made up, for you have cried out over your years for some presence, anything that can appear to come from someone other than your own."[16]

When I ask people about the word *God*, I find that it opens an avalanche of thought associations and most people want to close the door as fast as possible. "It's too loaded to talk about." But for me, it cannot remain unexamined. As long as it is left aside, there is a hole in our concept of spirituality, and what we think are spiritual pursuits can be just feel-good pastimes. It is spirituality without Spirit, substituting an elevated concept of the personal self for true acknowledgement of That which is beyond it. Unless we revisit the concept called God and re-examine it for a new day, the word that is supposed to connect us to the Source of our existence remains so laden with baggage that it becomes an obstacle to realizing the very state that it describes. I call this re-examining a rebranding because it requires changing our thoughts about the word, and likely changing the word, in order to access its essential meaning. Of course, what is rebranded in this process is not God but ourselves.

Those who worship God in churches, synagogues, and mosques do not have this branding problem. Their faith is part of centuries' old traditions in which the sacred word *God*—named or unnamed—is held in the highest regard possible. With this word at the centre, they enjoy a congruence of language, ritual, and community through their place of worship.

The rest of us feel impelled to reinvent because we still don't know the answer to our presence. There are many scientific explanations, such as evolution or mapping the genome, that help account for how our bodies and the planet appear today. But it is not our bodies, or the planet, that is asking the question. A material object is not enquiring about the nature of existence. My table is not wondering how it became a table. A rose bush is not asking how it is a rose bush. My elbow is not questioning why it is an elbow. Scientific explanations that address only physicality would be satisfying if we were solely matter. But it is the full comprehensiveness of being that is asking, What am I? Where did I come from? What is the nature of presence? What was I before birth? What am I after death? Why is there something and not nothing? Where and how does the universe arise? These questions stop thought and invite wonder. In the stillness, an inner knowing stirs that there is more to "being" than my mind can comprehend. If the totality of being were within the confines of my mind and body, it would be known totally. The fact that it is not is the mystery beyond the mind that inspires wonder and humility and is the releasement necessary to receiving a new understanding of the concept of God.

Dr. Mills had to release his former concept of God, as he explained one evening to a group of people at his home:

> God is the Force that IS. I don't call it so much "God" any more, because I used to always pray to my God as a white-haired man sitting on a throne; that's the way I was taught in Sunday school. I can't any longer; it's too far away. If I can think of God sitting on a throne, where is that happening but within me? So, where is it, then? To me, the Primal Cause is much more of a Force, an energy.

I was happy to adopt these words—*Primal Cause, Force, energy*—as synonyms of God, along with words such as *Consciousness* and *Creative Source*. These simple changes in language helped me to let go of thought-associations and sit in stillness, in wonder and gratitude of that Primal Cause.

Dr. Mills also changed the language in his use of a biblical statement that had bothered me for years. "I of myself can do nothing; it is the wonder of the *Invisible* that doeth the work." With the new wording, I finally realized that this statement is not about a worshipful suppli-cant calling upon a paternalistic *Father*; it is a statement of fact, literally true. Even on the level of physicality I do not exist without air, which is not "of myself." I depend on the spark of Life, on energy, on the ordered, principled coherence of the universe, on the gift of presence, and on intuition, ideas, and feeling that appear unbidden in my awareness. These gifts from the Invisible animate and enliven the person called me, even while they remain not subject to the limits of time and space, aging and death. Recognizing this was the only route that allowed me to let go of the wilfulness, the hunger for personal success, and the need for external validation that had defined my earlier years.

It reminded me of an exercise we did with Dr. Mills. He would take a piece of paper and draw perhaps a tree, a dog, a sheep, and a person and then ask, "What is common to all of these objects?" Eventually we would realize that what was common was the paper. Then he would erase the tree, the dog, the sheep, and the person and ask, "What remains?" The paper. When he illustrated this point to a young man in 1971, he went on to say: "Some people call this (the paper) Consciousness. There really is no division of the Consciousness into a consciousness of a tree, or a consciousness of a dog, or the consciousness of a sheep or a person. It just appears that way for the fun of the drawing, for your picture book, you might say." *

It is one thing to accept intellectually that Consciousness (or God-Consciousness) is fundamental; it's quite another to make the leap to no longer identifying primarily as the person or the object drawn on the page. From the standpoint of one Consciousness, everything I am, everything I do, is an expression of that oneness. There is nothing outside of Consciousness. My thoughts, words, and actions have agency and volition because I am not separate from that state. Where my attention is matters, what is included in my considerations matters, feeling love for those around me matters. This is all one body, connected not person to person but by the shared substance of one Consciousness.

Revisiting our concept of God, or God-Consciousness, is not an academic exercise; it is fundamental to our future as a society. How we conceive of ourselves determines how we conceive of God. In turn, how we define God determines how we define man. Our conception of a higher power, or lack of one, is a fundamental determinant in how we

---

* Another expression of this idea can be found in a 2005 commencement address given by David Foster Wallace at Kenyon College in Ohio. In the cinematic version of his address called "This Is Water," two small fish are asked by a large fish, "How's the water?" The small fish swim on, and eventually one asks the other, "What the hell's water?"

conduct our lives, how we define satisfaction and success, and how we treat our fellow men and women and the planet on which we depend.

Would we as easily go to war, or treat the Earth as though it were disposable, or be indifferent to each other's needs, or infuse words with negative emotional energy? A changed understanding of the real nature of what's going on here leads to a change in behaviour. Acknowledgment that "I of myself can do nothing; it is the Invisible that doeth the work" is an essential prescription for a world that is on a destructive path of ego and fear. Realizing our interdependence as one body of Consciousness is, to quote my friend Ian Mirlin, the new basis for civil society.

As I reflect on these ideas, a sliver of sunshine begins to glow pink on the horizon, signalling the beginning of a new day. It is a beautiful reminder that without the sun we do not live. I have done nothing to cause the sun to shine; life is a gift that we receive. We can so easily assume that we are animating our own bodies and minds, forgetting—until illness or impending death reminds us—that the Life-Force does not originate in the person.

> The Life-giving Force must be a consideration to you. What in your life can you control that is essential for life? What in your life are you master of that is Life-giving? And you deny a primal Source? Or allow it to be considered non-present? There is no one who is capable of controlling the Life-giving Force that sustains what appears as you and your world. (Kenneth G. Mills)

Home

WHILE WORKING AT BCG, I was living in what I called my "one dining-room apartment," the main floor of a house in the Annex neighbourhood of Toronto with my bedroom in the original dining room. I loved the homey feel of the big old house and back garden. It was a

welcome contrast to the offices in which I spent my days, and to the
hotel rooms in which I stayed on frequent business trips. I was ready
to buy a home and looked at many condominiums, but in my heart I
knew that wasn't what I wanted. I wanted a house with a deck, trees,
and gardens. But I had to consider security given that I was a single
woman and that the house would often be vacant because of my work
and travel schedules.

After months of searching in vain, I told Dr. Mills about this
dilemma. His response was immediate: "What a suggestion that you
could ever be separated from the idea called home!" I accepted the
truth of the statement, swallowing it whole, and sat quietly, not letting
my mind get involved. I knew that on a higher level metaphysical
work was done, and I waited to see what would happen, knowing that
I could never be separated from the idea called home.

Within a few days I received a call from a long-time friend, John
Arciuch, who also studied with Kenneth Mills. A "For Sale" sign had
gone up on the other side of his semi-detached house. He had heard
that I was looking for a home and wondered if I might be interested,
and even commented that if I lived there, he and his wife could keep
an eye on it when I was travelling. At the open house on the following
weekend, I walked through the front door as two people were coming
down the stairs. Looking up at them, I thought, "What are they doing
in my house?" I knew instantly that this was my home. The backyard
had the envisioned deck and flowers, a magnolia tree, and even a vegetable garden reminding me of my family home. The house was small
and manageable, and, best of all, there were friends on the other side
of the adjoining wall. I put in an offer, and the house was mine.

Having the idea "home" suddenly manifest in my life in this remarkable way is a reminder that precipitation of an idea into objective form
happens by claiming the idea as natural, inherent to what I am—not
something "out there," wished or prayed for. The three-dimensional
world is not a separate realm, with boundaries and limits, apart from
the unlimited possibilities of Being. What appears as the objective
is actually all arising in mind. We are co-creators, with the power to
change our experience. As Dr. Mills once put it: "Do not hold to what

you want. Hold to what you know you include." In an Unfoldment in 2004 he said:

> What you imagine, focus upon with clear intention, can't help but manifest and be precipitated provided you assume before it: "I will be responsible for what I precipitate into my life, be it another person, another place, or another thing, or the beneficence that comes with a divine recognition of essence."[17]

The responsibilities of my new house were fulfilled, and I lived there very happily for years until I married and moved into another home that is also surrounded by trees and flowers.

With the idea of home restored and brought into expression, I took time to appreciate and revel in an inner as well as outer sense of home, finding a place of peace where I could relax with no thought of work or the Unfoldment. In many ways, these years were my version of having it all: the stimulating adrenalin-fuelled world of consulting, the soaring releasement of receiving the Unfoldments, and the comfort of home. I loved it all and was able to savour moments of peace, joy, and satisfaction, even within the busyness of my life.

One day I admired Dr. Mills' elegant fur coat and he said, "You should have a fur coat." A simple enough reply but one that caused an immediate reaction of horror in me. I was willing to admire elegance and radical uniqueness in him, but appropriating it for myself was out of my comfort zone. Choosing to do this required me to go into stores I normally wouldn't visit and act out wanting to buy a fur coat. Then I would have to part with a substantial amount of money, and, worst of all, I would have to wear it proudly, claiming that I loved wearing it. Donning a controversial, pretentious, old-fashioned, and expensive garment was the perfect storm. Shyness, insecurity, wanting to blend in and not draw attention to myself, and preferring the kind of simple clothing that my family would approve of, were all on the line. The early lesson to "Do what you don't want to do and don't tell anyone you don't want to do it" was continuing, now in a new form.

While far from typical spiritual instruction, I trusted Dr. Mills' unconventional teaching methods and went shopping and, not surprisingly, didn't like the coats. I was about forty years old, and they looked like something a much older woman would wear. Then I found one that I truly did love; it was a beautiful rich colour and softer in design than the others and felt wonderful. It was very expensive and looked extravagant. I decided to buy it. Soon afterwards, I wore it to a dinner party at Dr. Mills' home. He admired the coat and even gave me a scarf to wear with it from his own front-hall closet.

From then on, I wore the coat on every possible occasion and gained some confidence in carrying it off. One day, my father saw it and was very disapproving, particularly of how "over the top" it was. ("Why choose *that* one?") But of course, that was the point, to stand firm in adopting a standard of elegance in the face of any disapproval—my own, my father's, or anyone else's. About a decade later, when I became chair of the board of the National Ballet of Canada, I thought, "Well, at least I have the coat to go with the role!" I still have it and wear it to this day and finally feel more at home in it. I still associate it with Dr. Mills' encouragement to let go of limiting patterns of personal identification and try on a new standard of elegance.

A Dead Season

DESPITE ENGAGING the idea of home in my cozy new house, in the rest of my life I sometimes still felt divided. I couldn't fully commit to corporate life and behave as though I believed this world to be the fundamental reality. But the long hours, travel, and demanding nature of the work meant that my life was largely spent in this environment. Despite my inner branding efforts, I still tended to alternate between two worlds, adopting the language and thought patterns associated with each one and allowing those to dictate my expression, rather than having one distinctive voice throughout.

Yet I knew that I was choosing to live in this divided world. The combination of business career and spiritual quest acted as a pressure-release valve on both sides. There were times with Dr. Mills when I felt completely at sea as he pulled the rug out from under me, puncturing my carefully prepared and over-thought questions and comments, leaving me having to face the shenanigans of my mind. Sometimes those moments led to an amazing flow of spontaneous creativity and feeling. At other times I would just sweat through it and think with relief about going to work the following day. There was nothing that the business world could throw at me that came close to the destabilizing and disorienting experience of being with someone for whom logic was secondary to intuition, and who was more interested in showing me where I was at than in accomplishing the apparent purpose of any meeting or gathering.

Working in business did draw me away from my involvement with Dr. Mills' work and the group surrounding him. Yet it gave me the chance to grow and mature as an individual. It also gave me a unique inside-outside perspective on my study with Dr. Mills, as well as on the corporate world. But as the childhood pattern of non-communication about what my life was really about continued, I wondered what toll the fracturing of my experience was taking on my well-being. Experimenting with branding and language to try to be more open had helped, but I still didn't want other people's opinions and judgements interfering with what was precious in my life. I assumed that people wouldn't understand my dedication to the Unfoldment. In fact, I could barely explain it to myself.

From a practical point of view, it was also hard to introduce the subject into regular conversation. After one particularly intense weekend of Star-Scape rehearsals and Unfoldments, one of the singers, Terry Stevens, turned to me and said, "When someone asks us on Monday at work, 'How was your weekend,' where do we begin?" We had been shaken up and transformed and had touched new levels of conscious awareness, and then been brought back to the practicalities of living according to Principle. How do you have that conversation at the water cooler?

In the late 1980s, I did a private consulting project for Naropa University in Boulder, Colorado. It was a fascinating window into Tibetan Buddhism, and I enjoyed being the "corporate suit" surrounded by the spiritual seekers who were my clients, instead of my usual feeling of being a spiritual seeker surrounded by corporate suits. The Buddhists initially showed great interest in Dr. Mills but then dismissed his significance when they found that he did not come from "a lineage." I talked with Dr. Mills about this, which led to him stating clearly that he did not come from a lineage, nor was he establishing one; his work was pertinent to his lifetime. This caused me to consider deeply my role in his life, and his role in mine. I was grateful for this clarity to avoid imagining that my future would be defined by continuing or representing his work. It left me asking, "What, then, is my work?"— another question that stayed in the background of my attention for years and eventually had to come to the fore.

By the 1990s, I was going into the third decade in which studying the Unfoldment was central to my life. My mind started asking if anything of significance was happening anymore in my association with Dr. Mills. Since doing the MBA, I often felt the absence of the fun, wonder, and sense of adventure that had characterized my early years with him. It seemed that I had fallen into a serious, busy, analytical life despite every opportunity to follow my heart in a new direction.

My primary BCG client at this time was in the Chicago area. I was commuting frequently across the border, feeling buried with work that was consuming but not satisfying. Sitting on the plane, reflecting on my life, I concluded that the hoped-for integration of spiritual quest and professional accomplishment had instead resulted in nothing but a lack of satisfaction in both spheres of activity. The habitual compartmentalizing of my life had to come to an end. I talked this over with my friend and long-time BCG colleague David Pecaut over lunch in the Chicago client's cafeteria on a Friday afternoon. David, who had met Dr. Mills on several occasions, urged me to go and see him and discuss it with him. It occurred to me that Dr. Mills was in Connecticut, and I could easily fly there before going home to Toronto. I gave him a call and soon found myself on a flight to Hartford. Even after arriving at the home of my friends, the Hoovers, where I had arranged to stay, my mind was still trying to catch up, wondering when I had made a decision to do this.

I was surprised to learn that Dr. Mills' schedule the following day was fully booked. I would only be able to see him at the Unfoldment he was giving at the Hoovers' in the evening. It was an odd turn of events given that I had flown in from Chicago to meet with him. But I trusted Dr. Mills and knew well his masterful way of throwing off balance the plans and expectations of the logical mind.

When Dr. Mills arrived at the Hoovers' home, he admired the spring garden that was starting to come into bloom, greeted the many guests, and then sat down to speak. The living room was filled to overflowing. I sat on the edge of my chair, wedged partway into the dining room, straining to see, but hearing every word:

> We are here watching the green leaves come to fruition from the bare trunks and the bare limbs of the past season. We have never doubted the constant Creativity of what appears as the dead season when nothing active, nothing of growth, nothing of beauty appeared on what appeared to be the dead limbs of the dead trees. It wasn't that they were dead; it was that they were resting to be prepared to receive the wealth of foliage: that green stuff! . . .
>
> I wonder how often we are entering, willingly, into that stream of cutting down our successes by allowing ourselves to be whittled down by the aggressive thoughts that would cause us to want to uproot all that we have done, thinking it was dead just because the foliage hasn't appeared. . . .
>
> If the dead season were really dead, the tree would never be filled with such newness that a whole new print job would come out in the spring! It's never counterfeit wealth; it's the Wealth that is inherent with Promise. It is the Wealth that is inherent with the Knowingness that you can't believe the appearance if you expect to see a new spring.[18]

The lecture was later published and came to be known as *Green Stuff*. Today it is obvious to me that this Unfoldment, spontaneously and universally given, was offering me a way to shift my attention to a new spring rather than dwelling on the apparently dead season that I was feeling. Nevertheless, a few months later I decided to let go my association with Kenneth Mills, at least for a while. It was a wrenching decision that I agonized over. But I had been involved since I was a teenager; I was now a mature adult, thirty-seven years old, and felt the need to know clearly within myself what I wanted in my life. I was building a career and finding my own voice as a business professional. I hadn't lost my appreciation of what Dr. Mills offered but felt the need to explore my own creativity and that of other artists and speakers.

When I pieced together the sequence of events in the 1990s, it was shocking to me to see how quickly I shifted in those years from receiving gifts such as the precipitation of home, and the considerations about an integrated brand, to feeling divided again and the need to move on. But such is the nature of the unreliable human mind.

As the months without attending Unfoldments went by, instead of finding creative freedom I found instead a dullness and an absence of the creative spontaneity and crackling tension that characterized the experience with Dr. Mills. I went to some lectures by other speakers, including one by a former student of Dr. Mills. As I sat in the lecture hall, the difference couldn't have been starker. Everything I was hearing was intellectual and derivative. What I had heard in an Unfoldment was original, creative, spontaneous, and life-giving. After a year or so, I began to think about returning to the Unfoldment and to stop worrying about whose mouth the creative expression seemed to be coming from.

At first, returning was very difficult, in part due to pride but also because the scene looked very different after an absence of a year. My friends Pier Paolo and Susan Alberghini invited me to accompany them to Muskoka to spend a day at Dr. Mills' summer festival. With some reluctance I agreed. When I arrived, I felt like a foreigner. We sat in a class, and the gathering around Dr. Mills seemed odd, unnatural, and unattractive. With new eyes, I realized that I would not be returning to an old role. If I continued any association with Dr. Mills, I had to reinvent the relationship on a new basis.

After the class Pier Paolo and Susan asked me to join them in visiting

Dr. Mills' cabin to say thank you before driving home. I didn't want to go, given my negative impression of the class, but knew that I couldn't come all this way to the festival as a guest of Dr. Mills without at least saying hello. During our visit Dr. Mills didn't mention the class; instead he told me that he had taken up fashion designing, an interest that had begun years before in designing the Star-Scape Singers' concert ensembles. He had created a line of elegant evening gowns and even had a fashion show at the Ed Sullivan Theater in Manhattan, which was filmed for high-definition television.

As I listened, I thought, "During the year when I expected to find some new creative freedom for myself, Dr. Mills took up a new art form and progressed all the way to a show in a prominent New York theatre."

Dr. Mills also told me that he wanted to establish an arts and cultural centre and was considering a symposium as the first step. I knew that he was enticing me to return and become involved in this and had to admit that this conversation was much more interesting than what I had observed in the class. When we left, he invited me to "come anytime."

I was torn between a natural attraction to what had always felt like home, and a desire to grow independently. I wondered if Dr. Mills would tolerate a different form of relationship, one that didn't fit what I thought was the definition of being his student. I decided not to overthink it, to just be grateful for what I had received from him over the years, and to hold a clear intention to have a more mature relationship.

Colours on the Mountain

A FEW WEEKS LATER I met up with Dr. Mills again, unexpectedly at Chicago O'Hare airport. I was returning home from my client in Chicago, and Dr. Mills and the Star-Scape Singers were on their way to perform at John Denver's music festival in Aspen, Colorado. The singers invited me to come along; after all, I was already halfway there. Given the surprising coincidence, in a rare moment of spontaneity I decided to join them. Dr. Mills seemed completely at ease with my unexpected presence in the group and was gracious and welcoming. I felt much more relaxed, with a freedom to define my role.

In Aspen the singers sang beautifully, but the festival was a busy, noisy event with no apparent standard of performance. Dr. Mills was asked to participate on a panel, which he declined. He decided instead that he would accept an invitation for us all to stay at a Colorado ranch owned by the Hoovers, the family who had hosted me in Connecticut. We left Aspen behind and drove out through endless acres of Colorado ranch land.

John Hoover met us at the door, welcoming us to what he called big-sky country. We felt the Alice in Wonderland experience of the huge open space shrinking our bodies to a smaller size and at the same time literally expanding our horizons. It was a world away from my usual city habitat, which added to the adventurous feeling of these unexpected few days. In the distance the horizon was defined by the Southern Sawatch mountain range, including Mount Shavano. The setting sun produced a spectacular light show on the mountains, which gave way to a silhouette against the dark sky. During the day the changing light transformed the mountains from green to brown to blue. At times they seemed close, accessible, and welcoming; at other times they were distant, remote, and even menacing.

Dr. Mills observed that the changing colours could be an analogy for thoughts and emotions arising on the surface of experience, while the mountain and the sun, the light source to this picture, remained untouched and changeless. I added that the apparently changing picture of the mountains could represent glimpses into Reality. The mountains are always the mountains, but they look different every time they are viewed. We may experience the transporting feeling of wonder, or the sharp edge of Truth, or the humility of acknowledging God, or the intuition of knowing without thinking it through. These are endless ways that "the mountain" appears, all due to the unchanging light of the sun.

The mountain range became my analogy of the spiritual quest and seemed to represent the multitude of experiences of the past few years.

It helped me to let go of trying to define in my life that "this is what the mountain range should look like," but to just enjoy the changing colour display, while also acknowledging the unchanging Light source that enables the picture to appear. It added an image to my concept about branding and spirituality. God, or the Light to the mountains, is always the same, but the mountain range may look different in every era, in every culture, in every phase of life.

At the ranch I sat in on a conversation that Dr. Mills had with the Hoovers' neighbour who was a war veteran. This man described in detail how he was struggling in his life and said that he had taken up art to help calm the emotional torment that he had felt ever since fighting overseas. He asked Dr. Mills for help in dealing with his inner anguish, but during a long conversation he continued to reiterate and give emotional energy to the negativity in his experience. Finally, Dr. Mills made the following declaration:

> There is only one Self, and the suggested imposter is "you." It is the divine Self that has never been in the conflict that allows you to talk about the conflict. You have to relinquish your hold on the belief system that you are this imperson-ation of a man who has been in conflict. You have to accept without reservation that you are the divine Fulcrum at which point man can balance equally the "suggested" and the Reality of Being so that the ministrations perceived by you and carried by you, through your writing or through whatever art work you may do, is a blessing to those who perceive its intrinsic nature.
>
> You are in essence the wonder of Man existing in form to offer unto all those who perceive your presence, the univer-sal solvent, Love.

I hope that this man was able to find some peace in these words, and in the love that surrounded the declaration of them, words that required him to shift his attention away from his mental and emo-tional state.

Sitting there, I too absorbed these words that seemed to be said to me as well. They deeply penetrated my awareness and showed in sharp relief how occupied my mind had been with personal thoughts about doing this or not doing that, which ultimately did not matter at all. Presence, as "the universal solvent, Love," was the only role. (In this declaration Dr. Mills used the word *Man* to describe a state of being, not a gender.)

To remain at and as the Fulcrum felt like a life mission. I once again acknowledged God-Consciousness, the only basis for a fulcrum that does not take the ego as its centre, and the only way to continue my life without being "an imposter."

Dr. Mills' words had acted as a tuning fork, aligning my awareness to a pitch where I was no longer identifying as the "imposter called me" but as the universal solvent, Love. This shift is felt in my experience as a reversal in which thoughts, emotions, and events that had seemed real and important become illusory and passing. Universal Love, or divine Self, which can sound abstract and intellectual, becomes tangible and fully present, filling my entire field of attention. It is very hard to describe this spontaneous shift in identity. It comes as a rare gift of releasement from limits, undefinable but experienceable. In the moment, the new awareness feels obvious, self-evident, and natural and even carries a feeling of relaxation. It was only hours later that it seemed fleeting and precious and I wanted to recreate the moment, but it is impossible to conjure on demand.

While revelling in this state of awareness, I knew that, regardless of my judgemental thoughts, this rarified experience was, at least for me, unique to being in Dr. Mills' presence. The shift from imposter to divine Fulcrum was why I had come to Dr. Mills in the first place, and it is the reason I decided to continue to study with him.

The weekend in Colorado was the beginning of a new relationship with Dr. Mills. Having left and chosen to return, I felt a new freedom of authenticity. During this transition I was grateful to have built a long-term trust with Dr. Mills. This quality supported me through the inexplicable, transcendent, and sometimes irritating moments that happened both before and after the year and a half of absence. Trust is essential to a teacher-student relationship. Without it, the student doesn't withstand the ego-disruption that is absolutely essential to any serious spiritual quest.

A deep teacher-student relationship is seldom entered into quickly, despite the flash of recognition at the beginning. Dr. Mills was always wary of people who, upon meeting him, immediately wanted to devote their lives to "being with him." The relationship usually didn't last, and the person moved on as soon as the initial shine wore off. In my case, it was a relationship built gradually over years, as I learned from experience that Dr. Mills was more than capable of seeing through whatever nonsense I had persuaded myself was true, and of getting to the heart of the matter. He was the one I could count on to hold up a mirror when I needed it. He was also the first to recognize and celebrate my breakthroughs in coming into the realization of my true nature.

Dr. Mills eloquently captured the nature of this relationship in the title of his poem "Someone Knew Me as I AM."[19] This phrase encompasses both the ego-disrupting sword that cuts through illusion, and the real prize—someone who knows me as I AM, perfect, complete now. This was the touchstone that enabled me to re-engage the relationship with Dr. Mills through what turned out to be the last decade of his life.

The Invisible Appearing Visible

SOON AFTER the trip to Colorado, the Star-Scape Singers were preparing to embark on a concert tour in Poland in 1994. Dr. Mills asked me if I would like to come along and see the response of the European audiences. I accepted the invitation and am very glad that I did.

After sold-out performances and critical acclaim in Warsaw's Philharmonic Hall and in Krakow, we went on to Częstochowa where Star-Scape performed at Jasna Góra, the seat of the Catholic Church in Poland, as part of the celebration of the sixteenth anniversary in Rome of the Polish pope, John Paul II. Thousands of pilgrims were gathered at the huge edifice, lining up to stand for a moment before the famous shrine of the Virgin Mary.

The singers performed their signature work, *The Fire Mass*.[20] The huge resonant hall was packed with people standing for the entire two-hour, a capella piece. You literally could have heard a pin drop. *The Fire Mass*, composed by Christopher Dedrick and Kenneth Mills, interpolates the traditional Latin Mass of the Ordinary with words of poetry by Dr. Mills. Some of the English-speaking priests and nuns standing near me occasionally appeared shocked by the new language and the contemporary music that had permeated the familiar Latin. It was audacious to perform this work in the seat of the Catholic Church in a deeply Catholic country. Nevertheless, Dr. Mills and Star-Scape were warmly embraced, and people couldn't thank them enough for bringing their music to Poland. Throughout the tour, including very successful performances in Warsaw, many audience members told us they were deeply moved and felt the power of this music and the words to elevate and transform the listener.

The father general told us that during the Soviet communist regime, Catholicism went underground and people relied on music as their church and their politics. In those extreme circumstances Poland's deeply musical culture gave its people an inner freedom. While Canada in the twenty-first century is wholly unlike Poland of the twentieth century, for some people the arts—and particularly music—is taking the place in our lives that going to a place of worship would have held. There were lessons to be learned from a country that out of necessity found in the arts a non-religious outlet for expressing spirituality.

Back in Toronto, inspired by what we had witnessed in Poland, and by what he and the Star-Scape Singers had encountered all over Europe on previous tours, Dr. Mills held a series of planning meetings for an arts symposium. He saw this as a first step to establishing a series of arts and cultural centres. These plans did not come to fruition in Dr. Mills' lifetime, but they planted seeds in me that bore fruit later in my life.

After returning to work at BCG, I mentioned to Dr. Mills that I was working on a consulting assignment that involved finding cost reductions in a large Canadian corporation. He expressed concern about my working with clients whose employees might view the consultants as threatening their job security. He asked me what inner work I was doing before going into the organization, to protect myself from psychic attacks, essentially the employees' negative thoughts that were fuelled by emotion. He reminded me to every morning "take time to be Timeless."

Soon after this conversation Dr. Mills met with one of my consulting colleagues and returned to this subject:

> Unless you know how to protect yourself, you can be inundated with the stream of tremendous riptides of force when you go into some situations.
>
> I am sure you enter situations where there are so many questions to be answered, and so many answers to be found to questions that are not even asked, because it may reveal the inefficiency of someone present. Always surround yourself in protection so that nothing harms you, and you move there with confidence.
>
> We should really be so wise with each other that we support everyone from the standpoint of the Invisible appearing visible. It is a big job when you take it on, because you cannot believe that error is real. It is a suggestion. It is a suggestion because it can be changed. Anything that can be changed is not real. That is why it is so wonderful to see the Changeless in the midst of the changing, being able to witness the changing but not in it.

Taking his words to heart, I decided that I was being too cautious and self-conscious in not bringing Dr. Mills together with a group of my consulting colleagues to hear these ideas. Even if they didn't understand or agree with the standpoint that Consciousness is fundamental, they would perhaps respect and appreciate Dr. Mills' guidance about how to protect ourselves in going into organizations.

A date was set for the gathering to take place at my home. A few of my colleagues had met Dr. Mills previously, but for most of them this was their first introduction to the man whose lectures I attended every week and whose festivals and workshops were my idea of a vacation. After some pleasant introductions Dr. Mills got right to work. He began by telling the group that I missed more Thursday night rehearing classes than anyone else did in his group, and that I had an obligation to attend them regardless of the demands of my job. As my stomach knotted and my hands got sweaty, I realized that this evening was not going to be my opportunity to demonstrate to my friends that this Kenneth Mills was a wonderful and insightful man. Instead, he seemed to go out of his way to make me uncomfortable with the fact of having a spiritual teacher. Perhaps he was simply being open and honest about how he saw what was important in my life—a stark contrast to the secrecy and the carefully contrived messages I tended to convey. But I was mortified, wondering what had happened to the intelligent, stimulating conversations we normally had. I don't recall the rest of the evening; I was too tied up in mental gymnastics to process what was going on.

While I can laugh about it now, at the time I could only rely on the wisdom of my friend David Nash who observed, "Dr. Mills does not live by a constitution." In other words, he will always spontaneously respond to the moment rather than follow any expectations or plan. We could never expect him to be predictable and offer in a new setting what he had given in another context the previous day. In the spontaneity of my living room he had no interest in impressing my friends or making me comfortable among these people about my dedication to studying with him. His interest was perhaps in showing me how tangled up I still was in needing to impress people, even to the point of using him to help me do that.

I heard recently from a colleague who was there that evening and who came to several other events with Dr. Mills. He said that when he reflected on his life, the greatest and most transforming individual he had ever met was Kenneth Mills. I have no idea what the rest of my colleagues thought of the evening; perhaps they also found it fascinating and valuable, even while I suffered through the humiliation of trying to make the wildness of the spiritual quest acceptable in the eyes of the business community. As always, unaffected by the setting or by my recent departure and return, Dr. Mills went to the heart of the matter and showed me where I was still personally and egotistically involved and how easily I became self-conscious in the situation. I wish I could say that I had had the fortitude and equipoise in that moment to have picked up the ball he tossed into the conversation, and respond with humour and clarity.

Some time later, Dr. Mills once again adroitly stopped my mind in its tracks at a board meeting of the charitable organization Patrons of Wisdom, which was raising money for the arts. At the time, I was serving as treasurer. The first item on the agenda was plans for a scholarship competition that Patrons of Wisdom was offering to emerging classical musicians. Dr. Mills, as president, was asking questions about the adjudicators and how the submissions would be reviewed, and he seemed very engaged in the conversation. But he also glanced down at the financial statements in front of him. With his pen, he put a large black tick mark beside one of the numbers.

Knowing how careful and rigorous Dr. Mills was about management of the charity, I surreptitiously went through my copy of the statements, trying to figure out which page and which line item he had marked. Sure enough, there it was, the only questionable number in the entire package. How did he know?

When we came to the financial report on the agenda, Dr. Mills turned to me expectantly. Out of nervousness, or perhaps the absurdity of trying to present financial statements to someone who could see through anything, I started to laugh. I said I had noticed that he had marked an item on the financial statements. He said, "Yes, I don't know why this number stands out for me, but it does." I told him that when I met with the bookkeeper to prepare the statements, we had wondered exactly what this expense was from a recent fundraising event, but I trusted the organizers of the event and was busy with other priorities, and so I had let it go through without further investigation.

He looked at his paper, as amazed as I was. Shaking his head, he said, "I don't know much about finance but I knew there was something questionable about this number." I promised to go back and verify the expense. It seemed to me that it wasn't necessarily that the number was wrong, or the expense not legitimate. It was perhaps my unfinished business of knowing that I should look into it and had not done so. Once again the invisible seemed to have become visible. I don't recall what happened about the expense but do remember feeling the relief of having full clarity about every number on the page.

I wish I had kept that page with its black tick mark as a reminder to not allow unclarity or unfinished business into my experience. It was also a profound lesson in following intuition, in the power of discernment without thinking it out, and a wonderful remembrance of Dr. Mills' uncanny ability to zero in on the spot that needed polishing, even when he was presented with pages of numbers in a financial report that a business person might have spent time analyzing and perhaps still not have noticed.

Regardless of what we were apparently working on with Dr. Mills, we were always only working on one thing: living according to Principle. Recalling these stories reminds me of Dr. Mills' definition of enlightenment. He was asked numerous times what enlightenment meant. On one occasion he replied that to him it meant being confined to Principle in thought, word, and deed. That was always the agenda, whether at a business meeting, a symphony concert, a dinner party, or a formal Unfoldment.

Presence Is the Happening

ON A TYPICAL DAY AT BCG in the mid-1990s, I was in my office reviewing a document filled with charts and analysis for a client presentation the following day. Some young consultants had been up late the night before to finish it, and we were racing to the deadline, trying to offer a substantive response to a company obviously in need. But sitting in my glass-walled office that morning, I also had a phone call scheduled with Dr. Mills. He was in Tucson, Arizona, and when he came on the line, he asked me about the weather in Toronto. The weather? I had barely looked outside for days. I noticed that it was a bright, clear February day, and my awareness started to settle, becoming more cognizant of the present moment. We covered the topic of the call, and the conversation leapt from there, and soon he was speaking in poetry. I quickly flipped over the document on my desk and scribbled down the poem as he spoke. Reading it back to him and enjoying every word, I told him what a relief it was to move into a poetic realm after days of being immersed in preparations for the client presentation.

The consultants were hovering outside my office, waiting for my edits. I mentioned to Dr. Mills that the client was a huge bureaucratic organization and that we had called our report "Making Change Happen." A new tone of voice came over the phone line, Dr. Mills' words ringing out: "Don't make anything happen. You don't have to. You *are* the happening! Hey! You don't have to make anything happen. *Your very presence is the happening!*" My pen kept up with the words, moving more quickly than my mind could process this message scribbled on the back of a report about making change happen.

The work done, Dr. Mills hung up, leaving me vibrating in an elevated state of awareness, reading the declaration in front of me. Looking at the pages of analysis and the stacks of research on my desk, I could only agree. He's right. What's needed is not analysis; presence is the happening. By now, the consultants were wondering what I was doing, and looking for direction. I took a few deep breaths and copied the statements into a notebook. I turned the report over and finished reading the now stale pages of charts and analysis. This was a classic moment with Kenneth Mills: disrupter, inspiration, and force of realignment.

We finished the report with few changes, even though I was inclined to throw it out entirely. I wondered if I would have the courage to walk into a room filled with the client's senior executives and present no report at all after weeks of work. I didn't have that courage but resolved to treat the analysis as secondary to evidencing presence, a force that could offer the kind of instantaneous change in perspective that Dr. Mills had just given me. I no longer imagined that our earnest consulting

136

team was going to transform with charts, analysis, advice, and plans an entrenched organization of tens of thousands of employees. Beyond the recommendations in the report, all that any of us could do was embody a presence that inspired new possibilities, a presence that did not accept as real the limits that the employees had imposed on themselves.

The next morning our consulting team met at the airport and boarded the flight to the client's head office for the meeting. I was aware of how relaxed and joyous I felt, completely untouched by the apparent negativity and serious issues at the client company or about the upcoming meeting. The presentation was well received, which perhaps means that I didn't challenge and disrupt their mode of thinking as much as I could have, or perhaps they appreciated a new perspective. I made the point that the answer didn't lie in our analysis or plans; it was in the presence that would require change in the realm of thought, not just in organizational processes and policies. After the presentation we moved on to meeting with groups of employees throughout the company.

In every meeting I simply perceived and magnified as often as I could their unlimited potential, which was readily evident to me, regardless of the negativity they presented. Many of them were incredulous and unwilling to let go of their problems in favour of a brighter future. I could see how their every thought and word was reinforcing the stagnation in the company, and how easily they could change their thoughts and thereby the company if they chose to do that. I didn't feel any need to persuade or convince them; I simply offered a living alternative in presence to what they considered the only reality.

There may not have been a profound transformation in the client that day, but it was a profound transformation for me. My habit had been to try to make change happen both in my life and in my work with clients, using analysis, willpower, persuasion, and sheer hard work to push through physical and mental obstacles to achieve something. Knowing that Presence is the happening is a very different standpoint. It requires being still and enjoying the moment, asking and expecting to receive inner guidance. Presence is not some future state to be achieved; it is actual, now. I stop and remember that I am not in charge; I am a recipient of gifts of inspiration, intuition, and insight. From the standpoint of stillness there is nothing to do, nowhere to go, only to Be. As Dr. Mills put it in my very first dokusan with him, "I AM . . . Now . . . done."

Recalling this event at BCG reminds me of how radical the standpoint is, how radical it is to adopt it in a society in which acknowledgement of the higher Self—let alone allowing that Presence to be the happening—is not generally known or accepted. It requires being a living challenge to society's assumptions. Dr. Mills, fearless in his stance, was often frustrated by my tepid attempts to take this stand. He would always notice when I was self-conscious or concerned about what other people would think. He had no patience with the tendency to say what other people wanted to hear, and advised me to make a point of saying what people would find challenging to hear. Whenever the old thought patterns of needing safety and acceptance reappeared in my mind, I appreciated this encouragement to stand in my own uniqueness.

In the decades since the "your very presence is the happening" conversation with Dr. Mills, the word *presence* has become widely used in spiritual practice, for example in mindfulness meditation. Returning to presence is desperately needed in this age of distraction with the twenty-four-hour news cycle, the internet, email, and social media always at our fingertips. Our mental focus is constantly externalized, immersed in everything other than awareness itself. The attention span of young people in particular has been "out-sourced" to an unregulated world of social media and online content that has no roots in their home and family or in an elevated standpoint of Principle.

Many authors and speakers today, such as Eckhart Tolle, Pema Chödrön, Thich Nhat Hanh, and Jon Kabat-Zinn, attest to the importance of presence to gain inner authority over the discursive mind. They urge us to focus on what is always and only in the present moment: the in-breath and the out-breath, the physical body, or one of the five senses, or just being in this present moment. When we do this, the fact of generic "being" takes its place at the centre of our attention span. With presence, we gain perspective as the observer of our thoughts, emotions, physical body, and circumstances rather than as the actor.

I may feel frightened, angry, or in pain, but it only takes a moment to realize that presence is not frightened, angry, or in pain. Presence simply *is*, untouched and unchanged. It is neither aging in time nor moving about in space. Returning to presence is the first step to realizing that this is a conscious experience primarily, and only secondarily physical and mental.

I find that the practice of being present releases force, the energy associated with being fully present. Using this energy to purposely disrupt mechanical and habitual responses by thinking, saying, or doing something unexpected is a marvellous way to reveal presence as the happening.

For those who haven't experienced this, *presence* is one of those words that makes spirituality outside of religion sound superficial and simplistic. It is easy to mock. It is also a word that's easy to drop into advertising and branding, promising presence in clothing, makeup, or expensive leadership training. In our culture we tend to assume that the serious pursuit of spirituality requires an ancient doctrine and the ritual of religions. How could something as self-evident and free as presence have any power or authority? Yet presence, unburdened by the baggage of any religion or belief system, is the evidence of what is substantial, and the practice of being present requires far more rigour than the pablum that often passes for spirituality.

At a time when religious beliefs have lost meaning for so many, and yet materialism has left many unsatisfied, returning to presence is the raw material for returning to meaning, joy, and satisfaction.

It is perhaps through presence as the happening that the old dichotomy of religion versus atheism can evaporate. Even the most rigorous atheist cannot account, within a purely material framework, for how it is that human beings are conscious of being conscious. Similarly, no religion can claim presence as its own. Presence is beyond the reach of both the rational mind and religious beliefs, making it the perfect focus in this post-religious and increasingly post-secular age. It is individual and experiential, yet at the same time global and unifying as we recognize within ourselves an essential nature that transcends all cultural differences.

Convergence

A HIGHLIGHT of my career at BCG was helping to create a youth internship program called Career Edge that was designed to address Canada's high youth unemployment in the 1990s. David Pecaut and I recruited Urban Joseph, then vice-chair of the TD Bank, to be the founding chair of the board of directors. Over the next two years Urban and I worked together, volunteering our time to implement and build support for the program.

One day Urban invited me to a white-tie, Three Tenors gala concert. I was surprised but accepted, and we began dating. A couple of years later we moved in together and then married. Urban is twenty-one years older than I am, but in our decades together we have seldom noticed the difference in age. Urban's youthful energy and love of life more than close the gap.

When I first met Urban, I discovered that he already knew quite a bit about Dr. Mills. Urban was chair of the board of PRIME Mentors of Canada, an organization that had recently selected Kenneth Mills to be the 1997 Honorary Prime Mentor of Canada. In being chosen for this award, Dr. Mills was in very good company with Sir Peter Ustinov, the Honourable Mitchell Sharp, and Sonia Bata, who had been the recipients in the previous three years.

As Urban grew to know Dr. Mills and more fully appreciate his renaissance nature, he decided that the planned PRIME Mentors' gala dinner was inadequate to recognize the many facets of his accomplishment. The occasion became a two-part gala, beginning at the Toronto Design Exchange to celebrate Dr. Mills' fashion designs and visual art, and continuing with dinner, music, and speeches in the glittering ballroom of the Royal York Hotel.

The event, on April 5, 1997, attracted five hundred guests from Canada, the United States, Europe, and Russia. Grammy Award–winning pianist Bob James and flutist Alexander Zonjic performed a new composition, "The Odyssey" by Bob James, dedicated to Dr. Mills. This was followed by a film about Dr. Mills directed by Rhombus Media partner Barbara Willis Sweete, called *The Rapture of Being*. Then the PRIME Mentor of Canada award was presented by CEO Conchita Tan-Willman and Senator Stanley Haidasz to "a man of vision, often called a Renaissance man, the 1997 Prime Mentor of Canada, Kenneth George Mills." Subsequently, Senator Haidasz also presented Dr. Mills with a "Senate award of excellence for outstanding achievement in humanities, education, philosophy and arts."

The occasion was a rare example of public recognition of Dr. Mills in Canada. While he was celebrated as a maestro in Europe, he was a controversial figure in Canada and kept a low profile. For me, it was an experience that brought together many of my professional colleagues, my new relationship with Urban, and my lifelong relationship with Dr. Mills. I felt, at least for a moment, the alignment of integration.

Urban and I together introduced Dr. Mills to a number of people in our combined circle of contacts. Urban is an excellent cook, and we often invited Dr. Mills and an unlikely combination of guests to dinner. I still hear from people who were there, remembering these unusual and lively evenings.

In 1998 we hosted a series of salons, continuing to introduce Dr. Mills to friends and colleagues. To one of these, Dr. Mills arrived with the *Globe and Mail* newspaper under his arm. He began by saying, "I know Urban believes everything in the *Globe and Mail* so I wondered if he had perceived, or if any of you had read, about being 'blissed out in the workplace.'"[21] He read: "In this climate of instability people have an inherent hunger for a sense of purpose and something they can believe in and commit themselves to body, mind and spirit.... As the wellness movement takes hold of the mainstream, religion and spirituality are slipping in behind, into boardrooms and staff rooms." The article described new workplace wellness programs incorporating yoga and meditation. The first annual conference on wellness and spirituality in the workplace had just taken place in Toronto, sponsored by "big guns" such as RBC, KPMG, and Bell Canada.

The journalist had interviewed Amy Cross, then health editor at *Chatelaine* magazine. As research for her article on this subject, Cross had organized yoga classes at her office. "Cross says it would be misleading to say she started the classes with any spiritual intentions, yet she had to strong-arm friends into joining. The general reaction was, 'Yoga?!? Yiiikes. Isn't that a cult?' 'Now they know it's a cult,' she quips. 'They're hooked.'"²²

After receiving this article from Dr. Mills, I began a clipping file of articles that occasionally appeared in the media about bringing spiritual principles and practices into the secular realm, especially the business world. Was the convergence I had longed for in my career finally beginning to happen? This question hung unanswered in the background, while life intervened with a new priority in the foreground.

At our Christmas party in 1998, as the guests were leaving, my mother took me aside to tell me some terrible news. My father had been diagnosed with advanced colon cancer and was unlikely to live more than a year. For hours I cried inconsolably. I couldn't fathom how my father, healthy and strong throughout his life, could succumb to this. The following day I had a long visit with my father, and felt somewhat calmer having run out of tears.

I called Dr. Mills with the news, and he offered me a metaphysical statement of fact to hold to, a statement intended not to be analyzed by the rational mind but to be accepted by the heart. Knowing the power of words, I repeated the words constantly, breathing into them and letting them flow over my body and mind. Here is an example of a metaphysical statement by Dr. Mills that is published in his book *The Cornucopia of Substance*:

> If there seems to be disease, you know that it's a lie because in the Light of what is known, there's nothing but divine Energy, and it can never run rampant or be misdirected. The Divine is declaring the non-materiality of what appears and the divine Presence in essence as the knowingness of the invincible nature of the Ineffable.²³

To take the metaphysical stance of perfection and know that the disease is "a lie" in the face of a family member's end-stage illness is difficult and can even feel heartless. Yet, doing this opens one up to the divine Presence and the "invincible nature of the Ineffable," thereby elevating the attention beyond the apparent situation and holding this door open for one and all.

For the next eight months I spent as much time as possible with my dad. I had always deeply loved this reticent man who had stayed in the background through most of my childhood and adult years. Now I feared losing him before I really knew him. We had never reconciled my choice to study with Dr. Mills, with Dad's scientific point of view, and now did not seem to be the time to get into it.

Many years before, I had given my father Dr. Mills' first book, *Given to Praise*. Handing it back to me a few weeks later, he had remarked, "Does Dr. Mills know he is an ecologist?" My father and Dr. Mills shared a conviction of the essential oneness of all things. However, their definition of the nature of that reality seemed to be entirely different.

Dad and I spent precious hours together, sometimes not talking much, just enjoying each other's company. In one of these quiet tender moments he commented that he could no longer understand why he had spent so much time learning all those Latin names and taxonomy classifications. I said that it seemed to open up the meaning of the natural world for him, understanding how it all fit together. Yes, he replied, but knowing the genealogy is not the same as experiencing the plant or animal, and appreciating its beauty and very existence. We sat there quietly in his room, the admitted limits of the intellect hanging in the air, and with it, acknowledgement of the vast uncharted realm of experience beyond it. I had seldom felt closer to my dad than I did in that moment. All systems of thought, whether scientific or spiritual, collapse in a moment of extremity when faced with the mystery of life and death.

In August 1999, Urban and I got married. My father was there, pushed in a wheelchair by my sister, and it was the last event he ever attended. When he passed away two months later, it was the first time I had had to confront mortality in all of its mystery. Trying to grapple with how someone I had known all my life could be here one day and gone the next showed me where concepts of heaven, reincarnation, and the afterlife must have come from. I desperately wanted to know where he was and if he was all right. Looking at the lifeless body on the bed, I knew that wasn't the man I called my father. The presence that made him Dad was no longer there. Where or what was his presence, his energy, now that it wasn't attached to this form? I searched for statements by Dr. Mills about death and found this one particularly comforting, from a conversation he had had with some doctors in 1992:

> Always hold to the fact that "this" [the appearance] is not
> Life; this is only the suggestion that Life could come and go.
> That blesses the one that is quitting the body because, after
> all, we birthed (so we're told) and we're dying (so we're told),
> so that is a "stereo": to be birthed and to die. When one is
> dying, they are just losing the identity with the limitation.
> That is all death is: a lessening of limits so that they can
> go on with that part of life that is in the awareness pattern
> beyond the verifiable objective framework.

The fundamental practice offered by Dr. Mills of seeing through the apparent picture of living as it seems to be is never more challenging than in the face of illness and death. It can feel "in denial" to go to an elevated statement of fact when one is overwhelmed with grief. Yet I knew that this was the raw opportunity to see through the illusion that life begins and ends with birth and death, and I spent hours meditating on this fact. I also surrounded my remembrance of my dad with love and affection and continue to do so to this day.

Assisi

IN 2002, Urban and I went to Italy on vacation. In Assisi we visited both the elaborate church built in honour of Saint Francis after his death and the small, plain building in which he is said to have lived and prayed. We heard about the controversy between those who had founded the new church and those who knew that such pretensions were contrary to everything he upheld in his life.

Then, having driven up the mountainside to the Hermitage, the spiritual retreat of Saint Francis and of many generations of monks, along with other tourists we entered the building. Urban and I went down some stairs that led to a small room. As soon as I entered the room, I felt an overpowering sense of familiarity. There was something about the dimensions of the space and the odd-shaped window high up on the far wall—so ridiculously high that you couldn't see out of it. To the left on the same wall was a door. Standing there, I realized that the room matched exactly the room in a recurring dream that had started when I was a teenager and lasted for years.

Night after night I had dreamt of being in an enclosed room with these exact dimensions and features. Sometimes there were other people in the room, but usually I was alone. Sometimes there were a table and chairs, sometimes not. It always felt tedious and confining. Eventually I would walk across the room, open the door, and walk up an outdoor staircase to a meadow with colourful wildflowers waving in the breeze under bright sunshine. The meadow was high on a mountain, and below were endless acres of green fields, forests, and villages. I would walk in the meadow, drink in the sunshine and fresh air, and gaze out over the long view. That was always where the dream ended.

As a teenager I analyzed the dream endlessly. The essence of it seemed to be the contrast between the confinement of the room and the wide-open meadow in the sunshine. My life in the city versus being out in nature? Teenage angst versus moments of confidence? Ignorance versus knowledge? After meeting Dr. Mills, I thought of it as my life before and after hearing him speak. When I started attending the Unfoldments, the dream became less frequent and finally stopped.

Looking around the room in the Hermitage that day in Assisi, I could only think, "In all of my theories and analysis, it never occurred to me that it could be a physical place. It's a place!"

I said to Urban, "If we open that door on the opposite wall and find a stone staircase going up to the left against the outside of the building, I don't know what I'm going to do." We walked across the room and opened the door, and there was my staircase, exactly as I had dreamt it. I walked up the stairs as I had done so many times in my dream. At the top was a manicured lawn, walkways for the tourists, and a magnificent view of the valley. I saw some stones marking a path that led into the woods. Walking over there, I sank down on large boulder and cried and cried. It was overwhelming to have a dream that I hadn't thought of in decades suddenly come to life.

Urban sat with me until I was calm enough to continue. We walked back along the path and looked at other parts of the Hermitage. Urban asked me if I would like to go back into the small room. I said, "We could go that way, but I know it so well that I don't really need to see it again." We did go back to the room, and this time it was filled with tourists and felt like any other room, although the dimensions of it once again seized me as familiar. I realized that the first time we were in the room, we were entirely alone, and how unusual that was on a busy summer's day in Assisi.

Back in Toronto, one evening after dinner, I told Dr. Mills about the experience, and he told me about his own remarkable and potent experiences in Assisi. We discussed the possible significance of these encounters and then sat quietly for a few minutes together in awe of the mystery of life and the possibility of connections beyond this lifetime.

I have always loved Saint Francis' story and his prayer for peace. I am also drawn to the simplicity and plainness of the life of Saint Francis despite decades of encouragement by Dr. Mills, and more recently by Urban to enjoy glamour and elegance. I had thought that my attitude about this was due to my parents, but now it seemed that it went back even further.

A great sense of peace came to me from the experience in Assis. Even today I sometimes image the room and walking up the steps to the meadow and feel the beauty of the moment and the much slower sense of the passage of time. Even in memory, it's a door to another world.

Releasement

THE SUMMER FESTIVAL OF 2003 took place at Far Hills Resort near Saint-Sauveur, Quebec. We had made the six-hour drive from Toronto in great anticipation. The Unfoldments in these years, especially at festivals and workshops, had become even more elevated and rarified.

After those lectures we would be unable to speak, revelling in what we had just heard. Marvelling at our good fortune, we might mouth the words "We were there!" I remembered Dr. Mills telling us decades before that we would know when the final years with him were at hand because the lectures would move to a higher level, a "recapitulation" (to use his musical term). It seemed that this time had arrived.

During one of the Unfoldments in the summer of 2003, I said to Dr. Mills that I felt as though a thought habit of fear or lack, which was causing me to look externally for the fullness of my experience, had finally entirely fallen away. I had written pages about this perception and read a portion to Dr. Mills. This exchange turned out to be the last time he gave me guidance on the subject that was central throughout the years of study with him: acknowledgement of God.

Dr. Mills asked me to reread what I had written and then stopped me after a paragraph that ended with the phrase "knowing that I AM the radiance to the sun." Here are excerpts from his reply:

> No. "Knowing that the Sun is the radiance to me, and I cognize it." You can't put the sun in you; you can't say, "I am the radiance to the sun," because I AM is the honorific title for the Sun, the Source of all Life. . . .
>
> You are assuming that you know I AM. That is what we do; we assume we know I AM. All we know is that the I AM, the Sun, the Soul, the Spirit, Mind, Principle, is never capable of being brought into a mind concept; it can only be tonally referred to as an awareness pattern of something other than the objective confinement. . . .
>
> It's a great, subtle, intoxicating consideration to put it into the terms of "I AM the Sun, I AM the Love, I AM the Truth," but it is the Truth, Light, and Love which appear as the substance of my objective being, contained in the realm of awareness.
>
> It's great because you'll still be freer than ever because you won't be out having to take the place of God for everyone else—let alone for yourself. . . .

I'm so glad you're on that; that's a very incredible spot to be at because at that very spot, right now, you can feel the releasement of being the container of something that you couldn't possibly contain, but being the recipient of the One who gives every good and perfect gift. Got it? [24]

I deeply felt in that moment the releasement from being a "container," and being the recipient of the unlimited gift of Life. Yes, I got it.

This exchange with Dr. Mills felt like a recapitulation of the themes in my life with Dr. Mills, answering once again my childhood question "Am I in the world, or is the world in me?" It was a powerful reminder to acknowledge God, or Sun, the Source of all life. One memorized phrase from this passage is my daily reminder: "Truth, Light, and Love appear as the substance of my objective being, contained in the realm of awareness."

Soon after this exchange with Dr. Mills, an astonishing, inexplicable experience of releasement happened—on a fly-fishing trip. I was back in Quebec a few weeks after the summer festival to go fly-fishing with Urban on a river in the Gaspé Peninsula, where he had grown up. I'm not a good fisher because I'm always rooting for the fish instead of the fisher. But I love the unspoiled beauty of nature in the region and the feeling of standing thigh-deep in the river, braced against the current, the river stones shining under the clear water. On either shore banks of evergreens rise sharply to create a tunnel of green through which the fresh breeze and birds travel. Now and then a bird or a moose appears. Fishing reminds me that we share this planet with many species—and thank God there are places where nature still seems to have the upper hand. When I am back in Toronto, stuck in traffic or a downtown office tower, I think of these rivers and relax.

That year, we stayed at a camp beside the Cascapédia River with about fifteen other fishers. Our room was on the top floor of an old white clapboard building, accessed by an outside staircase. The windows looked out over green hills and, beyond them, the river.

It was raining on our first day. I went out in the morning, my hip waders and rain jacket keeping me mostly dry, but then, with the rain continuing in the mid-afternoon, I decided to stay indoors. After Urban and the other fishers had left to go fishing, I went up to our room. The 2003 summer festival with Dr. Mills was still redolent in my mind. Taking out a transcript, I sat down on the bed and turned to the passage Dr. Mills had given to me about I AM as the honorific title for the Sun, the Source of all life.

Deeply absorbed, I glanced up at the cloudy sky. Suddenly I was in the clouds and the sky. The formerly objective world was a swirling field of energy, and I no longer had the sensation of being anywhere in particular. There was no distinction between me and the hills and the clouds; it was one swirling mass that consumed my entire field of attention. Then the clouds seemed to evaporate, the sky cleared, and bright sunshine blazed down, the wet surfaces already drying.

My attention eventually returned to my body sitting in the room. A personal thought formed in my mind: I would like to go outside and sit in the sunshine. But I had a feeling that if I moved, the clouds would return. After remaining still for a while, I decided to go out. Taking my transcript, I walked down the steps. By the time I had reached the lawn chairs, the sky had already closed in with rain clouds. I raced upstairs but still got wet.

Back in our room I sank down on the end of the bed in awe of what had just happened. I was still feeling a palpable energy, but ordinary perception had returned, with me a body sitting on a bed, looking out the window at hills and clouds. I wondered if anyone else had experienced the sunny clearing or if it had happened only in my imagination.

It reminded me of the childhood moment on the beach when suddenly I had been everywhere and nowhere. In both cases it was not a feeling of an altered perception of reality; it was more like a veil coming off to reveal what was the reality all along but just obscured by the mind and senses. As a child I had wondered why people didn't know this, why everyone seemed to behave as though the subject-object duality was real. Now I know how rare and precious it is to know this releasement, the experience of pure being with no identity of form or name.

When the fishers returned, I went downstairs to hear their stories and join them for a drink before dinner. The main topic of conversation wasn't about someone's catch; it was about that weird blast of sunshine. They were comparing stories of taking off their rain jackets, only to have to retrieve them again from shore. I learned that the sun had been out for about fifteen minutes over our camp and that the rest of the region had remained overcast. The only thing I added to the conversation was my experience of going down to the lawn and then running back upstairs.

When we returned home, I described to Dr. Mills what had happened. He smiled and nodded as though it were the most natural thing in the world. Over the years, I had witnessed dramatic changes in the weather in the presence of Dr. Mills, so I knew it was possible, but to find it actually happening to me was a mind-bending experience—especially while I was studying a passage about the Power that allows me to experience the radiance of the Sun.

I wondered what I might have said to the fishers as they drank their Scotch and exchanged stories after a day on the river. They would perhaps have thought I was mad to say that the clouds had cleared in a moment of deep contemplation and attunement to a higher frequency, that life is a conscious experience primarily, and that it is altered by what we are conscious of. Perhaps it would have intrigued them and opened their awareness to a new consideration. Or perhaps they already knew this and had had similar experiences. I will never know because at the time the experience was raw and precious and I just held it in my heart.

Now, after writing of this experience, I sit for a moment considering what Dr. Mills might say about the experience at the fishing camp. I open at random his book *The Cornucopia of Substance*, daring him to join the conversation. Glancing down at the page, I read, "What chased the clouds away?"[25] Once again, stopped in my tracks by what is not just a memory but absolutely present, I can only sit in wonder. "What chased the clouds away?" is the only relevant question, and the one that Dr. Mills might ask. To which he might reply: "I of myself can do nothing. It is the Invisible that doeth the Work." And now the cloudy morning sky has temporarily opened to bright sunshine.

Passages

JUST BEFORE CHRISTMAS 2003, my mother developed what seemed to be the flu, and it wouldn't go away. One awful day in January she called me to say that she couldn't move her legs. I called an ambulance, and my sister, Sue, and I met her at the local hospital. The diagnosis was very grim: Guillain-Barré syndrome, an illness so seldom seen that the emergency-room doctor had to look it up in a reference book to be sure of his diagnosis. Mum was transferred to St. Michael's Hospital in downtown Toronto, a hospital that specializes in treating neurological diseases.

It was horrible to see my tiny mother lying on a bed in the neurology ward, barely able to move. The doctors assumed that the eighty-two-year-old woman they were treating was typical of her age group and gender. The first doctor who examined her asked, "Do you know what you've got?" Mum said, "Yes." "We'll fix you up," he replied as he left the room. A few weeks later, when she had regained some strength, I told the doctor that his patient was a PhD biologist who had worked in medical research, including isolating eye bacteria to create new antibiotics. The doctor was impressed and asked my mother the name of the bacteria, which she remembered. He said he had learned about the antibiotic in medical school and it was still in use today. Whether he was being gracious or honest, I don't know, but this gave my mother a huge boost in confidence. After that, the doctors explained her recovery process in more detail, and in return received many more questions and challenges.

Managing the progress of the disease and her recovery was a chaotic mix of influences. There were the expert but busy doctors and nurses at St. Michael's, and the twenty-four-hour personal caregivers we hired, most of whom had recently come to Canada and brought caring traditions from their own cultures in Jamaica and Trinidad. My sister and I spent hours at her bedside, doing what we could to support her. There was Mum's dousing friend, Margaret, who was sending us, in effect, psychic messages. Mum's other friend, Kennis, had been a nurse in

England and she knew better than anyone how to arrange the pillows to make Mum comfortable.

Then there were my phone calls with Dr. Mills, who took up metaphysical work for her. After two weeks Mum and I were both exhausted from the roller coaster of pain, anxiety, progress, and falling back. I sought advice from Dr. Mills, who offered these words, saying them slowly enough that I could scrawl them in my notebook:

> At a time like this, it can seem impractical to offer the Absolute, but it is the only thing that is practical. We have to hold to the fact that Man is co-existent with the Father, which means that in essence Man is perfect. Since we acknowledge the Father, we have as our right to experience the expression which is wholeness, perfection, grace, and immediacy. You see, we should expect an immediate healing. It is NOW, not progressive. Look how the sensorial tries to take our attention, in this case as your mother.
>
> "What I [Lucille] have to know: She in essence is freed from the pain; in fact, she is not even in it." You hold to that, even though the suggestion is something! You tell her that I expect her up. With that spirit, I don't know how she could be kept down!"

Later that afternoon, my notebook reports, there was "a breakthrough on the food side. The doctor has approved tea with sugar on a spoon. She just had her first spoonful. A big smile, obvious enjoyment."

The following day brought even more progress. Mum was off painkillers, and she swallowed apple juice and even a piece of biscuit perfectly. The doctor said, "You have made my day! To see this spontaneous recovery is amazing."

I called Dr. Mills with the good news, which he was thrilled to hear. He reminded me that any healing is not personal; it is the Father that doeth the work. As he said in his book *Change Your Standpoint, Change Your World*:

A healing does not only point to the presence of God; it points to the lessening power of material suggestion. In God's kingdom in the Light, in the Energy that IS, there is nothing to heal. When you realize that in essence you are divine energy (not material, "no-thing"), then is it surprising that perfection or healing takes place?"[26]

Mum's rapid progress continued over the following week. Soon she was transferred back to the regional hospital near her home that, I feared, would have no idea how to look after her. However, Mum was happy to be closer to home and in a new place, putting the pain and anxiety of the last few weeks behind her. However, as she regained alertness, she began to realize the situation she was in and the mountain she had to climb to become functional again. She couldn't yet eat independently or walk, and she would have to relearn everything. It began to dawn on her that perhaps her former independent and active life had slipped away forever.

To counteract her mood, which was feeling dangerously like resignation, I brought in photos of her dog who was being lovingly cared for by my stepdaughter Kim. I hoped it would make her want to get well and go home. The plan backfired as she looked at the pictures and said, "Oh good, she's happy."

On February 28, 2004, she had an internal blockage that the hospital did not diagnose, and she died during the night. It must have been a painful, horrible death, and neither my sister nor I was there. Her fear of hospitals, that they were as likely to kill her as cure her, had come true. Ever since her mother had died on the operating table due to too much anaesthetic when Mum was fifteen, my mother had lived with this fear and distrust of hospitals all her life.

On what turned out to be the last day of her life I had a long visit with Mum and afterwards called Dr. Mills, who was in Quebec at the time. I don't recall the phone call except that, in describing to him Mum's precarious situation, I felt some comfort in Dr. Mills' words. What a surprise it was, sixteen years later, in 2020, to be listening to an Unfoldment and noticing the date it was given—the evening of

February 28, 2004. At the end of this Unfoldment, which was given to a group of people in Quebec, he said these words that, to me, will always be for my mother:

> Healing is not as important as perceiving Reality. Some people mistake healing as the evidence of attainment, but what healing *really is* is the lessening of the material confinement, the realization that you are more than this body. You are Love Conscious-awareness.
>
> Right now, she cannot be any more Love, more conscious, and more aware in the entire lifetime of ten thousand lifetimes than she is right now. It's only the mind which limits it. And neither are you! Yet, you behave as if you have not got the gift of God! You couldn't even say or consider the name of God if it were not, in essence, originating in your Conscious-awareness, because it has absolutely no meaning to the intellect, but it is known in the heart to be the essence of that Force field that allows you to return to your heavenly home, which is what? To the harmonic state of Being.

To me, this was a "send-off blessing" for my mother.

In the midst of our devastating grief after Mum died, my sister, Sue, and I tried to console ourselves with the fact that she would have hated living in a compromised state, dependent on others. It seemed to us that she had decided to let go. But this knowledge didn't lessen our pain at her loss.

In the spring we took Mum's ashes, as she had requested, to Nanaimo in British Columbia, where she had grown up and where her brother still lived. We scattered the ashes from a boat in Departure Bay, barely able to see the shoreline through our tears.

Back in Toronto, one evening I said to Dr. Mills that I didn't know how to make the pain go away; I felt even more grief in the spring than I had immediately after she died. His response has stayed with me ever since, and it helped me with another event that was just a few months away. He said: "Don't even try. The loss of your mother is now part of the fabric of your being, and it will always be there. Accept it; don't fight it." Relaxing in these words, I immediately felt calmer, and with time the sharp pain of losing her seemed to soften. It was strangely comforting to know that it was not something to be gotten over.

I had felt guilty calling on Dr. Mills during the ordeal with my mother because his own health was declining. All of us around him felt the poignancy of this time and the preciousness of the occasional visits we had with him.

The very last entry in my many notebooks of encounters with Dr. Mills were words of releasement that seemed to close the circle back to the expressiveness of my early childhood: "Stop feeling obliged. It's a word to get rid of. You want the joy of spontaneous movement."

On October 8, 2004, the phone rang. It was my friend Pier Paolo Alberghini. Wandering into the dining room with the phone in my hand, I began to joke about something that had happened the day before. Pier Paolo interrupted me, saying that this was no time for laughing—Dr. Mills had died. As I stared out the window, this seemed impossible to me. I thanked him for letting me know and went and sat with Urban in the living room, just looking at the floor. There were no tears, no emotion, just an inability to process this piece of information. The impossibility of presence, and now absence, engulfed me again.

My mother and Dr. Mills had been born within eight months of each other, on opposite coasts of Canada, and now they had died within eight months of each other. I no longer had living parents or a living mentor and had to face the future without these loved ones who had been such guides to me and whose presence had been fundamental to my life.

At this time I had been married to Urban for five years, and my new family of husband, his daughters, and his son-in-law was a great comfort. Thanks to them, at the age of forty-eight I already had two grandsons, Christian who was four and Nathaniel who was only a year old. As Nana, playing with them, and seeing them grow was a special joy at this tender time. It allowed me to experience the circle of life, a renewal happening before my eyes, and thereby hope for the future. Nothing could replace what I had lost, but the immediate, demanding presence of two small children brought me back into the here and now and helped me to get on with my life.

I was also ready to move on to a new job. After leaving BCG, I had spent several years as a bank executive and then three years as CEO of Career Edge Organization. The prospect of another career transition added to the sense of closing a chapter in my life.

I tried to reflect on what the years with Dr. Mills had meant to me. There was so much to process from the intense thirty-year relationship that, as it was happening, had left little time for reflection. But I found that I could barely begin while I was grieving. I needed time to just hold the relationship in my heart and let it be. I felt the absence of the man, even as my mind was helpfully reminding me that the energy and the transformative grace I had experienced were not in the body that had died.

The loss of Dr. Mills was much more than the loss of a friend. I would never again hear the sound of his voice live in the room, or listen to an original spontaneous Unfoldment as it was being given. My ever-present notebook was closed forever. The lectures, music rehearsals, dinners, meetings, and daily study of current material that had been a huge part of my life were over. This had been my grounding, my balance to being immersed in the secular world. Much of this activity died with Dr. Mills. At times it felt as if my access to higher levels of Being was also lost. I pictured living out the rest of my life in an indifferent world without the inspiring and challenging force of realignment that was Kenneth Mills.

As I found myself without his physical presence, I had to know deeply within myself what could never be lost. I had learned from Dr. Mills that the heights of releasement available to me with him were not in Dr. Mills; they were my experience. He always told us that "what you see in me is all within yourself." Yet, had I built a scaffolding within myself to be able to access this experience directly, without the physical presence of Dr. Mills? Only the years ahead would give me the answer to this question.

Meditation on a Rose

THE ROSEBUD APPEARS, blooms, and dies. This is its foretold fate before it even begins. Yet we confidently know that when a rose dies, "rosedom" continues and another blossom will surely come. The creative force, the principles, the mathematics, the elements behind the appearance of a rose haven't died. The small bouquet before me is the evidence of this coincidence of the eternal and the finite.

Why do I feel so drawn to these roses picked from my garden? How is it that I feel love for a rose? An analysis of its form, name, and variety leaves me unsatisfied. That is not the essence of the rose, and it doesn't explain why they inspire so much feeling.

When I look at a rose, I am looking at my own body in a different form. The principles, the elements of its composition such as carbon, and the originating force of creation are exactly the same. The artistry that makes the rose is the artistry of my body as well. I claim the beauty, harmony, rhythm, colour, delicacy—yet strength—and fragrance of the rose as the same substance that constitutes my beingness. I couldn't appreciate the rose if "rose-ness" wasn't inherent to my disposition as well. In essence we are one.

In form, my body and the body of the rose will come and go. But body is created and sustained by a Life-giving Force that is timeless and never comes or goes.

I photograph the vase of roses in an attempt to preserve their beauty and the poignancy of this moment, but the photos do not convey their delicate loveliness and beauty. It startles me that in the photo they look ordinary and imperfect.

I return to the living forms in the vase on the table. They have the bruises and rough edges of roses grown outdoors on a windy ridge. Each one is imperfect in its own perfect way; every curled or blackened petal is simply more evidence of the principles that shape its life.

These roses have life, as surely as I do. I have cut it short by bringing them inside, but outside the temperature plunges and soon the frost will kill the outdoor blooms.

We commune, these roses and I, about our short fleeting life and about the infinite layers of depth in the petals of a bud, each with a story yet untold. The roses seem to talk, to reach out and take my attention. Their voice is male, matter of fact, practical, battle weary, not delicate or whimsical. The velvet red of their surface is as inviting as a blanket, while the thorns warn me to keep my distance.

I remember that my mother grew the same variety of roses. Perhaps we are connecting via these ruby wonders, from generations ago when these roses grew in her garden at the end of each vegetable garden row. Those plants are long gone, but these new ones are here, freshly bloomed, bursting with life, defying the approaching frost and my garden shears.

It occurs to me that the rose was Dr. Mills' favourite flower. Perhaps he too is appreciating these blossoms, their ethereal fragrance and mortal bodies.

There are many buds on these stems that will never open—possibilities and potential never realized. Yet the completeness of the bouquet is undiminished, its form perfect from every angle. Some blossoms are dying, some buds are small and green, and some are everything in between. The gift of life in its perfection and frailty in a small bouquet of flowers.

Dedicated to my mother and Dr. Mills

IV

THE CREATIVE SPIRIT

If men and women were solely this materialization
they would not be prompted to find the great Creative
Spirit, because there is nothing within the environs of your
physical location – in body, mind or soul – to answer
satisfactorily your questing nature which arises as
a result of a feeling sense of incompleteness.

KENNETH G. MILLS

Facing the Future

IN THE MIDST of almost overwhelming grief at the passing of two loved ones who had been so central to my life, a new thought appeared in my awareness: this is my time and I need to walk it alone. After decades of influence by scientists and by a mentoring metaphysician, my life felt like a blank slate, as though I was graduating from one life into another.

Since the age of eighteen I had lived with the dichotomy of the scientific materialism of my parents and the metaphysical standpoint of Dr. Mills: "There is nothing but matter" versus "It is not mind over matter; it is Mind instead of matter." Both relationships were wrapped in love, guidance, friendship, and a feeling of home. Within a few short months both were swept away in a wave of upheaval that left me standing alone. I wondered if this would resolve the tension I had felt for so many years. It was time to reflect deeply on what was entirely mine, on what I *know*, regardless of external influences.

The radical nature of what I had been doing for thirty years—so unacceptable in the eyes of many people—combined with a tendency to seek acceptance had resulted in a life lived in parts instead of an integrated whole. I knew it wasn't healthy, yet accepted this as a necessary compromise. The Unfoldment was a precious part of my life, and I didn't want to subject it to the judgement of "others" who wouldn't understand. I didn't have the wherewithal to live openly and proudly as one who had studied for thirty years with a spiritual teacher, and to speak up to defend my choice. The actual experience with Dr. Mills was so natural, fulfilling, and satisfying but almost impossible to explain to a world that didn't understand, a world in which the thoughts of "cult" and "loss of personal freedom" overtook all other considerations. I had internalized this negative mindset and allowed it to co-exist in my mentality, sustaining it inwardly, whether or not anyone else actually held this view. It finally occurred to me: why not release it and expect everyone to be interested in what I've been doing and be innately drawn to the same essence? Why not finally break the impediment of otherness and claim Oneness?

It was an internal, not external, change that was needed. I had never fully let go of the "me" that was the serious, analytical child, skeptical of anything not based on observable fact. This "me" is constantly surprised by my interest in spirituality. The curiosity and intellectual rigour instilled by my parents had served me well in living what most would call a successful life, even while it seemed to compete with a knowingness that lay beyond its grasp. It's remarkable how easy it is to maintain more than one "me," and yet how harmful that can be to wholeness and well-being. Breaking the habit of living my life in separate buckets, pleasing one group after another, was my new priority. The point of reconciliation could not be found in family or mentor or personal success; it had to be an inner fulcrum. I needed to learn to live without the energy generated by the friction of having a foot in two worlds. Otherwise I would recreate the same tension all over again.

In my quest for wholeness I began to write down my life stories and drew a timeline of highlights to see more vividly what had constituted my experience. Tracing it over the years, I could see the unwavering commitment since childhood to find viability in the Invisible, despite growing up in a family that didn't acknowledge the existence of such a thing, and then living and working in a society that accepted only the rational mind and body as real. There was the spontaneous pull to artistic expression, always just below the surface, locked away by a fear of failure. At the age of eighteen there was the immediate and profound recognition of Kenneth Mills that extended for thirty years of my life and his. There was the initial discomfort with the influences in Dr. Mills' life—formative years in the Baptist Church, the decade in Christian Science, and his lifelong commitment to elegance and formality.

Despite these differences in appearance, there was so much in the encounter with Kenneth Mills that was truly home. At its heart was the transformative sound of the Unfoldment, a vibratory frequency that I recognized as the sound of Truth itself. That sound was garmented in deeply familiar ideas and in poetic language that poured forth spontaneously in every Unfoldment and always inspired wonder and awe. And then there were the many techniques I had developed thanks to Dr. Mills, such as an ability to see the overview, claim higher ideas, and allow the evidence of them to precipitate in my daily life. There was the recognition of music and the arts as being at the very centre of elevated experience, which had always been my prompting and which came vividly to life with Dr. Mills. Most of all, there was the direct encounter with Dr. Mills' presence, a transforming force of energy that rearranged my molecules every single time.

How do I take these elements and activate them in my life now? I decided to ease up on the business career and become more involved in the arts, which had always been my first love. I also began writing, to find my own words. And I continued to base my life on what had been gained in philosophical attainment, and studied daily to centre my experience in the timeless wisdom of higher ideas, regardless of what I was doing.

In these moments of reflection after Dr. Mills died, I asked that life might grant me another thirty years in which to fully appropriate what I had received and to articulate in words the deep knowingness that I was born with and that became so tangible thanks to Dr. Mills.

It was a rare gift to have met at the age of eighteen someone whose words and presence still inspired me thirty years later. Yet, this sustained relationship required me to have the initiative to grow and mature as the full recipient of the gift, rather than only as an adherent of someone else's work. I knew from conversations with Dr. Mills that he did not want us to be exponents or teachers of his work; we were to live and work from our own "God's green acre."

The Arts as the New Cathedral

THIS NEW PHASE in my life began right back at the beginning, with me as the small child dancing around the living room. In the years following the death of my mother and Dr. Mills, I returned to my childhood love of dance, becoming a board member and eventually chair of the board of the National Ballet of Canada. Serving on the board gave me the opportunity to apply my business experience in an organization I had loved and admired all my life. I've always been drawn to the beauty and magic of ballet, an art form that Dr. Mills, while attending a performance with me in the 1990s, called "an anti-gravitational force field."

Soon after I joined the board, the National Ballet conducted surveys of its audiences to learn more about the reasons they came to the ballet.[27] Was it to see familiar productions they knew and loved? To see daring new work? Ballet stars? The music? Spectacular sets and costumes? Or for a social night out? The respondents duly answered the questions, but it was the open comments that revealed their true motivation: "I come to the ballet to be transported out of my everyday life"; "To experience beauty and grace"; "To enter a different world." It was gratifying to know that I was part of a community of people who found in ballet an avenue for transcendent, anti-gravitational experience. In a post-religious era, when spirituality is more felt than defined, the arts are a perfect vehicle for both artist and audience. They offer a doorway to enter a new state and explore the territory, no doctrine required.

Through the National Ballet, I met Rob Binet, a young Canadian choreographer whose work opens this door. Watching his piece *The Dreamers Ever Leave You*, which was inspired by Lawren Harris's paintings, I saw a moving, swirling, interconnected energy field of rhythm and harmony. Afterwards some audience members described the performance as a spiritual experience. I asked Rob what *spiritual* meant to him. He replied that he was not religious, but that "I believe in people, the energy they create and the connection between them. The body is a physical manifestation of the soul, our non-material essence. I can feel it when the dancers connect to this and are not just moving their bodies. When it works, it makes me cry."

Whether we are participants or in the audience, the arts allow us to take on the vibratory frequency of something that is not "me," something that doesn't arise from personal experience. Paradoxically, the portrayal of someone we are not, or witnessing to someone else's story, helps us get in touch with who and what we are in essence, loosening our attachment to personal identity.

In our day-to-day life most of us present a superficial, polished persona, seldom allowing others to see us in a raw, unaffected state. We tend to keep our vulnerable, imperfect selves carefully in the closet. Yet, we are endlessly fascinated with what constitutes other people. The twenty-four-hour media, reality TV, YouTube, Facebook, Instagram, magazines, and so on are filled with images and stories about . . . ourselves.

Artists open their closet door through their creative expression and let us in to see their vulnerability and depth of feeling. When the door truly opens, a crowd forms. We strain to catch a glimpse into the depths of what can constitute being human. This is what draws us into theatres and galleries. We may think we are interested in seeing paintings on the wall or movements on a stage, but what we are really interested in is feeling the full dimensions of what it is to *be*. This perspective is what motivated me during the many non-artistic hours on boards of directors. It had been twenty-five years since my brief first job at the St. Lawrence Centre, and I was finally immersing myself in the arts, now with the benefit of business experience and the artistic adventures with Dr. Mills.

As an arts board member I was sometimes asked, "Why support the arts?" One answer to this perpetual question came to me on a fly-fishing trip in the Gaspé. Our group was sitting on the screened-in porch at the end of a day, listening to the river flow by, and one man said, "What would justify any government spending $100 million on the arts when the needs of health care and social services are so urgent?" There was a pause and a feeling among the group of not necessarily agreement but also of no ringing endorsement of the value of public support for the arts. Without knowing exactly what to say, I took the plunge: "It all depends on your definition of identity. If you believe that man is solely a physical body, you will direct all funding to food and shelter and to health care. If you also believe that man is mind, you will also support education. If you believe that man is more than body and more than mind, you will support the arts. This is the realm in which man's higher nature is nurtured and opened." Another man in the group jumped up and said, "Yes! That's the best explanation

I've ever heard for supporting the arts!"

I had an opportunity to put this conviction into practice in 2005 when I received an invitation from my friend and former BCG colleague David Pecaut to a meeting to discuss the possibility of establishing a large-scale arts festival in Toronto. David and his partner on the project, Tony Gagliano, CEO of St. Joseph Communications, outlined in the meeting their vision for a festival, which they hoped would someday rank among the top international arts festivals in the world. I was very interested in the idea, and it reminded me of the conversations I had had with Dr. Mills about establishing an arts and cultural centre. Pecaut, with his skillful way of drawing people in, soon had me involved.

I started as a volunteer. By late 2005 we had secured start-up funding, and I became the festival's first employee. This position was later referred to by some as the founding executive director of the Luminato Festival Toronto, but at the time there was no organization and no position. Just the thrill, chaos, and terrifying moments of a large-scale start-up, combined with the wonders and craziness of the arts. We had only eighteen months to translate a business plan on paper into a fully functioning charitable organization with an annual budget of twelve million dollars, and to have the first ten-day festival ready to go for June 2007. It was challenging, creative, and incredibly productive.

Luminato Festival was the perfect project for me while I was feeling my way through this huge life transition, seeking ways to put into practice what I had learned from Dr. Mills and at the same time moving on from that relationship. The compressed timetable made it the most intense assignment I had ever done, but it was also a remarkable experience of being carried. I never doubted that the festival was already complete in the idea realm, and what we were doing was helping it to land, like a spaceship, into the three-dimensional realm. It seemed to come together in one seamless flow with doors opening as a result of vision, intention, and collaboration.

A new festival with no reputation and no artistic director in these preliminary stages, Luminato presented extraordinary programming in its first year. We were offered and accepted two world premieres:

Leonard Cohen and Phillip Glass' collaboration *Book of Longing*; and Eric Idle's *Not the Messiah*, which was done in collaboration with the Toronto Symphony Orchestra. Atom Egoyan, Rafael Lozano-Hemmer, and other prominent artists created new work for the inaugural festival. I had no illusions that I was personally qualified to program an arts festival, and we drew on the advice and expertise of Toronto's arts leadership. In September 2006 the seasoned arts administrator Janice Price joined Luminato as CEO, and permanent staff were hired to mount the festival that was just nine months' away.

When the inaugural Luminato Festival launched on June 1, 2007, it was like being in a movie that I had watched many times before, having conceived and imaged every detail of the festival for the past eighteen months. Standing on the boardwalk at the edge of Lake Ontario watching Rafael Lozano-Hemmer's artwork *Pulse Front* light up the sky over Toronto, it was literally a dream come true. I had lived in Toronto all my life, and seeing familiar neighbourhoods and buildings transformed for ten days with music, dance, and art was so much fun. It was a chance to be part of painting my own city with the energy of the arts.

The first festival was a huge success, and we quickly began planning the second edition. During that year I switched from employee to volunteer and joined the Luminato board of directors.

In February 2008, I was standing in the lobby of a hotel in New York while attending the International Society for the Performing Arts (ISPA), when my phone rang. It was David Pecaut, calling with frightening news. The cancer that he had had five years before had returned and was already spreading. The busyness of the hotel melted away around me, and I stood there, wondering if my dear friend would survive and whether our beloved Luminato could survive without David Pecaut at its beating heart. David immediately began treatment, and for a while it seemed to be successful. But by 2009 the prognosis was grim. In the face of his illness David addressed the Massey Hall audience during the June 2009 festival. With characteristic grace he never mentioned his personal situation, but instead he channelled his depth of feeling into a speech about Luminato that captured perfectly the original vision and motivation for creating the festival:

Luminato is a hugely personal and collective enterprise. In a digital age, a festival like this is one dimension of human activity that must still be experienced in person. At its core Luminato is about the creativity in each one of us. We know that each and every child is fundamentally a creative being. Over our lives, some of that creativity is lost. Luminato is a time, a place and a set of experiences where each of us can reconnect with the creative in ourselves.

The dream of Luminato, a dream we can all dedicate ourselves to this week, is that each of us can discover and share our innate creativity. And in doing so, connect with one another as a community in the most powerful way we know.[28]

During the summer David and I made a two-hour audio recording in which he talked about his experience of co-founding Luminato. We both knew what was coming, but it was hard to admit out loud. He had been such a vital friend and mentor to me ever since I had joined BCG in 1986, and together we had launched the creative ventures of Career Edge and Luminato and had already been talking about a third venture.

David died in December 2009. Every political and business leader who spoke at his funeral used the word *love*, the first time I'd ever heard high-profile figures use this word in public. David had brought love—and with it, creativity, feeling, intuition, and fun—into boardrooms, government offices, and the streets of Toronto. He understood that we create our experience as individuals and collectively as organizations, cities, and nations. His irrepressible confidence and storytelling—as well as incisive thinking and apparently unlimited capacity for hard work—embodied the fact that we have agency to create the world we want to live in. While his life may not fit a conventional definition of spiritual, he offered a powerful example of the generating force of ideas and how to work in the idea realm and wrap it in energy and love to bring about change in the world. As I had learned from Kenneth Mills, harnessing the power of the imagination is very much part of the reinvention of spirituality today. David Pecaut's ability to do this was a powerful example of seamlessly bridging secular achievement with an inspiring presence.

David's death was especially hard for me because it was the second time in less than a year that I had lost a friend to cancer.

Susan Alberghini had first appeared in my life in 1975 when an impeccably dressed New York woman walked into the Unfoldment Hall at Sun-Scape Inn. From that day on, I had my model, making up for a mother who would rather be anywhere than in a clothing store and whose idea of cosmetics was putting coconut oil on her face at night. Susan was beautiful and refined in every respect, with a deep knowledge and appreciation of art, music, and languages. To me, she and her husband, Pier Paolo, were the embodiment of culture and elegance. Susan taught me so much just by being who she was, about how to be a woman and how to present myself in any situation.

Over the years we became great friends and did many projects together. Susan died of cancer in February 2009. I was alone with her when she passed, reading aloud a poem that she loved. It was an unforgettable experience of intimacy, and yet feeling oceans apart, and each one of us going on alone.

There hardly seemed to be enough time to fully process the deaths of Susan and David, to make these losses "part of the fabric of my being." The previous year, I had been elected chair of the thirty-member board of directors of the National Ballet of Canada. At the same time, I was vice-chair of the board of Luminato. I enjoyed the contrast between the exacting precision of a sixty-year-old ballet company versus the creative spontaneity of a festival start-up. Serving in a leadership role in both was challenging and time-consuming, while also deeply satisfying. These were unique opportunities that enabled me to grow. At times I felt exhausted and wondered where this was leading. Was I recreating the kind of demanding life that I formerly had in business?

But I knew that this time it was a step forward, not backward. My early intention to have a career in the arts was being fulfilled and had quickly come to fruition. Immersing myself in the arts in Canada opened a whole new world for me. It often felt like a step away from the three-decade investment with Dr. Mills, yet it was also the perfect context in which to integrate and make my own what I had gained in those years.

The opportunity for integration became even more evident in 2010 when I collaborated with Judith Macdonell to present an arts symposium in Toronto. It was based on a provocative question posed by Judith: Where does the impulse to create come from? Judith, now retired, was the chair of Arts at Upper Canada College in Toronto. She is an actor and theatre director as well as teacher and was a member of the Earth-Stage Actors, a group who performed dramatic settings of Dr. Mills' words. Like me, Judith had been looking for ways to continue the creativity we had enjoyed surrounding Dr. Mills' life and work.

Together we developed and presented a weekend workshop on creativity at the Young Centre for the Performing Arts in Toronto. The format drew on the vision for an arts symposium that Dr. Mills had outlined in 1994. The program culminated on Sunday morning in a panel discussion with all the speakers. As facilitator, I asked questions that Dr. Mills had posed, such as "Who are your heroes?" and "What is your counterattack to your current success?" These engendered a lively discussion. Then we turned to exploring the point of synchronicity across the presentations of the past two days. We agreed that it was being carried on a wave of creativity after hours of seemingly uncreative preparation, which was exactly my experience in that moment. Based on the enthusiastic feedback we received, the symposium turned out to be another way in which people could engage in higher ideas outside of any "spiritual" context.

Following the symposium, the question that had inspired it—"Where does the impulse to create come from?"—continued to unfold in my considerations. We are both created and creators. I didn't create myself, and yet I am. The Creative Force that produces the appearance of a person is not a one-time, historical event. It is the constant fact, constant presence. The impulse to create seems to come from the created—the dancer, the painter, the parent, the innovator— but in fact, our creative activity is acting out the universal creative impulse that is at the origin of our very being.

In 2011, I served as chair of the Canadian Arts Summit, an annual three-day event that brings together the CEOs, artistic directors, and board chairs of large arts organizations across Canada. At the time, there was a remarkable arts building boom going on in Toronto. One of our speakers was architect Bruce Kuwabara of KPMB, who had designed several of these buildings. In his remarks Bruce observed that what a society values most can be seen in the architecture in which it invests. For centuries, churches and cathedrals were the pinnacles of architecture, their grandeur and beauty the embodiment of the devotion of the congregation. In the second half of the twentieth century, downtown Toronto was transformed by the gleaming new bank towers as financial wealth and success became an object of secular worship. Now the city was transforming again, this time with concert halls, theatres, museums, and art galleries becoming the dramatic new buildings on the landscape. People were seeking nourishment and community through the arts and investing in new spaces for this experience. Each generation builds its own cathedrals based on what it values most.

Listening to Bruce, I realized that for me, and perhaps others who didn't find their place in a church or temple, the arts had become the new cathedral. Like places of worship, these arts buildings are accessible to the public, offering free programs and welcoming spaces to encourage people to come in, create community, and integrate the arts into their lives.

It seemed to me that we seldom openly acknowledge the spiritual role of the arts. We emerge from an auditorium moved, renewed, disturbed, or refreshed and then talk about the actors or the plot or where to go for dinner. I wondered whether, in this era in which spirituality in various disguises was being reinvented and becoming more mainstream, it might become a more explicit part of the arts-going experience? Or a more explicit part of everything? The arts, it seemed to me, would be a core part of the rebranding of spirituality.

In 2014, I had the opportunity to experience this as an actor by performing with the Earth-Stage Actors, the group founded by playwright and actor Barry Brodie. Earth-Stage had presented dramatic settings of Dr. Mills' words in many cities in North America. They invited me to join them in their performances in Windsor, the Muskoka area, and Toronto. This was my first experience of standing on a public stage and reciting Dr. Mills' words—a piece called "Green Light," and another favorite, "Be Still." It was a potent experience to perform on a stage for the first time since high school. There were the familiar backstage nerves, worrying about whether I would forget a line or do something foolish as an amateur in a group of seasoned actors. But there was also a profound feeling of the universal nature of declaring these words, heard by the audience in the room and felt in the ethers, a vibratory frequency sent out into the world. It was an experience of getting out of the way and letting the words do their work. The deep satisfaction that welled up within me caused me to wonder if I was more artist than board member or business executive.

As a child, I had devoted all my free time to creative expression, but this was the first time as an adult that I allowed myself to think that perhaps working in business, serving on boards, and supporting other artists was an avoidance of my own artistic nature. Admitting to myself that I might be an artist felt self-indulgent and risky. I could hear my mother's voice cautioning me about showing off. However, after all these years of study and in administrative roles it was more than time for my own creative expression. It seemed to me that writing might be a way for me to reconcile the various parts of my experience into an integrated whole, and it would require me to come out of the proverbial closet and be open about my life in all of its complexity. The idea was daunting and more than a bit frightening, but very attractive. With usual diligence I purchased books about writing and enrolled in creative writing courses at the University of Toronto. I began with writing exercises, and soon notebooks were piling up in the corner of my home office.

At the Camera Bar

WHEN KENNETH MILLS died in 2004, he left only a few guidelines about the legacy of his life's work. The Kenneth G. Mills Foundation was established to hold his intellectual property, including the library of his lectures, music compositions, and other creative output. The unpublished Unfoldments were to be culled, and selected lectures could be kept. There was to be no successor; his work was pertinent to his experience. We were not to teach his work or attempt to give Unfoldments. In a private conversation a few months before he died, Dr. Mills made it clear to me that any further gatherings or activities surrounding the Unfoldment were to come only from our own impelling; there was no obligation to him, or specific expectation from him, of anything to be fulfilled.

I did have an inner impelling of something to fulfill because I was one of the people who had urged Dr. Mills not to erase the thousands of unpublished lectures and to let us review them and select material for future generations. Preserving these powerful expressions of universal Truth was vital for a planet in need of more, not less, philosophical wisdom. I also wanted to be able to enjoy the Unfoldments for the remainder of my life and not be limited to the published books and audio recordings. Important material, including all the video recordings, was still unpublished.

Dr. Mills was not concerned with preserving recordings or transcripts and had often said that the library of recorded Unfoldments should be "wiped out" upon his death. Without his living presence they could be open to misinterpretation. In particular, Dr. Mills was concerned that the Unfoldment itself might be turned into a religious teaching, with doctrine and processes—the very opposite of the spontaneity he embodied. From the standpoint of God-Man-One, there is nothing to teach, nothing to study, only a fact to be accepted and lived accordingly. In the rarified atmosphere of his presence this was a self-evident truth. Nevertheless, at our request, he agreed to let us review and preserve selected material from the unpublished library, and this decision was reflected in his will.

The project took years and was completed thanks to the leadership of project managers, paid staff, and a large group of volunteers. The selected material was digitized for preservation and online access. The resulting library of Unfoldments is increasingly available through the Kenneth G. Mills Foundation's website,[29] some are on YouTube and other sites, and it provides the material for the ongoing workshops and events of the foundation. In doing this project, we were grateful to be able to take full advantage of the evolution of media technology. The twentieth century had brought to the public for the first time widely accessible audio and video devices, enabling the Unfoldments to be recorded as they were given. Twenty-first-century digital tools enable the work of twentieth-century teachers and artists to be readily accessed and shared.

These technology innovations shift power away from intermediaries—people who hear a teaching and pass it on to the next generation—and give it to the original speaker. Imagine if today we had original recordings of the words or music of Buddha, Jesus, Mohammad, Rumi, Shakespeare, Bach, Beethoven, or Mozart, or thousands of other speakers and artists. Thanks to new media and digital technology, the work of twentieth-century teachers and artists is now available online, which offers direct access to the original presence and teaching for private viewing and public presentations. I can watch Margot Fonteyn and Rudolf Nureyev dance anytime I wish, thanks to these innovations. This technology is central to the rebranding of spirituality. Sacred wisdom is no longer set apart for only those who are ready and willing to alter their lives to be present in person, and then to interpret and pass it on to future generations. While a recording is not the same as being there, it is much more direct than reading it in a book, or hearing about it from someone else. A recording points the way to what is possible in a live encounter.

For me, the project of preserving the library was an opportunity to gain some overview of Dr. Mills' entire body of work, something that was not possible as it was being given. I searched the library for my conversations with him over the years. Our librarian at the time, Frances Giles, was my "co-conspirator," setting aside my dokusans, questions and answers, private conversations, and meetings. Gradually the whole journey was pieced together, from tentative first questions in the 1970s right through to lengthy private conversations during what turned out to be the last five years of Dr. Mills' life. Seeing an overview of the entire tapestry, I was amazed by the consistency of message, as though it was one conversation unfolding over thirty years.

While we were culling Dr. Mills' library of lectures, my attention often turned to the obvious question hanging in the air: is there an audience for this material, and if so, how do we share it? The language is unusual and requires concentrated attention, yet the message is universal. The ideas are at least as relevant today as when they were given, and they come to life remarkably when the recordings are played. If it was worth preserving, it was also worth sharing.

One answer to this question had already appeared in the form of people discovering the Unfoldments in the years since Dr. Mills had passed and finding great value in them. It is remarkable to watch people who never knew the man find an attunement to his presence through the archival recordings and our collective presence in listening together.

Exploring this question, in 2010 my friends David Nash and Judith Macdonell and I decided to present to groups of young people the *Rapture of Being* film directed by Barbara Willis Sweete that had been shown at the PRIME Mentors event. The film follows Dr. Mills during three days as he works with musicians and actors, composes on electronic keyboards, paints, speaks spontaneously in poetry and prose, and talks about his life work. At one point he asks (and answers), "What is the rapture of Being? The uninterrupted flow of new inspiration." An apt description of the film and of the man upon which it is based.

We organized a series of film screenings and invited young people who were friends of friends, who in turn invited their friends. One of these screenings took place in June at the Camera Bar, a fifty-seat theatre and art gallery on Queen Street West in Toronto. Watching the packed audience arrive, I was surprised and impressed to see them elegant in dresses, high heels, makeup, jewelry, suits, and jackets. I remembered the reluctant compliance of our group in the 1970s to meet Dr. Mills' formal standard of dress. I thought, "Dr. Mills would have loved this young generation!"

The audience was deeply moved by the film. Their many questions and comments during the Q&A session told us that they were not drawn to religion but they were not content to be immersed in only their careers, friends, and family. Many of them meditated and had read books by spiritual teachers, but they wanted more. One young man in the middle of the auditorium stood up and asked: "Where do I find a Kenneth Mills today? Where do I find someone who will take the interest in me that I saw him doing in the film? Someone who will offer the kind of transformational words and actions that he did? Where do I find that?"

The world stopped for a moment. It was obvious that this was the relevant question. Where would he find someone today who was able to offer the deep insight, radical standpoint, and provocation that those of us who knew Dr. Mills had experienced? Kenneth Mills' work, through the archive of lectures, is a valuable and eloquent guide, but without the living presence could it be the direct intervention this man desired? Could we be that presence in people's lives? I knew that if this young man was sincere, the answer to his request would appear in his life in some form, as it had in mine.

At the end of the evening David, Judith, and I went out into the warm night on Queen Street, still awestruck by the responsiveness of the group and by their desire to have the rare relationship with a mentor that we had experienced. The clear night air and stars overhead seemed to witness this moment as we took in the enormity of what we had just discovered. Not only was the film meaningful to them, but they seemed to be starving for true nourishment. We now knew that we no longer lived in a world where what we loved was weird and off-putting to many people. We were in a world where what had been our primary interest was a precious gift that others wanted to find.

Remarkably, in my more recent meetings and interviews with people from many walks of life, the year 2010 has been referenced again and again as a turning point when there is suddenly new interest and openness to these ideas. Something was changing, and that change would only accelerate in the years that followed.

What Happens after Church?

FOLLOWING THE Camera Bar event, I kept wondering, "If these young people did find a Dr. Mills today, would they do what I did—devote decades of their life to philosophical study under the guidance of a mentor?" For those who wouldn't make that choice but who still want a philosophical and spiritual basis to their life, what avenues are available? At one time churches and temples filled this role. But what about today? What happens *after* church?

This question is not meant to diminish in any way those who continue to find religion vital in their lives. In fact, they are perhaps to be envied: they have an established avenue in which to practise and celebrate their deepest beliefs and values. The question for the rest of us is, What happens after church? Where and how will we recognize an originating Life Force, without institutions, dogma, rituals, or traditions?

Once this question occurred to me, it took root in my awareness and has stayed there ever since. I deeply wanted to know what would constitute the search for meaning in this post-religious and yet post-secular age. Where would people turn for answers and, importantly, for experiences, and how would that shape us as a society? Could right now be a moment in history in which we reinvent the age-old search for meaning? It felt like revolutionary change, shaking off the old and embarking on something new that was as yet unformed.

I became like Roy Neary in his living room in *Close Encounters of the Third Kind*,[30] rebuilding the same shape over and over again. In my writing, regardless of the topic I was supposed to be writing about, I was always exploring the same questions: What is the change that is coming and how will it happen? Could ours be a generation that rebrands God? Could this be a time of rediscovering meaning in a Higher Power and expressing this in new language relevant to the twenty-first century?

The questions were both intellectual and personal. I was strangely fixated on answering them in terms of a social trend. What could be more transforming to society than a new awareness of how we understand the nature of life itself? Just as urgently, in those years after Dr. Mills' passing, I needed to answer the questions for myself. What is my "after church" or "after Unfoldment"? What is my avenue to realize the fullness of what I have received and to make it my own?

The years with Dr. Mills now felt analogous to sitting in a restaurant immersed in the private bubble of a table for two, oblivious to the surroundings. But now that I was sitting alone, I was aware of the whole "restaurant." I became interested in the patrons at the other tables, wondering what they were "eating," and intrigued about their lives.

Starting in 2010, I began to pay much closer attention to the changes happening around me, by getting to know the young people who had attended our events and by tracking broader trends. The file that had started with the 1998 *Globe and Mail* article about introducing meditation into the workplace was now, twelve years later, an avalanche of clippings and online references. For example, in 2011 Google had invited Thich Nhat Hanh to speak to its employees, and the company was also offering ongoing mindfulness meditation programs. Meditation and yoga had already shifted from "cult" (according to the 1998 article) to a method of relaxation, and was shifting again to essential life skill. A few brave executives were publicly acknowledging the value of their meditation practice and inspiring their employees to try it. It seemed to me that meditation was the prow of the ship, reintroducing spiritual principles and practices to the "mass market," which would bring about a shift in awareness and restore acknowledgement of the beauty and wonder of life.

The change in the air was evident in the consulting industry. In 2009 a firm was launched by Rasmus Hougaard based on his foundation in studying the principles of dharma. The objective of the Potential Project company is to "enhance individual and corporate performance and well-being through skillful application of meditation and mindfulness in a corporate context."[31] Hougaard and a handful of other entrepreneurs, such as Michael Apollo with his firm Mindful Gateway in Toronto, were building consulting firms that offered timeless wisdom to corporations.

I recalled Dr. Mills' encouragement to me in 1992 to start a consulting firm on this basis. At the time it seemed too radical, impossible to do. Perhaps I was just too cautious, but the appearance of these new consulting and meditation training firms less than two decades later could be taken as a measure of how far we had come. This new generation was finding that in an accelerating world, working harder and faster by using the skill set of a former world was simply not viable. People were coming to an extremity of overwork and burnout and needed a new solution. A premise that embraced the full potential of the individual was no longer "nice to have"; it was a necessity.

I felt the excitement of a profound shift taking place. It had been a long gestation period, but now the signs of change were everywhere. Meditation in the workplace could spark a revolution with huge implications. What if business did change and embrace the full dimensions of the beings who walked in the door every morning, not just their rational mind and body? It would change the nature of the workplace and the way our society gets work done to keep the economy going. It would be a disruptive force. Feelings and intuition, compassion and cooperation, would be at the table alongside competition, logic, and analysis, causing all kinds of havoc. The supremacy of the rational mind would be challenged on its home turf. I could hardly wait to see how it would all unfold.

Interestingly, the new focus on spiritual principles and practices did not seem to include any evidence of acknowledgement of God—by this or any other name—and at times felt like spirituality without Spirit. No doubt some people did privately acknowledge a Higher Power, whether called God or Self, and many had grown up in families that went to church, but the entire realm of God-Consciousness was largely missing from the current conversation and articles about spirituality. I wondered if a new realization of God-Consciousness would be the next frontier.

Science was clearly playing a major role in the re-emergence of spirituality. By 2010, in some fields science was already an ally, proving rather than discrediting the emerging new perspectives. Alongside the breakthroughs in quantum physics and neuroscience, research into the nature of consciousness was requiring scientists to work right at the seam of the visible and the invisible. The proposition that this is a conscious experience primarily, that what appears to be "out there" is in fact arising in mind, has been part of wisdom teachings for millennia. What was new was that scientists and others with no interest in spirituality were exploring this possibility.

In another facet of science, appreciation of nature was coming to the fore, with "forest bathing" and rediscovering the mental and physical health benefits of immersion in the natural world. Our awareness of and respect for the life of other species was expanding, as more people became cognizant of the harm we do to the animals raised for our food supply, as well as to those in the wild.

By 2010, health-care workers, fortified by the recently published research on the benefits of meditation, were applying it and discovering that not only did it help their patients relax, but it was a healing modality, sometimes more powerful than drugs. People had begun asking if children should be taught meditation in school or if that would be introducing a cult into public education. At the University of Toronto, thanks to founder Michele Chaban, courses in applied meditation at the School of Continuing Studies were attracting hundreds of health-care and education professionals into new certification programs.

The concept that the mind is a tool that needs to be trained is not new. It is the basis of every education system and even civilization. But now, instead of training the mind to acquire knowledge and skills, people were interested in the subjective experience of the mind itself. As more and more people sat down with their own mind in meditation practice and observed its fluctuating contents, a freedom was being gained in not identifying with every thought that appeared on the screen of awareness. Dr. Mills' instruction in the 1970s to adopt the standpoint of the observer, to "be the watch," which had felt so radical to me at the time, was becoming widely accepted.

Principles and practices of spirituality were breaking out of houses of worship and small set-apart gatherings and moving into the workplace, health care, education, and even government. This seemed to offer great hope for the future and paralleled my own journey to greater integration.

By the 2010s, the stigma and cult label surrounding spirituality outside of religion was being replaced by a new openness and curiosity and a desire to find meaning and satisfaction beyond what the material world or religion had to offer. Centuries-old patterns of seeking certainty in religion seemed to be falling away, as was the certainty of rational thinking, leaving nothing to turn to except the breath, awareness, presence, wonder, nature, life itself. This releasement was the blank slate upon which a new chapter could be written.

It occurred to me that researching these trends could be a way to understand the events of my life, put them into context, and see my life from a broader perspective. I could apply my strategy consulting skills not only to explore what's happening "out there" but also to continue my own journey. The recent encounters with young people had woken me up to the realization that my thirty-year investment in the Unfoldment had given me something to share. Dr. Mills had made it very clear that we while could share the Unfoldments we were not to be teachers of his work. This left only one avenue open: to come into the full realization of what I had received, to be that which had poured into my tilted cup.

This plan momentarily raised the old fear of otherness and of a family heritage of Christian missionaries imposing their beliefs on the people of India. By some magic, I remembered something that Dr. Mills had said to me years before: "You are never imposing as long as you're not posing." This felt like cosmic permission to just be authentic and put myself forward. Taking this step would be my releasement: by letting go of old thought patterns of insecurity, and trusting in the present moment to express myself.

At first it seemed like a crazy plan to do interviews and conduct market research to understand spirituality today and advance my own journey. Yet the idea appealed to me. It would give me an avenue to investigate the subject, bring me into contact with inspiring individuals, and require me to find my voice. I decided to give it a try.

As I was about to begin the project, an unexpected health crisis inserted a long pause between the Camera Bar event and embarking on the research program. However, the illness gave me a first-person insight into spirituality and health care, and how much attitudes had changed in the eight years since my mother's illness.

A Prescription for Health

IN JUNE 2011, while working out at the gym, I suddenly lost strength in my right leg and sunk to the floor, shaky and nauseous. I had been experiencing odd symptoms for several months but there was nothing I could put my finger on. I was shedding a lot of hair and seemed to tire easily, especially when walking quickly or going up stairs. A dermatologist told me that the hair loss was due to stress, and I was inclined to agree. I was still processing the intimacy of being with Susan when she died, and feeling the loss of David Pecaut, and I was juggling numerous work and volunteer projects.[32]

The symptoms gradually got worse, and a year later, on May 24, 2012, while most people were going off to work, I was in my living room barely able to move. The previous evening I had been a judge for a business plan competition in my new role as CEO of the Pecaut Centre for Social Impact. As our group of judges walked quickly through the huge Metro Toronto Convention Centre, my body was telling me that I would be paying for this extra exertion. By the time I got home, I was too weak to go up the stairs. My husband came home an hour later and found me slumped in a chair in the kitchen and helped me up to bed.

Sitting almost immobile the next morning in the living room, it occurred to me that in this state I couldn't even go to a grocery store. I was completely dependent—a very frightening thought, not knowing whether it would last a day or a lifetime. Whatever this health problem was from a medical perspective, for me it was a signal to stop running around, looking for my life in outside pursuits. It was time to look within.

Over the days and weeks that followed, while confined to a wheel-chair, I saw several doctors in Toronto and then went to the Mayo Clinic. Through the many medical tests and the uncertainty of it all, I often repeated to myself a statement by Dr. Mills that I had written down and taken with me:

> What is *body* to you? This physical form? . . . Body is *an idea*, and you make it up to be "you" with a body. But if it's an idea, why do you let it drop to materiality? Why don't you restore it to the realm of ideation? And what is that realm of ideation? *Where harmony, rhythm, and perfection abide.* Body is the natural rhythmic movement of conception unconfined and not at all interfered with by intellectual hypotheses.[33]

"Restore body to the realm of ideation where harmony, rhythm, and perfection abide," I silently repeated, lying on yet another examination table. Another favourite statement helped calm me as I lay on the bed in my hotel room, wondering what had happened to my life:

> The Light will never shine more brightly than it is at the moment, and it will never be dimmed by the suggestion of a time-space suggestion and a continuum of limitation.[34]

These words saw me through the darkest days and illumined the ones that followed.

The crazy collection of symptoms—muscle weakness, a "buzz" all over the surface of my body, nausea and headache caused by the slightest exertion, sweating and chills, and an autoimmune scarring hair-loss condition—didn't add up to any known malady. The extensive testing at the Mayo Clinic revealed only one issue, "autonomic dysregulation," a condition of the autonomic nervous system. The prescription was to gradually rebuild strength, which they predicted could take eighteen to twenty-four months. I was to start with two minutes a day on a recumbent bicycle. As my sister said when I returned home, the Mayo Clinic was expensive and a long way to go to be told to get some exercise. But after spending two weeks in a wheelchair, I was ready to try anything.

My life seemed to be a list of things I was not doing—not working (I had to quit my new job), not going to concerts, not driving, not going out with friends and family, not even making those trips to the grocery store. If I went downstairs in the morning, I would pack for the day because I couldn't manage any extra trips back up the stairs.

We rented a recumbent bike, and I started on the two minutes a day. At first, even this was impossible. Within a minute I would feel ill and have to stop. After months of trying, it seemed that the weakness could be permanent. To counter this suggestion I returned to one of the very first statements Dr. Mills had said to me: "Rejoice in the ever-newness of Being." The ever-new quality of Being is how any seemingly intractable situation in the three-dimensional realm can be dissolved in an instant. The ever-newness of Being is how my body will heal.

In September I had a telephone appointment with my doctor at the Mayo Clinic and told him I still wasn't improving. He said, "Don't give up. Just don't give up." I persisted and very gradually regained some ability to exert and was able to slowly increase the minutes. With every additional minute I counted my blessings and declared, "Rejoice in the ever-newness of Being!"

Now that I knew I could slowly regain capacity, I resolved to take a positive approach to this sudden change in my life. Life had handed me a clean sheet of paper—nothing to do, nowhere to go. How will I fill these solitary hours? How do I make the most of this interlude? I thought deeply about what I love most, and to my delight I realized that these were things I could enjoy even in my current state: words and music. They became the nurturing core of my restoration program, along with a renewed meditation practice. Jon Kabat-Zinn's book *The Full Catastrophe* was a godsend. Using the instructions he had developed for his patients, I could lie in bed, do the inner body scan, and meditate.

I began my words and music program with Jane Austen and Chopin's nocturnes. Spending my days in this way reminded me of how much I loved doing so. As the months went by, in addition to reading, I was able to write. In addition to listening to music, by 2015 I was able to sing in a choir. Increasingly I couldn't remember why I had spent so many years working in business; I couldn't even find the "me" that was the business executive anymore. I knew that this change was permanent. Even if I fully regained my strength, I would not be going back to work in business.

All stimulants—coffee, tea, wine, sugar, noise, bright lights, chemicals in products, EMF from devices, and even being with more than one or two people at a time—were way beyond my scope. We had thought that visits from my grandsons would be the best tonic, but at first even they were too much. It was a gentle, quiet time, and as I relaxed, I grew to love it.

My other preoccupation, during what turned out to be a journey of two years, was getting to know my body. I realized that despite having had it for over fifty years, I hadn't paid much attention to it and really didn't know what it wanted and needed. When dealing with an acute disease such as cancer, doctors and patients often describe themselves as being in a "fight." Fight wasn't the right word for my situation. I decided that mine would be a love-in. I would love my body, laugh at the symptoms and funny things happening to me, and bring as much warmth and goodwill as I could to the situation. It wasn't easy, especially at first.

One of the most distressing symptoms was hair loss. Most of my life I had had thick wavy hair; it was probably my most distinctive feature. Now I had lost my eyebrows, my hairline was receding, and every time I washed or brushed my hair, handfuls came out. Worse, I was told that this condition was permanent. For a woman, hair loss is emotionally traumatic. It dramatically changes and ages the appearance. I tried every medication and ointment that was offered, and had steroid injections in my scalp. With time the rate of hair loss finally slowed down enough that I was able to relax, laugh at it, and love this part of my body. I kept telling myself that "I am not my hair," and if it all falls out, I will simply wear a wig. I remembered and reaffirmed to myself that mine is a body that grows hair easily. Abundant hair is natural to me; that innate ability must still be present.

Getting to know my own body seemed like an odd project, but as I did this, I realized that I had to learn to love and protect my body. I became sensitive to the effect of foods, water, medications, exercise, activity, and thought—my own and the thoughts of those around me. I couldn't believe how much I had not seen before. My body had been constantly sending me messages but I wasn't listening.

Spending time daily enquiring into the state of my own body deepened the realization that I am not the body. I have a body, for which I am very grateful. I use it to be in the three-dimensional world, but this body is not what I am in reality. If it was my identity, it would be much easier to understand. Instead of trying to pick up signals and fathom what they might mean, I would be those signals.

I was discovering firsthand insights about the body-mind connection that reinforced what I had learned from Dr. Mills. I knew that what was held in thought affected the physical realm and that any change had to start first in mind. Now I had evidence in my own body, from day to day, of the power of that fact. I had to return to the basics and consider once again what constitutes life, what is necessary for health and well-being. On one level, it is shelter, food, family, friends, and financial stability. I had all of that. What I hadn't had enough of in recent years was "taking time to be Timeless." I hadn't been taking time to be aware of and furnish my inner room with the attributes that I wanted to constitute my experience. Without a strong internal reference point I was too subject to the energy fields, thoughts, and opinions of those around me. I was still very sensitive and able to adapt to almost any situation. I had been doing too much adapting, apparently present but only superficially conforming to the situation of the moment. I vowed that with whatever precious days I had left, I would bring my whole self to each and every day.

Through this journey I had to learn to relax and accept that "I am not in charge"—the releasement of being "the recipient," as Dr. Mills had put it. It was obvious to me that I couldn't heal my own body. What I could do was acknowledge the infinite Intelligence and Light of the universe that creates and sustains this entity called me, and simply rest in that. I held to statements of truth and then used my imagination to let them literally fall over my body. I reminded myself constantly of the body's exceptional healing and restorative ability, including that of growing hair.

I tried various healing modalities such as energy medicine, acupuncture, vitamins and minerals, massage, mindfulness meditation, Transcendental Meditation, nerve conduction exercises, and diet. Most of all, I held to the absolute statements I had received from Dr. Mills to remind me what is Real and what is unreal.

It was surprising to discover how much my new attunement to the body was a doorway to experiencing non-physical presence. My tendency had been to go through the mind, thinking about ideas, making declarations, and redirecting my attention to the Higher Nature. This was still in my awareness, but now I mostly just focused on the breath, on the body, and on presence.

I learned, as a result of not being able to exert, that bodies are designed to move. The heart, lungs, nervous system, digestion, muscles, and skin all work best in a body that is in motion. As my stamina grew, I enjoyed the freedom of being able to move again. Working out on an elliptical machine was fun—I was feeling good instead of ill! Walking in the woods felt like a miracle. A capability lost and regained is very precious.

Eventually the other symptoms settled down. I seldom felt the buzzing on my skin. There was no light-headedness when I stood up, and no nausea and blood rush when I tilted my head down. Even my hair was thickening again, despite the "permanent hair loss" diagnosis. I took none of it for granted.

In July 2016, I had a doctor's appointment at the Environmental Health Clinic at Women's College Hospital in Toronto. I had been on the waiting list for so long, I was almost embarrassed to go: I was too healthy. However, I didn't want to miss the chance to learn something new and couldn't assume that I might not need them again someday. Dr. Kerr reviewed my history, handed me a sheet of paper, and said, "Based on your symptoms, it appears that you had a classic case of chronic fatigue syndrome." Reading the printout, I was amazed to see my oddball collection of symptoms listed on a page and constituting a known ailment. As I said to Dr. Kerr, "I'm glad I didn't know this in 2012, especially with the word *chronic* in the diagnosis." I didn't want to give it the dignity of a label, which would have only made it harder to dispel. Dr. Kerr replied that I had done everything they recommend to their patients. In her experience, if a patient doesn't regain strength within the first three years of symptoms, they likely never do. Flashing back to that morning in my living room, unable to even walk around my house, shivers went up my spine in thinking about what the alternative could have been if I hadn't persisted and rebuilt strength.

(There was a relapse in 2018–19, and this time the doctor diagnosed that this type of illness is likely due to an immune system reaction to a virus. The symptoms of so-called chronic fatigue syndrome are similar to those of "long Covid.")

Looking back from the other side of the chasm since the initial illness in 2012, I'm grateful for the journey. It caused me to stop and reset and to reflect seriously on what is truly important to me and what is only important to the false sense of ego. It brought me back to reading, to writing, to music, to singing, and to meditation. It brought me back to myself.

I compiled a lifelong "prescription" for myself to maintain health on every level:

- Study and meditation

- Writing and reading

- Music, dance, singing in a choir, going to arts events

- Friends, meaningful conversations

- Spending time alone

- Enjoying the wonders of nature

- Daily exercise

- Discrimination in thought, word, and deed; making wise choices about the intake of food, media, and associations

- Purposeful activity that fulfills a sincere intention

I still use this list as my prescription for health. In recent years I have added three more points, and although they have turned out to be harder to implement, they are equally important:

- Lexicon: finding my own words for talking to myself and others about the realm beyond the mind, and about practices to keep these higher ideas foremost in attention

- Conversation and community: using these words in conversation with other people to build deeper connections and community

- Acknowledging God—by this or any other name

As I write these words, a bird has started to sing in the tree right outside my window. It startles me because it is dark outside at six o'clock, the beginning of another chilly April day. The bird isn't wondering about its lexicon, who to talk to, what to say, or whether it is acknowledging its creator. It is just singing, regardless of the dark and cold, singing as though it were the middle of a beautiful, sunny, spring day. I had my model.

V

REBRANDING GOD

*I don't believe in the God I grew up with,
but I believe in a feeling of God. There isn't anywhere
in my life to have this conversation. Church was that, and
it was where you could sing in public. Now I go out and find
a choir, and I have a running group, which is all great, but
we still aren't having the conversation. I wish we could have
church without church, where we can talk about
what constitutes a life well lived, while
having a sip of wine and a snack.*

CHRISTINA, FOCUS GROUP PARTICIPANT

Embarking on the Project

WITH MY HEALTH mostly restored, in 2015 I hired myself as my own volunteer consultant and began the research project that I called Rebranding God to explore how we were rediscovering and reinventing spirituality and the acknowledgement of a Higher Power. How were ideas and practices formerly confined to sacred spaces moving into the secular mainstream? What has been the impact of this in various fields of endeavour? How were people using language, including synonyms of the word *God*, and remaking those words for a new day? As I delved into the research, I found remarkable evidence of a rebranding taking place and signs of a new integration between spirituality and science, business, and the arts. It felt as though the universe was conspiring to meet me halfway as I attempted to build a bridge in my own life between a sacred inner knowingness and an aligned external life.

As a former business consultant, I started the project with data analysis, which turned out to be surprisingly revealing. In 1971, Statistics Canada had added a new category to its population-census question on religion, the option of "No religious affiliation." In this first year, 4 per cent of Canadians had selected it. It is likely that most of the 4 per cent were atheists like my father. In 1971, spirituality outside of religion was still the domain of cults and exotic spiritual paths. Fifty years later, in 2021, 35 per cent of the population selected "No religious affiliation," despite atheism (as measured in other surveys) remaining below 10 per cent. A new category of "spiritual but not religious" had implicitly emerged.[35]

It intrigued me that the question on religion posed by Statistics Canada read, "Which religion do you belong to?" It seemed to me that this wording would elicit answers that blended family heritage with current beliefs. I asked a few friends who were raised Catholic but hadn't been to church since childhood, which box they had checked on the census. They all replied, "Catholic." Without minimizing the importance of family heritage, I was more interested in where people stood today.

I was excited to find an Angus Reid poll that reframed the question of religious affiliation. This survey separated religion and spirituality and asked Canadians to select one of three choices. It produces a very different profile of Canada.

Spiritual but not religious (SBNR)	37%
Religious	34%
Not spiritual or religious	27%

Source: Angus Reid Institute, Religion and Faith in Canada Today, November 2015. The figures presented here are derived from Angus Reid's research and were approved by the company's staff, but they are not presented in these categories in the report.

The awkwardly named "spiritual but not religious" category—defined more by what it isn't than by what it is—was already Canada's mainstream choice in 2015. The predicted secular society into which late-twentieth-century Canada appeared to be heading constituted only 27 per cent of the population. After a lifetime of being identified in small minority categories of "atheist" and then "spiritual group member," I now appeared to be in the mainstream with a majority of Canadians. I could hardly believe it.

Some might speculate that the SBNR box was the default choice of those who seldom, if ever, thought about this subject and didn't want to select the third box, which might imply they were atheist—"atheists in denial," as some journalists call them today. In my research I wanted to investigate what constituted SBNR and whether there was a substantive conviction behind the label.

The Angus Reid poll also probed the subject of belief in God. It found that 78 per cent of Canadians say that they believe in God or a Higher Power. This figure is consistent with other surveys on the subject. At the same time, regular attendance at church, as measured in the Statistics Canada census, was indicated by only about 20 per cent of Canadians.

Combining these two findings—78 per cent belief in God and 20 per cent regular church attendance—yields the conclusion that more than half of the Canadian population believes in God but does not go to church. This led to my creating the one consultant-style chart in the book to show visually the size of the "white space" that is increasingly filled by the spiritual-but-not-religious category.

The "whitespace" between belief in God and church attendance is more than half of Canadians, opening the way for spirituality outside religion.

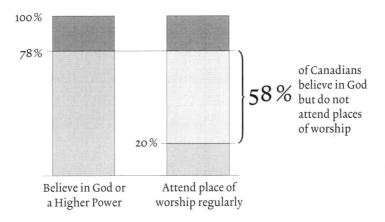

Source: Statistics Canada 2011, Pew Research 2015.

This bit of statistical analysis made me even more intrigued to know what half of the Canadian population was doing to acknowledge or nurture their belief in God. What does a Higher Power mean to them, and how does it affect their lives? Surely acknowledgement of God cannot be a passive piece of information at the back of the mind, only brought to the fore when filling out surveys.

Before seeing these statistics, one might imagine that the long decline in church attendance indicated a rejection of the entire proposition of spirituality. But it now appeared that many were not going to church, not because they had lost the conviction that there was a Higher Power, but because the institution of church no longer satisfied this impulse. For churches, this presents a serious market-share problem: how do we bring people back to religion? For the rest of us, it raises the interesting question: What are we doing, if anything, to nurture our awareness of a Higher Power? What happens *after* church? This question became a priority for my field research.

I wondered what factors were fuelling the sudden rapid growth of spirituality outside of religion, and I thought back to my own family. My grandfather had sparked the shift in our family from religion to atheism a century ago. He was passionate and vocal in his revolt against Christian ministers and missionaries in India. His stance would have been a radical move that probably alienated some family members. Rejecting religious affiliation can cause an emotionally charged, fundamental upheaval, especially in families where it has been the very basis of stability for generations. My father, the second generation in our family, inherited and adopted the atheist world view of his father, but with less emotional intensity. He accepted it as the way things were.

As the third generation, I grew up inheriting this view. I questioned it because by the time I was born, it had become only an intellectual conviction. My grandfather's original impetus, and the missionaries in India that had caused him such concern, were remote from my experience. I was drawn to exploring spirituality without institutional religion. I've since discovered that the three-generation pattern of the re-emergence of spirituality plays out in many families. Perhaps my family just got there sooner.

If the three-generation pattern continues to hold true, we can expect more growth in spirituality outside of religion as the burst of emotion surrounding the rejection of religion fades further into the past, and more people grow up without religion and feel prompted to seek answers to their presence.

This places us at a unique inflection point in history when many are hungry for a life lived in full recognition of its essentially non-material nature, but without an institutional affiliation. It feels like it will not be about perpetuating or re-establishing a shared belief system; it will be individual realization. We are witnessing today the chaos and turbulence of the transition from these established traditions to something new that is as yet undefined on the level of the rational mind, even as we are seeing undeniable glimpses of what is to come.

The turbulence of the transition can cause disruption in families and create a profound generation gap, especially in the absence of new language. My friend Kevin grew up in the United Church and raised his children with no religious or spiritual education. When Kevin's twenty-year-old son was about to undergo his third round of cancer treatment, Kevin yearned to connect with him on a deeper level. "How do I talk with my son about the big questions and the big answers? All the great lessons of morality and mortality that I know are in the Christian Biblical stories. Yet even I find the rituals of the church no longer comforting, and the doctrine no longer believable. How can I go back to this framework to talk with my son? In the face of his illness, I feel outrage that I have no words to express what I want to say."

The early-twenty-first century is not the first time that a spiritual movement has arisen from outside of religion. There have been many examples such as Plotinus, Marcus Aurelius, Ralph Waldo Emerson, Martin Heidegger, Ramakrishna, and Ramana Maharshi. What is unique to our time is the direct, unfiltered access by millions of people around the world to these ideas, all at the same time, through the global technology now available. It is exciting to consider that rather than the presence of lone voices teaching a select few, followed by books and eye-witness accounts to slowly widen the circle, people across traditions and cultures are responding to these ideas and changing their lives.

The next step in my research plan before beginning the interviews was to scan the environment. This revealed a great deal of apparently superficial "lifestyle" spirituality. Now that the word had become trendy amongst a younger generation, it seemed everyone wanted to be spiritual. Marketers of products and services were taking full advantage of the trend. A new clothing line promised to make the impossible possible, and makeup ads promised to make the invisible visible. A few days at the spa would reconnect you to your soul. The wellness industry was in full flight, with billions of dollars at stake. Slipping in behind it, just as had been predicted in the 1998 *Globe and Mail* article, was meditation and spirituality.

I wondered if it was the absence of new branding, language, and organizing principles that made spirituality outside of religion appear to be so superficial. Just as I had done, people were avoiding the word *God* and anything else that sounded religious or New Age, and they didn't have the words (or perhaps the courage) to express acknowledgement of a Higher Power other than to say, "I'm spiritual."

Two fundamental characteristics emerged from this phase of the research. The first is that in this revolution the beliefs associated with religion and atheism are being uprooted at the same time. The Christian religion is losing adherents as people turn to a secular world. However, the predicted secular world is also being disrupted as people return to spirituality, but without the traditions and infrastructure of institutional religion. People are questioning their religious beliefs but are also dissatisfied with purely rational thinking. Spirituality outside of religion may still appear to be flakey and superficial, but both religion and materialism are losing adherents to something new that is still being defined.

The second characteristic is that this new wave of spirituality is integrated, not set apart. Spiritual principles and practices (especially meditation) are flowing away from churches, temples, and Zen centres and into health care, the workplace, and education. While this observation is almost ordinary today, it was a revolutionary change to someone like me who had lived a divided life just decades before.

For example, my hairdresser and I, over thirteen years, had never had a conversation about spirituality. In 2022, I told him about my book, and he told me that during the pandemic he had taken up meditation. Then, he said, he started going to Othership founded by Harry Taylor and Amanda Laine, which offers guided wellness programs using saunas, ice baths, and breathwork. Ethan is not given to exaggeration and he hesitated over the words but finally said, "I've found it life changing." Furthermore, he continued, he had learned to clear his chakras, and this had resulted in physical as well as emotion healing. Startled, but keeping my head still as he cut my hair, I asked him where he learned to do this. He replied, smiling, "From a client who is a senior partner at the one of Canada's largest law firms. He meditates with monks: it's what sustains him in his intensive career as a lawyer. He taught me how to clear chakras." A hair salon, a law office. This is where insights about spiritual practices and principles are being discovered and shared today.

I have found in conversations like this one that there is growing acceptance of a key point: the reliance in recent decades on only the rational mind has already revealed its insufficiency in a society that is more fragile and fractured than ever. Many are recognizing the need to honour and utilize the wholeness that we are in totality, not just the intellect. Agreement with Crick's assertion that identity and will are no more than "the behavior of a vast assembly of nerve cells and their associated molecules" had not led us into an enlightened age but rather into a devolution of behaviour and decision-making that is putting the human race and possibly the entire planet at risk.

The extremity of our time is leading us back to exponents of wisdom. With this has come a growing awareness and appreciation of the Earth as sacred, and of the value and sanctity of all life, of which we are but a small part. Even the proposition that life is not "out there" but is a conscious experience primarily is no longer a dubious, fringe idea.

Despite the superficiality seen in some of the SBNR findings, this phase of the project had already uncovered the fertile ground in which something new was definitely growing.

The Field Research

IT WAS FINALLY TIME for the field research. From 2016 to 2019, in between board work and consulting projects, I had the joy of attending workshops led by Pema Chödrön, Eckhart Tolle, Thich Nhat Hanh, Caroline Myss, Jon Kabat-Zinn, Daniel Siegel, Jack Kornfield, Jeff Warren, and Shinzen Young, among others, as well as online events by teachers such as Joe Dispenza. Interviews were conducted with leaders in the meditation and mindfulness movement, in the arts, in health care, and in business who embraced wisdom principles in their work. Putting on my consulting hat, I even conducted a series of focus groups to investigate what people were searching for and what they were finding. I read articles by physicists and neuroscientists to try to understand current scientific thinking about consciousness and the fundamental nature of life.

In all, I met hundreds of people, learned a great deal, and made remarkable new friends. These are the people who motivated me to continue my journey, and despite the passage of time, their stories continue to inspire me today. My original intent was that their accounts would be a significant part of this book. Then the pandemic arrived, the research ended, and the world changed. The findings are still relevant today, but, recognizing that anything pre-Covid was of a different time, the research is included here in a much abbreviated form. The full report of *Rebranding God* can be found online at www.gemhouse.ca.

I found that despite the diversity of individuals and initiatives, something pervasive and unified was happening—a collective shift as people everywhere found acceptance of ideas and practices that just a decade or two before would have been relegated to fringe groups and cults. It was all the more remarkable because there was no new single leader or body of work to point to and say, "Adopting these principles or beliefs is what accounts for the change." My pile of field notes kept growing, filled with excitement about what was happening.

Here's a brief impression of the scope of change encountered in the research:

AT THE Art Gallery of Ontario the *Mystical Landscapes* exhibit was attracting the second-largest attendance of any exhibit that the AGO had produced in its one-hundred-year history, despite the institution's initial hesitation about the "spiritual" theme.

Just a few blocks away, Dr. Susan Abbey, the psychiatrist-in-chief of the University Health Network hospitals in Toronto, was offering a seminar for her colleagues on loving kindness and compassion. Meanwhile, in the hospital's operating room, everyone was still, focusing on their breath before beginning a complex surgery.

In France neuroscientists and physicists were sitting down with the monks at Thich Nhat Hanh's Plum Village monastery, exchanging insights on the nature of mind.

At the University of Toronto a student was working on a doctorate in meditation and mindfulness, while at the School of Continuing Studies more than forty instructors were teaching this subject to over a thousand students.

In New York, at McKinsey & Company, client CEOs were attending a three-day silent retreat in a former monastery, led by one of the consulting firm's partners.

In California twelve-hundred people packed a hotel ballroom, with another thirty thousand online, listening to Eckhart Tolle tell them that they were conscious being primarily and only secondarily a person.

Here are some highlights from the research.

In the Arts

One of my favourite artist conversations was with singer-songwriter Sarah Slean. Talking with Sarah was like interviewing a songbird. She perched on her chair, a bundle of energy and wonder. She had just released her album *Metaphysics*, a word that describes how she perceives life: there is a Light source that could be called God, the filter that is us, and the imagination that produces all that we see. She experiences songwriting—the music, lyrics, and even the artwork—as a gift of inspiration. She makes no distinction between her career and her spiritual quest.

Sarah was quick to dismiss my questions about religion versus spirituality outside of religion. "Those distinctions are arbitrary. What really is the difference? The great traditions of all of the world's religions are the source of wisdom and guidance for today. Why would we separate ourselves from this source and from those who have kept it alive over centuries?" She talked about her belief in God. "Because the word *God* is a noun, we objectify it. God is not a noun."

Evidence of change within arts organizations was most dramatically found in the exhibition *Mystical Landscapes from Vincent Van Gogh to Emily Carr* at the Art Gallery of Ontario (AGO), Toronto, organized in conjunction with the Musée d'Orsay, and featured in both institutions in 2016-17. After seeing the exhibit, I arranged to meet the highly regarded curator of the show, Dr. Katharine Lochnan. Over lunch across the street from the gallery she told me that it all began with a mystical experience she had on the Burren in County Clare, Ireland, the ancient territory of the O'Lochlainn clan, where she felt a powerful sense of belonging. While trying to paint her experience she began to wonder whether there was such a thing as a mystical landscape painting. This led to the idea for an exhibit which involved a team of art historians, theologians, historians and scientists. In a rare departure for a public institution, following positive feedback from the lead sponsor and a marketing focus group, the AGO's leadership supported Katharine in making the mystical content of these paintings the central theme of the exhibit. Even though art, spirituality and theology have had a long relationship, most public arts institutions avoid explicitly spiritual exhibitions. Katharine recalled that at the AGO there was a time when "we weren't allowed to put the word *God* on a wall label." In 2016 it took a lot of wordsmithing to arrive at accessible language to convey the spiritual message. Quotes by artists were featured on the walls, and an elegant book was published in conjunction with the exhibition investigating the subject in greater depth.

When the exhibit opened, it was clear that the message and the paintings resonated with the public. Many people went more than once, and some saw it as a place to meditate or as a respite from terminal illness. There was a dramatic increase in AGO memberships, as well as an increase in tickets purchased by people who had never been to the gallery before. The run was extended to the last possible day before the exhibit was due to be sent on to the Musée d'Orsay where it was retitled *Au Delà des Étoiles*. By then, *Mystical Landscapes* had attracted almost 300,000 people, making it the second-largest attendance for an exhibition organized in house by the AGO. In Paris it brought in 450,000 visitors and broke all previous attendance records at Orsay. In both venues people exiting the exhibition reported that they found the experience "deeply moving."

Katharine was told by members of the public in both Toronto and Paris that it is vitally important to open up a public conversation about the role of spirituality in our lives today. She said: "People are starving for this. We need this desperately at a time when our values system is not working, and people are not experiencing happiness and peace. We need to rethink the whole human project, where we are going, and how we get there."

The Focus Groups

When the idea of conducting focus groups first occurred to me, it took a while to adjust to the thought of using this technique to explore spirituality, in contrast to the consumer and corporate focus groups I had led at BCG and Career Edge. But one of my findings in this project was that there are very few places in which to convene today to talk about our inner spiritual convictions and share our experiences. It seemed to me that there might be interest in getting together to discuss this unusual subject. I asked friends to invite friends to broaden the circle beyond my personal contacts, and reached out to a few organizations, and soon the planned series of focus groups was full. Two more were added. There was great interest in convening to have this conversation. Each focus group was different, and the full details can be found in the *Rebranding God* report. Here are a few highlights.

"There must be Something greater"—words so abstract that they seemed almost devoid of meaning. Yet for Andrew, an actor and playwright and the first speaker in the series of focus groups, they described what was impelling his search for meaning. Andrew was reluctant to define the "Something greater" to avoid conjuring up old associations with the word *God*. As he said this, heads nodded in agreement around the meeting table in the TD Bank tower in downtown Toronto.

The focus groups found again and again that people were sensing a fundamental change, dropping old beliefs and language, being drawn to "Something greater," and yet feeling somewhat groundless. As the conversations continued, we found that there were two "somethings." In addition to "Something greater," many also described a feeling that "there is something missing in my life." These two somethings were rubbing up against each other, generating the restless energy that is fuelling the search for meaning today, sparking curiosity, openness, and reinvention.

Although most in the focus groups were reluctant to define the something missing, a wide range of modalities and techniques were being engaged, including meditation, breathwork, long-distance running, forest bathing, singing in choirs, watching videos of spiritual teachers, chanting, and attending retreats. The participants found all of these valuable but wanted more. They were motivated to establish within themselves a foundation that was not subject to the vagaries of the changing world—of both their own mental and emotional fields and those of the world around them. They saw it as an answer to the chaos of our increasingly fractured world. It is a search for Something enduring on which to base our lives.

Most people drew on a wide range of influences from different traditions as inputs to their individual spiritual path. The challenge for them was how to go deeper, without signing on to any religion or teaching. In my experience, after years of self-enquiry, it was essential to fully commit to a path and come under the guidance of a mentor. If I had only sampled the work of the various teachers in the 1970s and 80s, and tried to make the journey alone, I would not have found the releasement and inner freedom that has become my experience. But it is not for me to say what should be anyone's path today.

After conducting the focus groups, I came to think of this time as a cleansing of our spiritual palate. Our collective shrug to shake off religious and institutional affiliations has made us wary of almost any form of teaching or doctrine, yet Something remains. Many of those who are searching for meaning are finding greater satisfaction in a lack of answers than they do in actually hearing an answer. Religion starts with answers. People today are starting with questions and the wonder of the mystery of life. Perhaps palate cleansing is the first phase of rebranding God.

Community and the Consciousness Explorers Club

Some in the focus groups identified *community* as the something missing in their life. In an era when many have an aversion to becoming a student of a teacher, community can be the teacher.

One of the focus-group participants had discovered community in the Consciousness Explorers Club (CEC) founded by Jeff Warren. I had interviewed Jeff about the CEC that he had started in his living room in 2012, wanting to meditate with a group. Since then it has grown to a large weekly gathering for meditation practice and exploring topics drawn from humanist and contemplative traditions. Jeff uses humour, honesty, and an irreverent style to ensure that he isn't seen as a teacher. As he put it, "CEC is intended to empower people to arrive at their own insights."

After attending some CEC sessions, I convened a focus group of regulars who confirmed that community was a prime reason for participating. I asked them what made it a community. After some discussion they agreed that it was a safe space in which to feel vulnerable. "We find we all have the same doubts and fears; we can ask crazy questions and learn from each other." Another added, "In these dark times, tackling challenges needs to be done at the community level, and the CEC is a unique way of doing that."

Spiritual Teachers Today

This is a brief look at a few of the leaders in spirituality today whose work deeply moved me while attending their workshops and retreats.

The first workshop was with Eckhart Tolle. There were 1,200 people in the ballroom at a California hotel and another 30,000 participating online—quite a contrast to the small interactive events I was accustomed to with Dr. Mills. Listening to Eckhart Tolle speak spontaneously with no notes reminded me of Kenneth Mills. However, Tolle was wearing his signature sweater vest and appeared on stage with the simplicity of a man walking into his own living room and unexpectedly coming upon 1,200 people asking him to speak. Quite a contrast to the formal and elegant presentation of Dr. Mills who entered a room with the stride and energy of a classical pianist walking onto the stage. Nevertheless, the content of their message was remarkably similar: we are conscious experience primarily and only secondarily a person.

At many of the events I attended over a four-year period there was a primary focus on mindfulness meditation and on how to self-regulate thoughts and emotions. This was fascinating to me because Dr. Mills had simply expected us to drop thoughts that were not commensurate to Principle or an ideal and to superimpose thoughts that were in keeping with the Divine. Today whole systems have emerged on exactly how to manage the inner room of our thoughts, supported by a growing body of work that combines scientific data and spiritual practice.

Teachers such as Eckhart Tolle, Jon Kabat-Zinn, Pema Chödrön, Tara Brach, Jack Kornfield, Joe Dispenza, and many others are offering vital how-to guidelines with tools and instructions. Widespread access to these teachers, in person and on line, has democratized this core element of spiritual teaching, making it available to all, rather than set apart for a select few.

My research found that the meditation and mindfulness movement is the one aspect of spirituality outside of religion that literally meets the test of a new brand, in this era of "rebranding God." Being affiliated with it communicates that one is open to exploring non-rational approaches to well-being without carrying the baggage of a specific religion, teacher, or organization. The brand is growing organically, locally, using the infrastructure on the ground—which presents it own challenges in terms of quality control and regulation. Communities of interest are springing up without anyone being in charge. The brand is defined by being "everywhere." Individual practice and experience are the guides, yet it has a shared quality that makes it a brand.

It is a brand that is evolving. The founding leaders, whose work in the 1990s and early 2000s shaped the brand of mindfulness meditation, are now redefining it by expanding the definition from sitting-meditation practice to a more comprehensive premise. Dr. Richard Davidson, who scientifically demonstrated the beneficial effect of meditation practice on the brain, has since determined that meditation practice alone is insufficient. His new prescription for "flourishing" includes four elements: awareness (with meditation as a component), connection, insight, and purpose. Dr. Jon Kabat-Zinn emphasizes that mindfulness is not just a breathing practice; it is about bringing mindful awareness to every moment, to change and heal our planet by healing ourselves.

I met Dr. Zindel Segal at the University of Toronto. A recognized leader in mindfulness meditation for cognitive behaviour therapy, he led a meta-study in 2019 that reviewed the large body of research on using meditation to address depression, addiction, and other cognitive issues. He and his team made a surprising discovery. The research found that there was no statistical correlation between a participant maintaining a regular sitting practice after their therapy had finished and not having a relapse of symptoms. However, there was a strong correlation between a participant mastering the skill of observing their thoughts without identifying with them and a much lower rate of relapse.[36] Achieving the serenity of the standpoint of the observer is the real prize of meditation.

Dr. Daniel Siegel is another pioneer whose work with mindfulness started with exploring the neurological processes associated with meditation and then blossomed into a holistic world view, as is evident in his recent book *IntraConnected: MWe (Me + We).*[37] I attended a workshop with Dr. Siegel at the Omega Institute. He led us in what he calls "the wheel of awareness" practice and then asked participants to describe their experience. His research has surveyed and documented hundreds of people describing their experience of doing this meditation practice. When the practitioners come to the point in the exercise where they turn their attention inward to become aware of awareness itself, they often report experiencing joy, love, or happiness.

To Dr. Siegel this is the hallmark of integration, a state of well-being and harmony in one's own individual experience and as part of the larger whole. His conclusion is that love and joy are not emotions; they correlate with a universal state of integration and the intraconnected nature of reality. This finding illustrates what Dr. Mills had always said: love and joy are not personal emotions, they are evidence of the essential Oneness of all life. Dr. Siegel's research has brought to life this essential truth.

It was perhaps inevitable that the meditation movement—an accessible brand that had seized the Western world—would also become the engine for going deeper. It is continuing its role as the prow of the ship, now enabling millions to take the step from a breathing-meditation practice to a more comprehensive way of being and flourishing. Making this shift can lead to questioning implicit beliefs about the nature of life, of identity, and even our concepts of God, and inspire a whole new leap into the unknown.

At the same time as biologists and neuroscientists such as Jon Kabat-Zinn and Daniel Siegel are becoming increasingly important voices in the spiritual community, spiritual leaders have become important voices in the field of science. They confidently look to science to prove, rather than discredit, the wisdom of their religion. For example, the Dalai Lama is a leading champion of scientific research into the nature of consciousness and is the founder of the Mind & Life Institute dedicated to the integration of science, contemplative practices, and wisdom traditions. In addition, there are numerous other research programs underway investigating the nature of consciousness applying cutting edge science to explore this still largely unknown frontier.

It was thrilling for me to realize that the choice I had made as a teenager between my family heritage in science and Dr. Mills' metaphysical standpoint didn't have to be made by young people today. A scientific career no longer limits one's sphere of research to the material realm. Spirituality doesn't require abandoning scientific facts. In the confluence of this new world I can embrace my upbringing in a multi-generation family of scientists, while remaining true to what I have come to know within myself.

A highlight of my research into spiritual teachers was attending a retreat at Thich Nhat Hanh's Plum Village in France. On one day of the rich week of experiences at the monastery, during a group walking meditation through the orchards of plum trees, I noticed that three monks—a cellist, a violinist, and a guitarist—were beginning to play in the adjacent poplar grove. I slipped away from the "river" of walking and went to listen to the music. Eventually the rest of the group joined us, and everyone settled on the ground for a picnic lunch. Pachelbel's canon wafted up through the poplar trees and filled the air. Out of the corner of my eye I saw some movement at the edge of the grove. There was a wheelchair carrying a small monk, accompanied by a group of attendants, slowly making their way down a path. It was the first time I had seen Thich Nhat Hanh and I was riveted by the sight. It surprised me that no one else seemed to be aware of or acknowledge his approach. It was all I could do to keep from standing up out of respect for this man. I stayed where I was, which was a good thing because the wheelchair stopped about two feet from where I was sitting. I realized then that the spot I had chosen was next to a small platform designed for a wheelchair, where Thich Nhat Hanh could enjoy the music.

From the close vantage point I watched this dignified man whose gaze took in the full scope of the scene before him. He was able to turn his head and move one arm but was otherwise paralyzed due to a stroke. This circumstance in no way diminished his powerful presence and obvious love and compassion. I was deeply moved and honoured to have had this memorable experience of proximity to his presence. The feeling was different from being in the presence of Dr. Mills, but there was the same combination of steely inner discipline and total freedom.

Not long after visiting Thich Nhat Hanh's traditional spiritual community I was on a train travelling from Amsterdam to Paris. As usual, I was writing and I was probing within myself the value of studying with a living spiritual teacher at a time when so few people seemed willing to enter into this relationship. At that moment an elderly man with a long white beard and wearing a black suit walked slowly up the aisle. No, I thought, smiling to myself, not necessarily that kind of teacher. Moments later, three young men and a woman with exposed weapons on their belts suddenly burst into the train car. They stood in the aisle with an aggressive air about them, staring at the passengers. They were not wearing uniforms, and the writing on their arm bands was in Dutch. Just a week before, there had been an attack on a similar train, and I couldn't tell if these people were security or terrorist. All conversation in the train car stopped, and the passengers barely moved. This could be it, I thought. Too panicked to compose my own declaration or recall a memorized one, I surreptitiously glanced at the papers on my lap. With relief I read Dr. Mills' words: "Light, Truth, and Love appear as the substance of my objective being, contained in the realm of awareness." Immediately I felt calmer, more ready for whatever might happen. After a few minutes, which felt like forever, the young people swaggered out of our car into the next one. Everyone returned to their conversations, and I concluded that the four must have been a security force.

But I had answered the question for myself about the value of a teacher. Thanks to having Dr. Mills' words in the notes on my lap, I had somewhere to turn in a moment of extremity. Reading them realigned my attention to a different state of awareness, knowing that I am not just a body with a mind attached, sitting on a train. Light, Truth, and Love are the substance of my being and cannot be touched by terrorism. I was able to revel in this fact, even in the midst of fear. This wasn't because of beautiful words; it was because of the investment I had made over decades that made the words meaningful to me. This is the magic of words as symbols to open a different level of awareness.

Many people have words they turn to in moments of extremity—a religious text, a poem, a love letter. I am deeply grateful to have known Dr. Mills and to have his words as that tuning fork in my life.

In Health Care

Much has been written about the revolution in health care as it incorporates new modalities such as meditation based on the premise that we are both material and non-material beings and what we think in our minds affects our bodies. As Dr. Susan Abbey, psychiatrist-in-chief of the University Health Network, put it, "When a patient undergoes a heart transplant operation, we are not just putting in a new battery. Hospitals need to recognize and treat the whole being that comes into our buildings at these liminal moments, not just parts of their body."

Meeting Dr. Abbey was the highlight of my research in health care. She had learned mindfulness meditation from Jon Kabat-Zinn in the 1990s and for decades had attempted to introduce it where she worked. We laughed our way through the interview as she described her skeptical colleagues who were questioning why she spent time on this project. She also spent time searching for unused rooms in the hospital, figuring out how many bodies she could fit on the floor for meditation. Today, demand for this instruction far exceeds the supply of qualified people, rooms available, and hospital resources. Mindfulness meditation has become a recognized healing modality, as health practitioners discover that changes to the mind change the body chemistry. As Dr. Abbey said, "It's such an exciting time to be human!"

Sitting at my computer a few weeks after interviewing Dr. Abbey, I couldn't decipher one of the words in my notes. The word was unusual and captured perfectly her extraordinary outlook on health care. Soon afterwards I went downstairs to the kitchen and glanced at the newspaper that was open on the counter and read in large letters "Liminal," referring to an upcoming band concert. That was the word! I ran back upstairs and filled it in. It seemed that a cosmic dictionary had come to my rescue.

When editing the previous paragraph a few months after that event happened, I questioned whether the word *liminal* had appeared in the newspaper exactly when I was searching for it, or several days or weeks later. When I went downstairs for lunch, my husband was reading the Saturday morning newspaper. As usual, I picked up the Arts section. The above-the-fold front-page story read: "Jordan Tannahill's debut novel, *Liminal*, was released last month."[38] In this mind-stopping moment I could only think, "Oh, it is instantaneous!" Before going on, let's pause here to acknowledge the mystery of the Unseen.

In Business

There are many well-documented examples of meditation and wisdom practices appearing in the business workplace. I wondered if BCG had such a practice, and I contacted Nina Abdelmessih, BCG Canada's chief operating officer. Nina said no, there wasn't one as yet, but her son's high school class had just learned to meditate at a leadership training program at McKinsey & Company. Astonished, I quickly got in touch with McKinsey, BCG's primary competitor in strategy consulting, and made a remarkable discovery.

When I met Bruce Simpson, a senior partner at McKinsey's Toronto office, we quickly got past the BCG-McKinsey rivalry and exchanged stories about what had led to our interest in meditation in the workplace. I had thought that meditation at McKinsey might have been introduced by its employee-benefits provider, as had happened briefly at BCG. It turned out to have much deeper roots. McKinsey's first meditation program had been developed over a decade before by Bruce and his colleague Michael Rennie, building on earlier work Michael had done in Australia with Gita Bellin, a well-known practitioner in the space. Bruce and Michael encountered a bit of resistance at the office and some said that it was not real consulting. Undeterred, Bruce, and fellow Canadian colleagues Zafer Achi and Kathleen McLaughlin, sought out CEOs who they felt might be interested in exploring it, and began to incorporate meditation into their work for these clients. When other McKinsey colleagues realized that clients were adopting—and paying for—consulting that included meditation instruction, they accepted it as part of Bruce, and his colleagues', unorthodox approach. An internal program for consultants and staff started to grow, and it has since become a core part of leadership training at McKinsey.

When a client wants to go deeper with meditation and principles drawn from wisdom traditions, Bruce calls in Johanne Lavoie. Johanne is a senior McKinsey partner who lives in Canmore, Alberta, in the Rocky Mountains. When I spoke to her, she had just returned from a three-day hiking trip with a client team. Johanne described her earlier life as "disconnected from the body and from anything non-rational." She had graduated in electrical engineering, did a master's degree in business administration at Harvard, and joined McKinsey. In 1997 she lost her first child. To help her heal, a social worker gave her a book about mind-body connection. The book started with quantum physics, and from there she began to read widely and reassess her understanding of the nature of reality. This took her into what she describes as the "nexus of spirituality and psychology" and the science of how we learn and grow as human beings. She has since built at McKinsey a body of knowledge to integrate developmental practices in culture change, leadership, and team effectiveness which enable deeper and more sustainable transformational change. As she tells her clients, rational and logical thinking is no longer sufficient to survive and thrive in today's fast-paced, complex business world; creativity, stillness, grace, and agility are essential tools.

It was very gratifying to find Bruce and Johanne applying spiritual principles and practices in corporate consulting, as I had dreamed of doing at BCG in the 1990s. Then I heard that Manish Chopra, a senior partner at McKinsey & Company in New York, had just taken his client CEOs on a three-day silent retreat in a former monastery. Amazed by this, I was soon in Manish's Manhattan office to find out more.

Manish told me that in 2010 he went on a meditation retreat in India and found it to be a life-changing experience. Soon afterwards, he wrote a book on those ten days called *The Equanimous Mind,* sharing in vivid detail the personal transformation he had undergone. For several years he worked on gradually becoming comfortable in talking about this new facet of his life and incorporating it into his work. To his delight, at the same time all around him meditation was becoming increasingly mainstream. Manish introduced bite-sized mindfulness training programs into a dozen McKinsey offices and embraced meditation and its attendant benefits into his professional life with increasing ease. In 2018 he conducted Inner Wisdom Retreats for senior leaders, a three-day program teaching contemplative practices in a monastery outside New York City, up the lower Hudson valley.

Like others with whom I spoke, Manish described corporate leaders as being at an extremity. "They are at the limits of an entirely intellectual and cognitive approach. The pace and complexity of the workplace has become untenable. People know that working harder won't help. They have realized that they need something more. They need to find and take a dip into the well of stillness and silence within themselves. They need to rewire and reboot the operating system of the mind and connect with their inner purpose to find more joy, meaning, and flair in what they do."

In 2013 Manish wrote an article on the benefits of meditation for senior executives and submitted it to the *McKinsey Quarterly* magazine. After a couple of years of processing the relevance of this to the target readership, the editor agreed to publish the article as a personal reflection rather than as a McKinsey perspective, fearing that clients might wonder if the firm was losing its business-mindedness. The story ran with this title and subhead: "Want to Be a Better Leader? Observe More and React Less: Overloaded Executives Need Coping Mechanisms; This Personal Reflection Shows How Meditation Can Help." The article quickly became the *Quarterly*'s third-most-downloaded article in the year of its publication. Reflecting humbly on this surprisingly development given the initial hesitation from the publishers, Manish said, "People are clearly yearning for this."

Manish has developed a skillful use of language, blending teachings from the Buddha and other masters with business terminology. With his clients and colleagues the subject is approached from a range of perspectives: from productivity gains, to work-life balance, to connecting with an inner purpose, to becoming a more spiritually aware being. He is happy to relate with them on any level to advance the concept in their minds in their preferred way of understanding and readiness, while retaining his own grounding in what is clearly, for him, a deep spiritual practice.

During the pandemic, when Manish saw colleagues and clients struggling with fear, anxiety, and isolation (and feeling challenged himself by managing work and life from the confines of a New York City apartment despite his years of training the mind to be well balanced under all circumstances), he launched a widespread campaign to promote the notion of "cultivating one's well-being" as an essential life skill, especially for those in high-intensity professions where it is easy to fall off the saddle given the continuous demands of time and the strains of the work itself. To promote the message beyond his own story of change, he invited Bill George (from Harvard), Adam Grant (from Wharton), and others to help generate inspiration and optimism in forums with clients and colleagues.

After speaking with Manish and other business professionals, I too felt inspiration and optimism. My enthusiasm for the work of these business leaders is not about bringing religious teachings and spirituality as we know them today into the workplace. It is about both spirituality and the workplace evolving to create something new that integrates a higher standpoint with professional activity. A different understanding of what is fundamentally going on here as we live out our lives taps into a different kind of human potential, one that acknowledges the limits of the purely analytical mind that rules most workplaces, and one that embraces the whole being. In all of my research the adoption of these principles and practices in strategy consulting—where it had seemed impossible to me just two decades before—best epitomizes the dramatic shift that has taken place.

The field research came to an end in 2020 with the start of the global pandemic. Although in some ways the pandemic seems to have changed everything, the same trends continue and are even accelerating. It seemed evident from the field research that what we think of as the future may be characterized less by places set apart for worship and more by the motivating force of a higher principle infusing our words, decisions, and actions in every walk of life. While this has always been the purpose of any place of worship, the difference today is that both the prayer and its desired effect are taking place on what would once have been thought of as secular ground. This integration of the sacred and secular in no way precludes continuing to enter and enjoy any house of worship or spiritual gathering.

During my years of studying with Dr. Mills the gap seemed impossibly wide between what I was learning and the world I encountered every day. Now it is as though time is folding over itself, and ideas put forward thirty or forty years ago are meeting the world just where it is today.

The Possibilities of a New Brand

THE PURPOSE OF THE RESEARCH was to explore the ways in which we are rediscovering and applying the principles and practices of wisdom teachings and to see if we are returning to acknowledgement of a Higher Power, perhaps with new language and imagery. I call this "rebranding God" because only the garment is changing. The essence is unchanged and can be clothed in an infinite number of ways. Life itself is expressing and fulfilling itself, always new but in essence unchanged. This continuous dance of life can appear as the promptings and the yearning for realization that we feel and express in our lives.

The research found that many people feel these promptings and, with an expanded appreciation of the nature of life, bring a new perspective to their work, whether it be in the arts, education, health care, or business. Spiritual principles and practices have gained a surprising new place in the mainstream despite a secular society and a decline in religious affiliation. There appears to be a shift in our collective awareness that is bringing about a profound change in our understanding of who and what we really are. Concepts and language that in the 1970s many people found strange or impenetrable—such as, "What you are conscious of constitutes your experience," or "It is not mind over matter; it's Mind instead of matter"—are finding new meaning and acceptance today. As we encounter these ideas in unlikely places—from hair salons to consulting firms—we are discovering how radical and yet how natural they are.

The research revealed that we are in a palate-cleansing phase as we release old thought patterns and become aware that the prompting still remains that there must be Something greater. In this receptive state we focus on the in-breath and the out-breath, on simply being present, on being aware of being aware.

From the premise of individual practice it seems unlikely that new institutional dogma and infrastructure will emerge. Religions have well-developed, centuries-old beliefs and infrastructure—institutions, buildings, hierarchy, doctrine, rituals, training, certification, centralized leadership, and financial management. Adopting the standpoint that Life in essence is non-material, for most people, has none of that. In fact, it doesn't even have a name, except "spiritual but not religious," which primarily describes what it is not. In its ethereal state it permeates the infrastructure on the ground: hospitals, workplaces, schools, and homes. Its brand character is its pervasiveness and yet invisibility.

Invisibility is its greatest strength. There is no target to aim at, no leader to cut down. There is no bookkeeping to speculate about, no anxiety about leading or following. Just individuals going about their daily lives with a deep acknowledgement that the mind-body complex they appear to be is only a small part of what they are in essence.

Out of this palate-cleansing state of "beginner's mind"—dropping beliefs and being open to newness—there might emerge a renewed appreciation of the world's great religions. Unencumbered by institutional expectations, a new generation would encounter the religious teachings of the West and the East with fresh eyes. Given the subtlety and complexity of the holy books there is always the risk of dumbing down and misunderstanding material taken out of its usual context, and yet there is also the hopeful possibility of receiving it anew via the heart as well as the head.

From this standpoint a multiplicity of activities is possible: going to a place of worship or not going to a place of worship; Eastern teachings, Western teachings, both, or none; meditating at home, the office, or in school or hospital; joining a weekly gathering or starting one; forming a community or engaging in a private quest at home; singing, dancing, breathwork, cold plunges, long-distance running; serving others and the planet. The people I met who are doing these activities are approaching them with a remarkable openness to the wonder and mystery of life, refusing to let the scope of their experience be circumscribed by the intellect.

It should be noted that the absence of structure and and definition of spirituality outside of religion is also a vulnerability. Today almost anything can be labelled spiritual to exploit the sense that many people have that "something is missing in my life." A day at the spa or a hike in the woods comes with a side of spirituality. Discrimination is essential to separate authenticity from superficial imitations.

In interviews, people sensed that they were part of a broader movement and wanted to know who else was feeling as they did, and where to find them. We all wonder what it is that we are part of, but few seek brand affiliation in a "wear the T-shirt" kind of way. There is no sign-up. Mentors, guides, speakers, retreats, and forums allow us to deepen, express, and enjoy what we already intuitively know, and to form communities.

The research findings make me optimistic about the future despite the divisiveness and chaos that seem to surround us today. But the potential for change suggested by these findings is not inevitable. It needs to be nourished in our attention and intention—in our communication and in our communities.

The global pandemic that brought the research to a halt provided a unique opportunity for us to realize, in vivid colour, that we are interdependent and we cannot pretend anymore that the apparent separateness perceived by the senses is real. The worldwide response to the pandemic could be understood as a struggle to regain control on a planet where as humans we thought we were in charge. The lesson of the pandemic might be to teach us a new awareness and respect for one another, all species, and this small planet's balance of nature on which we depend. Mother Nature (as Michele Chaban puts it) sent us to our rooms. There we had an opportunity to reflect and arrive at a new understanding of what is going on here as we live our lives. Perhaps it isn't about chasing after the pleasures and perils of our busy lives, but about discovering what is still present when almost everything that constitutes those lives is removed. It is a dramatic example of a global "palate cleansing."

It is tempting to try to define what a new world could look like, a world that takes as its centre and motivating force the high ideals of wisdom teachings, rather than ego and one-upmanship. However, knowing that "Presence is the happening," I have learned to not attempt to make change happen through the objective. A change in standpoint will inevitably bring about change in what appears as the external world. As we gain the awareness that we are responsible for our thoughts, for where our attention is, the world picture will change because we have changed how we direct the energy of thought. When we know that the multiplicity and diversity we perceive is attributable to one undivided Source, the basis of so much conflict in our world today is dissolved.

Crucial to making this shift is the restoring of acknowledgement of the Source. When in a moment of realization we perceive the illusory nature of the passing picture and begin to understand how it manifests, and yet do not recognize the Power that enables us to discern this fact, we are left with nothing substantial on which to stand. This state opens the door to manipulating thought energy and emotion for personal gain with no commitment to a higher purpose. We see examples of this in government and in technology that is taking us ever closer to hacking into the operating system of the mind without the guardrails of an elevated standpoint.

People I spoke to who identified as spiritual but not religious expressed a wide range of views in response to the question about acknowledging God or a Higher Power. Some people have gracefully translated their childhood understanding of this word into an acknowledgement of God that serves them in their quest today. Others said that they rejected the concept of God altogether. Many felt conflicted and had unresolved feelings about the word; a few refused to even discuss the topic. Thoughts about a judging God, or what Caroline Myss calls "an off-planet God," interfered with being open to acknowledging an unknown source of our presence and of Life itself. Unravelling this knot of unresolved tension is the next frontier in the project I call rebranding God.

Rebranding God is an activity, not an answer; it starts with excavation before any reconstruction. Rebranding is not about "selling God" or promoting any particular teaching or religion. It is the palate-cleansing experience, as expressed by those in the focus groups, of having an awareness of Something greater and not defining it intellectually. It's being able to feel in deepest humility the wonder of the unknown source of life without the mind stepping in and saying, "I don't believe in that." The effect of rebranding is a change in our understanding of identity—we are the ones being rebranded.

Language is important to shaping any brand. The phrase *Life-giving Force* is currently the most meaningful expression for me, perhaps because it cannot be conceived of as an object, only as the creative source of Life itself. In the lexicon of my mind, this phrase is inseparable from synonyms such as God-Consciousness and Something greater.

Metaphors and symbols are also vital in defining and redefining a brand. There are many analogies that can be used to acclimatize the mind to awareness of Something greater. The language, metaphors, and symbols from the great religious teachings through the ages find resonance in every generation and have become deeply meaningful to me. New analogies and symbols appearing today can help bring these timeless truths to life. For example, Dr. Mills' illustration by sketching and erasing drawings on a page, with the paper representing the unchanging backdrop of Consciousness, gave me an eye-opening new perspective. Another moment of realization came with an entirely different metaphor: the scientific finding that light is simultaneously wave and particle, as a way to express that we are both invisible and visible, energy and matter, at once indivisible as God-Consciousness yet appearing separate.

A circle is another powerful symbol found in many teachings and in nature that inspires awareness of Something greater. Everything that constitutes a circle is relative to the dot in the centre. Without a centre point there is no circle. A piece of the radius or circumference wouldn't have an identity as radius or circumference unless the centre were known. The centre is simultaneously a dot and the entire circle.

Just as the sun is at the centre of our solar system, we could think of the Life-giving Force as the centre point of the circle of life. When we identify as only the particular spot on the radius or the circumference where we find ourselves, we are unaware that we are actually one with the entire circle, that our our existence and identity is entirely due to the centre point. As a piece of the radius, we might try to puff up our little part to make it seem as real and important as possible. But we will never find peace, joy, and satisfaction based on a part. It is only when we realize that the Life-giving Force is the substance to the entire circle—including what appears as me—that we feel the releasement of being one with the source of all life. Then we are ready to tilt our cup and receive.

This is the leap that opens the door to the realization that there is nothing outside of God-Consciousness. From this standpoint, what we experience as "rebranding God" is recognized to be the Life-giving Force expressing itself, forever new yet always constant.

Acknowledging the Life-giving Force as the substance of my being, and allowing that fact to shape my experience, is what I call learning to dance with life. As Dr. Mills said to me, you cannot put the greater into the lesser. I can enjoy the gift of life as a seemingly separate self while recognizing the Life-giving Force that must exist in order for me to be. This realization has been the foundation of my experience of rebranding God.

I still wonder, Why is it that so many of us never talk about this most important fact of existence? Perhaps because the word *God* gets tangled up in politics, in divisiveness and greed, and attached to belief systems we no longer hold. Yet it seems to me that acknowledgement of the Life-giving Force, by this or any other name, is the only sustainable source of harmony and unity in our world. We will never come together by parsing our similarities and differences as people. Generic being itself is the shared basis of civilization. A citizen who acknowledges the unity of one Consciousness (or circle of Life) is very different from the one who pursues personal gain as though the abundance of life were their private storehouse. The project of rebranding—new ways to hold in thought and to communicate that there is Something greater—is key to a harmonious future with one another and with the planet on which we depend.

I cannot say how anyone else might approach rebranding God, I only know that it is worthwhile to do. It opens up access to ideas and possibilities that previously the mind would have shut down before they had a chance to blossom. Rebranding God is not primarily about reformulating words and images, although these are helpful to loosen up mental associations. Rebranding God begins by going to the origin of all the words and images by asking a question such as this one posed by Dr. Mills in an Unfoldment called *A New Heaven and A New Earth*: "How is it that I seem to have a beingness and yet seem to be nothing but surfing this life stream of world-living?" There's enough there for a lifetime of enquiry and excavation.

VI

LEARNING TO DANCE
WITH LIFE

*No one was born knowing how to
high kick or plié. You got there by practicing.*

RADIO CITY ROCKETTES,
5 Life Lessons You Learn from Dancing

Returning Home

AFTER COMPLETING the research, I found that I was able to see my own life from a new perspective. The natural sciences heritage, the love of the arts, the business career, and the decades studying with Kenneth Mills all took on new colour and definition when seen through the expanded lens of the profound shift that appears to be happening across these fields of activity. I am grateful for the multi-faceted nature of my life that enabled me to investigate and appreciate the diverse avenues of exploration.

My genuine interest in other people's journeys while doing the research also opened up an unexpectedly rich avenue to talk about my experience, which in turn has helped me find my voice. Ever since that morning with my family at the campsite, stirring Tang into a pitcher of water and pretending to be a normal child after a powerful experience of transcendence, I had been living an inner life separated from an outer life. Releasing the obstacles to expressing myself has taken decades and is absolutely essential for feeling a sense of peace and wholeness. Now that I was finally speaking up, I discovered how interested and responsive people are to what held my attention all these years.

The decades with Kenneth Mills now felt like a universal journey. I felt connected with everyone I met. In interviews, at events, and in other conversations I could see my quest in everyone, and their quest in me. The wholeness I had sought within myself now seemed to embrace the entire world—this was revolutionary change for an introvert who had previously found any social encounter painful. It also felt like a reconciliation with my family, with science, with business, and with Kenneth Mills. I no longer felt divided.

When the research project ended with the arrival of the global pandemic in Canada in March 2022, a surprising new journey began. The following month the Kenneth G. Mills Foundation started playing via Zoom each week an Unfoldment drawn from the digitized archive of Dr. Mills' lectures. In the first week, people from various cities in North America and even Europe tuned in. Since then the Gathering Place has become an ongoing and much-loved weekly event.

Realizing how easy it is to share the online library over Zoom, I began a weekly "conclave" to listen to Unfoldments with a small group of friends, both new and lifelong. It continues to this day and has become, as we often observe, a highlight of the week. Then another online gathering sprang up for those discovering the work of Kenneth Mills for the first time, called the Forum for Wonder. This forum also continues its weekly rhythm and is rich in discoveries for all of us. The participants' dedication and their appreciation of what they have found are a constant source of wonder for me. It is tremendously satisfying to engage with these remarkable individuals, while curating and presenting material from the Kenneth G. Mills library. Two more forums were added that are not specifically drawing on the work of Kenneth Mills, exploring inspiring themes and ideas that remind us of our true nature. Now immersed in convening these forums, the relatively intellectual research project was left behind as I leapt into hosting conversations that were elevating and heartfelt. My considerations over years about the need for places to convene to have conversations about fundamental ideas had precipitated four of these forums into my life.

I was listening to Dr. Mills' Unfoldment again with an unexpected result. It was all new, as though I had never heard it before. Over and over, I thought, "Oh! That's what he talked about. I didn't hear that until now."

How surprising to find that after I had moved on into the arts and then had several years of research into other teachers and paths, the place I thought was familiar and past was suddenly teeming with newness, excitement, and meaning. It was exactly as T. S. Eliot put it: "We shall not cease from exploration, and the end of all our exploring will be to arrive where we started and know the place for the first time."[39]

I sat back and laughed. How improbable, how incomprehensible, that the more I travelled away from what I thought of as "Dr. Mills' work," the more it is right where I am when I arrive home. When I stripped away all pretence of being an adherent of anything and focused on my inner room, there was never any separation.

Surely this is the ultimate releasement from the impediment of otherness. I had once again discovered the circular or holographic nature of life by moving away from Dr. Mills to find my own centre and then found that what I thought was in Dr. Mills was actually within myself. The further I travelled "within," the more I was at one with what Dr. Mills represents for me. Not an outside intrusion, not a retreat into familiarity—just home. This is a home that I have built over a lifetime, furnishing it within myself, a place of peace, joy, and satisfaction.

Somehow a new lightness of being has emerged from this releasement. Everything feels lighter, more fun. When I share something of Dr. Mills or from my life, the primary feeling is one of joy. A spontaneous laughter arises every time I start. The reluctance to speak up has evaporated along with the personal involvement in doing so.

What a cosmic paradox. Here I had wrestled with individuating, with reconciliation, with finding my voice and bringing the parts of my life together, believing it was necessary to quiet the voice of Dr. Mills in order to hear my own. And now, in the inner room of my soul, there is only one voice, and it has no name.

Continuing the Journey of Releasement

IN 2000, I went on a riverboat cruise with my mother and Urban into the Amazon rainforest in Brazil. Our point of departure was Manaus, where the great Amazon River and the Rio Negro come together. Each river has a different temperature and travels at a different speed. Their point of confluence is alive with energy, a turbulence of eddies, waves, and continuous bubbles that attracts pink porpoises and other creatures. This perpetual source of oxygenated water is a dramatic illustration of different levels of density coming together and releasing energy, which in turn supports life.

It felt like a metaphor for our time. Different levels of awareness are coming up against each other, creating what looks like chaos but may be releasing energy to move to a higher level of being and doing.

The Meeting of Waters, as this point in Brazil is called, could even be an analogy for the coincidence of the human and the Divine, the perpetual releasement of energy at the confluence of visible and invisible levels of density.

It also reminded me of my experience with Dr. Mills. For years I was immersed in the highly oxygenated atmosphere of his presence, with the chaos and release of energy that came with that encounter. At times it was choppy, all waves and eddies, as the ordered comfortability of my thoughts and beliefs were stirred up and tossed around. But the released energy elevated my experience, opening up my awareness to be able to receive and appropriate the gifts of life.

Kenneth Mills' work now appears prescient and leaps over developments happening today. He lived from the standpoint that "it is done" and refused to accept the slowness of a process of change. His vision, and his eloquent expression of it in every aspect of his being, is the basis of my hope for a new world. Through conversations with him I began to see what could be possible when more than just a few radical individuals choose to live this way.

The experience of having a mentor was transformative for me. No doubt some are seeking and hopefully finding this kind of relationship today. It is often said that when the student is ready, the teacher will appear. Kenneth Mills described himself not as a teacher but as a "force of realignment." He accepted a total state of releasement when he agreed within himself to give the Unfoldment and to share his experience with anyone who asked to be there. I'm grateful to have been one of them and for his kindness and fearlessness that opened up my experience in ways that I had not dreamt possible.

Writing this book revealed that what drew me to Dr. Mills and kept me coming back was not primarily the events or the words. It was not about feelings of bliss or renewal or irritation. It was not on that level of thinking and emotion. The essence of the experience was not stored in memory, because it did not take place there. It cannot be remembered as a past happening, because the Essence is only happening now, in the present moment.

What, specifically, have been the releasements in my life? What was received and incorporated as a result of tilting my cup? I don't claim perfection in anything on the following list, and my journey of releasement is far from over, but here are some of the gifts received in learning to dance with life.

First is the gift of an artistic life, rich in feeling, expression, ideas, joy, inspiration, creativity, and appreciation of art in its many forms. It is releasement from a purely intellectual life, from leading primarily through logic and strategic thinking. It is a return to the freedom and joy that I felt dancing around the living room as a small child.

I find myself happy in my own company without needing to prove anything to anyone. The insecure young woman who was chasing success while claiming self-realization has finally gone. In her place is a mature soul with a lifelong investment in rarified teachings of wisdom. I spend more time now as a human *being* and less as a human *doing*. I still observe the arising of old thought patterns of needing success, seeking approval, or compartmentalizing my life in order to belong, and I go within to confirm that the only validation I need is my own heart.

The techniques learned from Kenneth Mills, especially "be the watch" (witness the thoughts and emotions without getting caught in them), have given me far greater freedom to be in the world and not of it. This journey is ongoing, and life never seems to tire of producing more opportunities for me to practise. In those moments I'm grateful to have learned to have fun and treat lightly the inevitable ups and downs of daily living.

A most important releasement for me has been the letting go of the "impediment of otherness" and the shyness that produced. Today I find myself surrounded by a remarkable and growing community of like-hearted friends. This freedom enables me to have the artful fun of hosting forums and sharing the joy and discovery of philosophical attainment.

For most of my life there was a great deal going in, but hardly anything coming out in expression; it was a contained bubble of deep experience. With the willingness to open up, the contained bubble entered the flow and fluidity of releasement. I have gained the right of expression, the courage to tell my tale, and the willingness to do so.

It is a great gift to learn to enjoy the magnificence and perfection of life in every moment, regardless of appearances. I'm deeply grateful for the rarified moments of releasement when all thoughts of person, place, or thing have gone and only Being remains. "Presence is the happening," as Dr. Mills said.

Thanks to Dr. Mills' Unfoldments, I have a lifetime of precious words and reminders of Principle on which to stand, including in times of extremity such as illness or death.

Perhaps the greatest releasement I have received is receptivity itself: learning to be the recipient of the gift of life, rather than trying to be a self-sustaining personal container of life. From my first Unfoldment, it was startling to hear Dr. Mills' constant acknowledgement of God in all its many synonyms. As a self-absorbed teenager raised without religion, I was smug in the implicit belief that the abilities, talents, sounds, words, feelings, and creative inspiration that constituted my experience were somehow produced and sustained by me alone. Acknowledging the Life-giving Force has been the key to my whole journey. It was not a conversion from atheist to worshipful supplicant, but rather the humbling and liberating experience of knowing that I am not separate from the Life-giving Force, infinite source of being itself. This realization has wiped away the childhood anxiety of always wondering whether I had enough talent or would measure up and be worthy. Talent and worthiness are the evidence of the abundance of Life and its generous pouring forth of inspiration and wisdom.

The journey of releasement, of receiving and giving in the dance of life, continues. I am forever grateful for the limitless abundance of the Life-giving Force that sustains all that is, and enables me to share what comes to me as in keeping with its magnificence. This is the joy of tilting the cup to receive and then getting out of the way by giving it away.

The only way the cup can be filled is by keeping it empty.
How is yours?

KENNETH G. MILLS

For resources and guidance on putting these ideas into practice, visit www.lucillejoseph.ca.

ACKNOWLEDGEMENTS

FIRST, SINCERE GRATITUDE to Samantha Haywood, president of the Transatlantic Agency, for her support and encouragement to write this book. Her early guidance and her willingness to read drafts along the way was invaluable.

Author David Macfarlane helped me to see myself as a writer of more than business reports, and his feedback and guidance along the way has been invaluable. Editor Christine Pountney coached me through the early stages of compiling the book. Rosemary Kent's rare discernment of language commensurate to the Absolute kept the writing on point. Filmmaker Barbara Willis Sweete brought her eye for storytelling to the manuscript. Michele Chaban's insight and encouragement was instrumental in its birth. The expertise of copy editor Angela Wingfield and designer Brian Morgan brought the book to completion. Any shortfalls in the book in any of these areas are mine alone.

The interviews and focus groups were an integral part of the project. I'm grateful to the many people who gave of their time to explore the questions raised in this book and to offer their experience and wisdom, and for the friendships that blossomed as a result of these encounters.

Susanne Boyce was the first person to say to me, "You have something to say. You should write." In 2014 this radical idea caused shivers up and down my business-person spine. Susanne persisted, every now and then asking me how it was going, and giving me positive feedback on my early efforts to express on paper. When we met over tea more recently, she appeared with my manuscript under her arm; it was marked up with dozens of sticky notes, and I thought I was in for a full rewrite. But it turned out that she had marked those pages for herself—the passages she wanted to go back to and enjoy.

When it came time to release the manuscript into the world, the astute advice and enthusiastic response of readers including Eli Taylor, Angela Blumberg, Ian Mirlin, Naheed Hassan, Phil Taylor,

Judith Macdonell, and Lorraine Steele enabled me to finally let it go.

Many thanks to my husband, Urban, for his support and encouragement and for patiently waiting for the day when he would exchange his trademark fedora for a beret to celebrate a literary accomplishment.

Deep gratitude to Kenneth Mills for his willingness to share his realizations with a teenager who appeared at his door in 1974, which opened up my experience in ways I had not dreamed possible. His radical dedication to what he found to be true is what inspired me to find the words and the courage to write this book.

Lastly—and first—I offer thanks to the Life-giving Force that enabled me to seek out, recognize, and receive what is offered into my tilted cup.

KENNETH GEORGE MILLS was born in 1923 in St. Stephen, New Brunswick, the son of a candy maker at Ganong Brothers. Despite growing up in very modest circumstances in a small Maritime border town, he knew from an early age that he wanted to be a concert pianist. His evident talent for music and his dedication to it carried him through his childhood. He was raised a Baptist, instilling a lifelong appreciation and knowledge of Christianity. However, he refused to be baptized until he was about twenty years old and had found some meaning in the ritual. Growing up, he questioned the ministers and priests in his town, but they had few answers to his many questions. He studied hard and won a scholarship to Mount Allison University.

Thanks to the sponsorship of a mentor, Guy Murchie, along with other wealthy patrons who summered in nearby St. Andrews-by-the-Sea, Kenneth Mills was able to pursue his musical dreams. He moved to Toronto to study with Mona Bates, one of the finest piano teachers in Canada at the time. The patrons from New Brunswick connected him with wealthy friends and family in Toronto, who offered their homes, grand pianos, and support to this brilliant young talent. In turn, he gave piano lessons to their children, including the four Eaton boys, John, George, Fred, and Thor. In 1952 he made his debut at Eaton Auditorium in Toronto, and a decade later in New York.

Dr. Mills had learned a formal, almost Edwardian style of living from Guy Murchie. At Mr. Murchie's request, he agreed to keep alive in his own life this formal approach to the art of living, regardless of his financial means. As a start, he covered the orange crate in his Toronto student apartment with an elegant Turkish bath towel.

Dr. Mills married in 1952. His wife was also a pianist, and she was a Christian Scientist. For a time Dr. Mills attended the Christian Science church and studied with a metaphysician in New York, Dr. Hendrik J. de Lange, who influenced him greatly. As an exercise, Dr. Mills would write answers to metaphysical questions and send them to Dr. de Lange for adjudication, thereby developing his skill in the language of metaphysics. He dedicated many hours to training himself to use the dualistic English language in a way that was commensurate with an absolute, non-dualistic standpoint. These efforts exasperated his friends and family who used to say, "Ken, why can't you just speak naturally!"

In 1962, Dr. Mills left his marriage, Christian Science, and his concert career behind and chose to live alone, teaching piano and enquiring deeply into the meaning of life. He attended lectures by Eastern teachers who came to Toronto, most notably Maharishi Mahesh with whom he met privately on several occasions. Afterwards he meditated on the mantra he had been given by Maharishi for hours each day and had a series of dramatic mystical experiences, including the vivid presence of Saint Francis of Assisi appearing in his living room.

On two unrelated occasions Dr. Mills was given a mysterious message by people he barely knew, telling him that he "must learn to speak the Word again." He was astonished by this and wondered what it meant. Kenneth Mills was a shy man who communicated primarily through his music. However, he inwardly agreed to speak if asked, although he did not know what he would say.

By the mid-1960s, people were arriving at his doorstep, not for music lessons but to talk with him about their deepest considerations. At this moment and in the years that followed, Dr. Mills adopted the statement from Psalms (19:14), "May the words of my mouth and the meditations of my heart be acceptable in the sight of the One altogether lovely." Thus began, to his surprise, a journey that resulted in his meeting with thousands of people and giving thousands of hours of eloquent spontaneous lectures in poetry and prose that he called Unfoldments. He was fully present when he spoke, not in trance, and clearly listening to an inner prompting. He never ceased to wonder at the gift of speaking in this way, and he studied his own lectures with diligence and curiosity. The archive of audio and video recordings of his unique art form, one that reflects his artistry and discipline as a musician as well as his deep realization, is his legacy today.

The gift of the ability to speak in spontaneous poetry and elegantly structured prose is almost unknown today but has been documented in history. Most famously, the Sufi mystic Rumi was a spontaneous poet. Some who met Dr. Mills told him that this was perhaps the first time it had ever appeared in the West and in English.

When I met Kenneth Mills in 1974, the group around him had grown to several hundred people. He was still carrying a full-time piano teaching schedule, juggling this with an increasingly full-time commitment to meet with people and give Unfoldments. In 1976 he gave up piano teaching to devote himself entirely to what he called a "new keyboard of sound."

Dr. Mills rarely spoke publicly, the first time being in 1973 at the University of Toronto. He realized in doing so that it wasn't his work to speak publicly. From then on, people heard of Kenneth Mills only through word of mouth. He never advertised or publicly announced his lectures and events. Even his business card simply read, "Man is a Song." He knew the deep commitment necessary to appreciate what he was giving, and that it was not for the casual listener. Even to understand an Unfoldment on an intellectual level required deep commitment, let alone the journey it opened, which required letting go of beliefs and adopting a radical new standpoint.

Dr. Mills once defined the Unfoldment™ as "a projection from another dimension or plane of consciousness, causing those prepared to hear to awaken to the higher possibilities of living beyond the limits of three dimensions and translating what seems to be the ordinary into another level of consideration" (*Words of Adjustment*, 1992).

Addressing him as "Dr. Mills" (or in the years prior to receiving an honorary doctorate, as Mr. Mills) was part of the atmosphere of formality. It was out of respect for the transpersonal State that his presence represented, as he increasingly let go of any semblance of a normal personal life. The title greatly irritated those who had known him as Ken, who probably saw it as pretentious and arrogant. As a teenager I had no problem referring to a man of my parents' age as "Mr." (and I had had some practice by then with Mr. McGrath). Over the years, as I matured and came to know Dr. Mills as a friend and a mentor, I appreciated the doctor title. It kept the relationship on a footing that was respectful and in keeping with the purpose of spending time together. In Europe, where he became known primarily as a choral conductor, people called him Maestro Mills.

Dr. Mills' work did not come from a defined spiritual lineage or religion, and he made it clear that he was not establishing a teaching or appointing a successor to continue his work beyond his lifetime. His work had none of the trappings of a recognized spiritual tradition or religion. This was, for me, one of the most attractive aspects of Dr. Mills as my mentor: it was spontaneous, direct, and unstructured. In fact, as soon as we tried to adopt something as dogma or ritual, he would inevitably pull the rug out from under us, destabilizing our beliefs and requiring us to go deeper to find a solid foundation.

Over the years, Dr. Mills received many books about teachings both Eastern and Western, from people he met who recognized in his Unfoldments the same message as another great teacher such as Ramana Maharshi or Nisargadatta. As Dr. Mills learned about other teachers and traditions, he often quoted these while remaining true to his own unique lexicon. To Dr. Mills, it was all one multi-faceted garment pointing to what is beyond words. In fact, as those who do not speak English discovered, the stream of sound that constitutes an Unfoldment can be experienced purely as a tonal vibratory frequency that alters the energy field of the attentive listener. He described it as a "force of realignment," an apt description for the work of one who disliked the word *spiritual* and did not consider himself a teacher, but *spirited*.

Despite his reluctance to be called a spiritual teacher, there are many who would describe Kenneth Mills in those terms (with either a positive or a negative connotation). However, Dr. Mills knew the difference. When he taught piano, he sat in a chair while the pupil sat on the piano bench, presenting their pieces for his adjudication. In giving the Unfoldments, Dr. Mills sat in the chair at the "keyboard of sound," a place where he was as much artist as teacher. We had many occasions throughout the years to present to him our own efforts to write and speak, and to evidence in our lives what we had learned. In fact, he was always creating opportunities for us to see where we were at, and whether ego or Principle was ruling our lives. But the point was not to teach us to give Unfoldments—that was Dr. Mills' art form.

Dr. Mills did not fit the archetypal image of a 1970s spiritual teacher. Formally dressed in a suit and tie, he lived a disciplined, elegant lifestyle. No one who was taking drugs was allowed to attend his lectures. He championed the value of tension, knowing as a concert musician that it was a necessary ingredient for performance. There were standards of dress and behaviour to be adhered to. Commitments had to be fulfilled, quickly. There was no tuning in and dropping out around Dr. Mills.

Historically speaking, the unique blend of Christianity, Eastern influences, and spirituality outside of religion that characterized Dr. Mills' Unfoldments placed him in the context of late-twentieth-century Canada. This was a time when most people still knew their Bible stories, and yet many were moving away from traditional beliefs, looking for something new.

The absolute, non-dual standpoint offered by Dr. Mills did not require a change in beliefs, for example from atheist to the faith of a believer. It required a radical shift in awareness, away from the standpoint of being a mortal looking up to the stars to the standpoint of living "out from the star." This was the theme of every Unfoldment and every encounter with Dr. Mills.

Kenneth Mills' upbringing in a Baptist family in a small Canadian border town in New Brunswick in the 1920s, his career as a concert pianist and music teacher, and his journey (including Christian Science and teachings from the East) was entirely different from my background, in which I grew up in an academic natural sciences family in Toronto in the 1960s, wondering about the meaning of life. Yet, in my studies with Dr. Mills, that which had always been unspoken and elusive for me came vividly to life which enabled me to find my own voice.

Dr. Mills passed away in October 2004. His legacy lives on in those whose lives were touched by him and in the Kenneth G. Mills Foundation, which offers access to his library of Unfoldments and hosts a weekly "Gathering Place" on Zoom as well as an annual calendar of events.

NOTES

I   AM I IN THE WORLD, OR IS THE WORLD IN ME?

Roots in Science

1   W. A. Clemens, *Fishes of the Pacific Coast of Canada* (Fisheries Research Board of Canada, 1949).

Encountering Religion

2   Francis Crick, *The Astonishing Hypothesis: The Scientific Search for the Soul* (1994).

3   David Hume, "Enquiry Concerning Human Understanding," (1748) section XII, part II.

II   THE JOY OF BEING

At My First Unfoldment

4   Unpublished quotations of Kenneth G. Mills are printed with the permission of the Kenneth G. Mills Foundation. Most can be found in the online library of the Kenneth G. Mills Foundation at www.kgmfoundation.org.

5   Kenneth G. Mills, *The Candymaker's Son* (Toronto: The Kenneth G. Mills Foundation, 2007), 293–4.

A New Name

6   "You Picked a Fine Time to Leave Me Lucille," words and music by Hal Bynum and Roger Bowling.

Meditation

7   Kenneth G. Mills, *A Word Fitly Spoken* (Toronto: Sun-Scape Publications, 1980), 135.

8   Philip Kapleau, *The Three Pillars of Zen* (Beacon Press, 1965).

9   Kenneth G. Mills, *The Key: Identity* (Toronto: Sun-Scape Publications, 1994), 41.

Where Success Belongs

10 Kenneth G. Mills, *The Candymaker's Son: Memoirs of Kenneth G. Mills* (Toronto: The Kenneth G. Mills Foundation, 2007), 365; italics added.

11 Mills, 12.

12 Kenneth G. Mills, *The Cornucopia of Substance* (Toronto: The Kenneth G. Mills Foundation, 2008), 267–8.

Wisdom Isn't Clad in Form

13 Kenneth G. Mills, *The Key: Identity* (Toronto: Sun-Scape Publications, 1994), 133, 140.

The Science of the Invisible

14 Robert Lanza explores the historic separation of religion and science in *Beyond Biocentrism* (BenBella Books, 2016).

III LIFE-GIVING FORCE

A Chapter on God

15 Leonard Cohen, interview, quoted in Michael Harris, *Field Notes: Prose Pieces, 1969–2012* (Signal Editions, 2013).

16 Kenneth G. Mills, *The Key: Identity* (Toronto: Sun-Scape Publications, 1994), 155–6.

Home

17 Kenneth G. Mills *The Cornucopia of Substance* (Toronto: The Kenneth G. Mills Foundation, 2008), 307.

A Dead Season

18 Kenneth G. Mills, *The Key: Identity* (Toronto: Sun-Scape Publications, 1994), 334, 335.

Colours on the Mountain

19 Also known as "Palette of Light," in Kenneth G. Mills, *Words of Adjustment* (Toronto: Sun-Scape Publications, 1992), 68.

The Invisible Appearing Visible

20 For a performance of the "Gloria" of *The Fire Mass*, see
https://www.youtube.com/watch?v=IxNjmNLWDoc.

Convergence

21 Siobhan Roberts, "Blissed Out in the Workplace," *Globe and Mail*,
October 6, 1998.

22 Roberts, "Blissed Out."

23 Kenneth G. Mills, *The Cornucopia of Substance* (Toronto:
The Kenneth G. Mills Foundation, 2008), 160.

Releasement

24 Kenneth G. Mills, *The Cornucopia of Substance* (Toronto:
The Kenneth G. Mills Foundation, 2008), 196.

25 Mills, 372.

Passages

26 Kenneth G. Mills, *Change Your Standpoint, Change Your World*
(Toronto: Sun-Scape Publications, 1996), 94.

The Arts as the New Cathedral

27 Strategic Market Research for the National Ballet of Canada,
Secor Consulting, December 2005.

28 A version of David Pecaut's speech may be found at
https://luminatofestival.com/about/.

At the Camera Bar

29 kgmfoundation.org.

What Happens after Church?

30 *Close Encounters of the Third Kind*, directed by Steven Spielberg
(Columbia Pictures, 1977).

A Prescription for Health

31 See www.potentialproject.com.

32 The "prescription for health" in this chapter was pertinent to
my situation, and anyone with health concerns should consult
their doctor.

33   Kenneth G. Mills, *The Cornucopia of Substance* (Toronto: The Kenneth G. Mills Foundation, 2008), 309.

34   Mills, 310.

Embarking on the Project

35   Statistics Canada, *The Canadian Census: A Rich Portrait of the Country's Religious and Ethnocultural Diversity*, October 2022.

The Field Research

36   Zindel V. Segal et al., "Practice of Therapy Acquired Regulatory Skills and Depressive Relapse/Recurrence Prophylaxis Following Cognitive Therapy or Mindfulness Based Cognitive Therapy," *Journal of Consulting and Clinical Psychology*, February 2019.

37   Daniel Siegel, *IntraConnected: MWe (Me + We)* (W.W. Norton, 2022).

38   David Berry, "Jordan Tannahill, a Life Measured in Seconds," *Globe and Mail*, February 3, 2018.

Returning Home

39   T. S. Eliot, *The Four Quartets* (New York: Harcourt Brace, 1943).